IRELAND

THE COMPLETE GUIDE AND ROAD ATLAS

IRELAND

THE COMPLETE GUIDE AND ROAD ATLAS

APPLETREE PRESS

Published by
The Appletree Press Ltd,
19–21 Alfred Street, Belfast BT2 8DL

© The Appletree Press Ltd, 1995

Gazetteer: Hugh Oram. Additional text: Fergus Mulligan. Illustrations:
Stephen Hall. Photographs: William Caddell, Peter Zöller, the Slide File
and the Northern Ireland Tourist Board. Maps: Engineering Surveys
Reproduction Ltd.

The publishers gratefully acknowledge the assistance of Bord Fáilte
and the Northern Ireland Tourist Board.

The information given in this book is believed to be correct at the time
of printing. However, the publishers cannot accept responsibility for
any loss, injury or inconvenience sustained as a result of
information contained in it.

ISBN 0 86281 507 X pb
ISBN 0 86281 566 5 de luxe

A catalogue record for this book is available
from the British Library.

Printed in EU

Contents

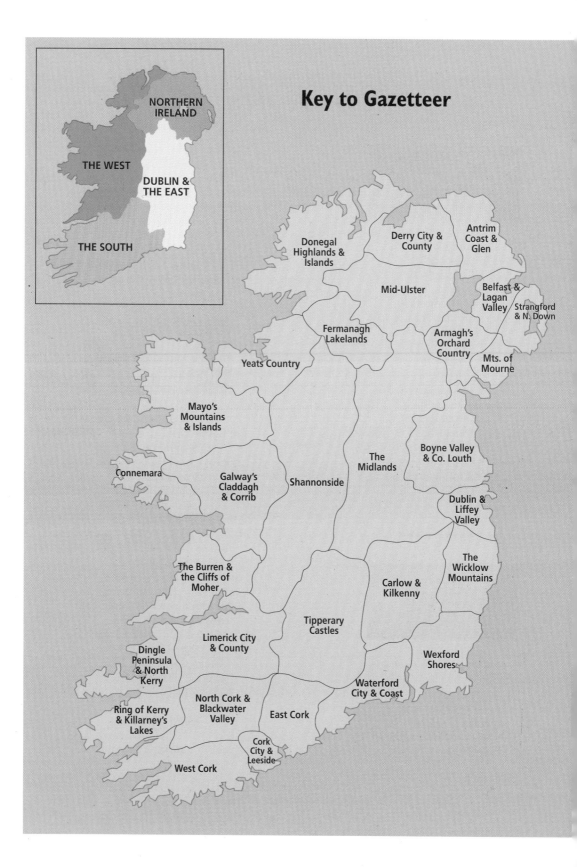

Key to Gazetteer

NORTHERN IRELAND

THE WEST

DUBLIN & THE EAST

THE SOUTH

Donegal Highlands & Islands

Derry City & County

Antrim Coast & Glen

Mid-Ulster

Belfast & Lagan Valley

Strangford & N. Down

Fermanagh Lakelands

Armagh's Orchard Country

Mts. of Mourne

Yeats Country

Mayo's Mountains & Islands

Boyne Valley & Co. Louth

Connemara

The Midlands

Galway's Claddagh & Corrib

Shannonside

Dublin & Liffey Valley

The Burren & the Cliffs of Moher

The Wicklow Mountains

Carlow & Kilkenny

Tipperary Castles

Dingle Peninsula & North Kerry

Limerick City & County

Wexford Shores

Waterford City & Coast

Ring of Kerry & Killarney's Lakes

North Cork & Blackwater Valley

East Cork

Cork City & Leeside

West Cork

INTRODUCTION

Ireland has a wholly justifiable reputation as a desirable destination for travellers and holiday-makers: the scenery is spectacular and the roads are among the least crowded in Europe; along its 5,600 km (3,480 miles) of coastline are some of the best beaches to be encountered anywhere in the world, while its interior, with some 800 rivers and lakes, makes it a centre for anglers and naturalists. Its varied landscapes and rugged, yet accessible, mountain ranges are a walker's paradise and for those whose interests are cultural or historical, Ireland has a wealth of fine buildings, museums and galleries which help preserve a fascinating, if frequently turbulent, past. Above all the renowned welcome that Ireland affords its visitors ensures that many return year after year.

Local Information

Tourists and other visitors are strongly advised to check opening times for buildings and sites before they set out. Quite often, opening times can vary slightly from those given although, especially with country locations, a certain flexibility is shown. Whenever possible, the telephone numbers of individual tourist attractions are listed; during the peak summer period most larger towns in Ireland have Tourist Information Offices (TIOs) in operation with full access to information on local opening times. If you are using boat facilities, it's worth checking with the local TIO that the boat operator is licensed. Local TIOs will also tell you which accommodation is registered, a useful consumer safeguard.

Telephones

The telephone systems in both the Republic of Ireland and Northern Ireland are fully automatic for both national and international calls. In this book, area codes are given in brackets; they need only be dialled when phoning a number outside your own area.

Public Holidays

In the Republic the following are public holidays: 1 January, 17 March (St Patrick's Day), Easter Monday, first Monday in June, first Monday in August, last Monday in October, 25 and 26 December.

In Northern Ireland the holidays differ slightly: 1 January, 17 March, Easter Monday, first and last Mondays in May, 12 July, last Monday in August, 25 and 26 December.

Currency

Northern Ireland uses the pound sterling (£) while the Republic uses the punt (IR£). Until 1979 the punt had parity with sterling but the two currencies are no longer interchangeable.

Banking hours in the Republic are 10am–12.30pm, 1.30pm–3pm, Mon–Fri. Some banks also stay open through lunch and until 4pm daily. In most towns there is opening until 5pm one day a week (Thursday in Dublin). In Northern Ireland banks are open 9.30am–12.30pm, 1.30pm–3.30pm Mon–Fri. Some central Belfast banks now remain open over the lunch-time period.

Electric Current

In Ireland the usual voltage is 220v, AC current. Visitors should note that 13amp, square-pin plugs are generally used: adapters are readily available from shops if required.

HISTORY

The first people who settled in Ireland were hunters, who arrived in Co Antrim c. 7000 BC. By 3000 BC tribes from the Mediterranean were building megalithic tombs all over Ireland which reveal a high degree of civilisation. The most spectacular are the passage graves at Newgrange in Co Meath, Carrowmore and Loughcrew, all of which can be visited. The National Museum in Dublin has a collection of masterpieces from this period: gold collars, torcs, dress fasteners and hair ornaments.

The Celts arrived around 300 BC bringing their distinctive culture, laws and customs. The Irish language derives from a

Mellifont Abbey, Co. Meath

dialect of Celtic, and The Táin is an epic account of Celtic life at the time.

In the fifth century St Patrick brought Christianity from Britain, establishing monasteries which became not only centres of learning but in effect small towns. Places associated with Patrick include Slane in Co Meath where he lit the Paschal fire in defiance of the Druids, Tara, where he used the shamrock to convince the high king about the Trinity and Downpatrick where a crude slab marks his grave. Irish monks produced a large number of beautifully illustrated manuscripts, among them the Books of Durrow, Armagh and Kells, which can be seen in Trinity College Dublin. The monasteries of Clonmacnois, Glendalough and Kildare drew scholars from all over Europe. In turn Irish missionaries

took education and religion to every corner of Europe. At the same time craftsmen were producing exquisite reliquaries, brooches, belts, and personal adornments made of gold and studded with precious stones (see the Ardagh Chalice and the Cross of Cong in the National Museum). This period is rightly known as the golden age.

The wealth of the monasteries and their towns attracted the Vikings, who swept in, burning and killing. Distinctive round towers and bell towers were built as a refuge from them. Later the Vikings settled around the coast and founded towns such as Cork, Waterford, Limerick and Dublin. They were finally defeated by Brian Boru at the Battle of Clontarf in 1014.

On his death, inter-kingdom

rivalry led to a century of chaos until the Normans arrived from England and brought order and prosperity. They were so well assimilated into Irish society that the English crown decided a reconquest was needed. Ulster put up fierce resistance under Hugh O'Neill and Hugh O'Donnell but they were finally defeated at the Battle of Kinsale in 1601. Their exile and that of the Gaelic aristocracy is known as the "Flight of the Earls". The systematic dispossession of the natives and settlement of migrants from England and Scotland followed. This division of Protestant settler and native Catholic has had repercussions ever since.

The campaign of Oliver Cromwell in Ireland is infamous and lives on in folk memory as the "curse of Cromwell". His approach o the Irish problem was drastic: the remaining Irish land-owners were stripped of their property; those who could prove themselves loyal were exiled to Connacht, those who could not were put to death. The incompetent James II was deposed from the English throne (for trying to impose Catholicism on the English) by William of Orange in 1688. William then defeated him at the Battle of the Boyne on 12 July 1690. This battle is celebrated each year as Orangeman's Day, a public holiday in Northern Ireland.

James was replaced by Patrick Sarsfield, and the war dragged on until the signing of the Treaty of Limerick, which was accompanied by the imposition of harsh penal laws. This oppression, coupled with grinding poverty and recurring food shortages, continued for more than a century. A series of revolts at the end of the eighteenth century culminated in the French invasion of Killala, Co Mayo. Although initially successful it was finally suppressed with great slaughter.

The Act of Union in 1800 abolished the Dublin parliament and removed power to London. Daniel O'Connell's election to Westminster (which, as a Catholic, he was forbidden to enter) led to the repeal of the more oppressive laws and to Catholic emancipation. A firm believer in non-violence, he came near to the repeal of the union but his final years were clouded by the Great Famine when nearly a million died and two million emigrated.

Parnell became leader of the Home Rule Party in 1877, and with Gladstone's support, a home rule bill nearly succeeded. Other leaders followed: Arthur Griffith founded Sinn Fein as a non-violent movement and James Larkin and James Connolly became key people in the labour movement. In 1912 the Commons passed the home rule bill. Ireland was to have self-government after World War I.

There was no rejoicing among the Protestants in Ulster. They quickly armed themselves to fight to maintain the link with Britain. In Dublin a group of volunteers decided they could not wait for the end of the war, and began the Easter Rising of 1916. Although unsuccessful and condemned by most Irish people, the execution of its leaders changed public opinion. The Anglo-Irish war lasted from 1919 to 1921.

The treaty of 1921 gave independence to 26 of the 32 counties; six of the Ulster counties remained under British rule with a parliament in Belfast. A sector of the Republican movement opposed this compromise and a bitter civil war followed, culminating in the death of Michael Collins, the brilliant young Corkman who masterminded the war of independence. World War II imposed great strains on the Free State (economically stagnant for many years) which stayed neutral. Sean Lemass later adopted a more vigorous, expansionist economic policy which brought new prosperity and paved the way for Ireland's entry to the European Economic Community (EEC) in 1972. The EEC has since become the European Union (EU).

Today the Republic of Ireland is a parliamentary democracy with a president as head of state. There are two houses of parliament, the Dail and the Seanad, and three major political parties, Fianna Fail, Fine Gael, and the smaller Labour Party.

Northern Ireland continued to suffer some unrest. In 1968 the Civil Rights movement called for power sharing and equality in jobs and housing. Since then there has been an upsurge of extremist republican and loyalist para-military violence. However, despite its beleaguered image, it is quite safe to visit.

GEOGRAPHY

Ireland has an area of 84,421 sq km (32,595 sq miles). At its greatest it is 486 km (302 miles) long and 275 km (171 miles) wide and consists of a central lowland surrounded by a broken range of hills and small mountains.

The climate is mild on account of the Gulf Stream, without extremes of heat or cold. Average temperatures in January are 4–7°C and in July 14–16°C, rising occasionally as high as 25°C. May and June are often the sunniest months, and North American visitors in particular will notice that there are many more daylight hours in summer than in the US. Rainfall is heaviest in the mountainous west and lightest in the east but the weather is at all times very changeable. A day of prolonged drizzle can end with a clear sky, a spectacular sunset and the promise of a sunny day to follow. Even so it is wise to have a raincoat or umbrella to hand while touring.

There are thirty-two counties and four provinces: Connacht,

The Burren, Co. Clare

Leinster, Munster and Ulster. Six counties are part of the United Kingdom and the other twenty-six form the Republic of Ireland. The population of the Republic is 3,500,000 and of Northern Ireland 1,580,000. Dublin is the capital of the former, with an urban population of about one million. The principal cities and towns are Dublin, Belfast, Cork, Derry, Limerick, Waterford and Galway. Of these only the first three have a population in excess of 100,000.

Food, drink, tobacco, engineering, textiles, chemicals and electronics are the chief manufacturing industries. The recession has caused many redundancies but exports show a steady increase in real terms. The Industrial Development Authority (IDA Ireland) conducts a vigorous campaign to attract foreign companies to the Republic with a package of financial incentives for foreign and Irish firms. Many firms from the USA, Britain, Germany, the Netherlands and France have located in Ireland. In the north the old reliance on linen and ship-building has been largely replaced now by light engineering and textiles, most of it from Britain and located in the east of the province.

Ireland does not have great mineral resources. There are some small coal deposits, cement is made at Limerick, Drogheda, Larne and Cookstown, and there is a large lead and zinc mine at Navan. Natural gas was discovered off the Cork coast and brought ashore in 1979. It now counts for 14 per cent of Ireland's primary energy. While oil exploration goes on there has not yet been a major find. Other minerals are dolomite, gypsum, barytes and salt.

Turf is one natural fuel found in abundance. Bord na Móna, a state company, produces over million tonnes of peat and million tonnes of moss peat annually. Production is highly mechanised and much of the peat is used for electricity generation as well as by the domestic and industrial consumer. Other sources of electricity are oil, natural gas, hydroelectric systems and coal.

Farming is a major industry being mainly of a mixed pastoral nature. Irish beef, lamb and pork along with dairy products such as cheese, butter, yoghurt and cream are famous. Output and profitability have greatly increased in recent years, largely as a result of Ireland's entry into the EU.

The main types of sea fish landed are herring, cod, mackerel and plaice. Shellfish include lobsters, mussels, periwinkles and oysters. Much of this is exported to Europe, where pollution-free Irish seafood is greatly prized. Salmon and trout are taken in large numbers, particularly from inland waters, and are also highly valued.

About 6 per cent of Irish land is under forest and coniferous trees grow particularly well in Irish soil. Over 350 forests are open to the public, and many are laid out with car parks, picnic areas, nature trails and walks. Among the loveliest are Glenveagh (Co Donegal), Lough Key (Co Roscommon), Connemara, Lough Navar (Co Fermanagh) and the John F. Kennedy Park (New Ross, Co Wexford).

Ireland, as everyone knows, is very green. This is caused by the mild, damp climate which encourages growth. Two areas of great botanical interest may be cited. Around Glengarriff, Co Cork, which enjoys the full benefit of the Gulf Stream, there is a luxuriant growth of tropical flora such as arbutus, fuchsia and other delightful flowering plants. A trip to Garinish Island, just offshore from Glengarriff, with its beautiful plant collection is well worthwhile. By contrast the Burren is an area of Co Clare which resembles a lunar-like landscape of bare, carboniferous limestone. It is 40 ha (100 sq miles) in size but in spring and early summer produces a host of exotic orchids, ferns and rare plants.

There are at least 380 wild birds to be seen in Ireland, for migration goes on all year. The most common species are blackbird, thrush, goldcrest, starling and curlew. Among the indigenous animal species are the Irish hare (once seen on the old three-pence coin), the Irish stoat, fox and red deer. Wild deer roam the Kerry and Wicklow mountains and are also

to be seen in the Phoenix Park, Dublin.

Irish horse breeding is world famous, being centred on counties Meath and Kildare. The national stud at Tully, Co Kildare (near the Curragh) can be visited at certain times of the year.

There are seven distinct breeds of Irish dog, the best known being the giant Irish wolfhound, the Irish setter and the Irish water spaniel. There is only one reptile, the common lizard, and, thanks to St Patrick, no snakes!

ANCIENT MONUMENTS

All archaeological remains in Ireland are under state care and most can be easily visited, including those on private land. Please take care to close gates, not to disturb farm animals and to respect the landowner's property. A good detailed map, a pair of stout shoes or boots and occasionally a torch will be useful, especially for the more remote examples. Once you are in the area ask the locals for directions. They will tell you exactly where to find the monuments – and a lot more besides.

There are vast numbers of ancient monuments including dolmens, crannògs, forts, clochàns, tumuli, cairns, passage graves,

stone circles, round towers and high crosses. It is well worth visiting at least some of these, as they reveal much about how people have lived in Ireland over the last 5,000 years.

Forts were ramparts built of clay (raths) and stone (cahers or cashels). They have given their name to many Irish towns, for example Rathdrum, Rathfriland, Cahirsiveen and Cashel. Since there are said to be 40,000 forts it would be hard to miss them. This term was used for any strengthened structure including stockades and cattle enclosures. Staigue Fort in Kerry, Garranes in Cork, Grianan of Aileach in Donegal and Navan Fort near Armagh City are among the best. Tara, once the palace of the high kings of Ireland, has a number of raths.

Dolmens are tombs dating from about 2000 BC and consist of two or more unhewn stones supporting a flat capstone. There is a huge one at Kilternan, Co Dublin. Others are at Proleek, Co Louth, Knockeen, Co Waterford and Legananny, Co Down.

Passage graves are set in a mound of earth or stone with a passage leading to the central chamber, and often have side chambers. Many are 4,500 years old and show a sophisticated knowledge of construction, design and astronomy. They are often decorated with geometrical motifs, spirals, concentric circles, triangles, zigzags, the human face and, of course, the sun. Their meaning has not yet been deciphered but presumably they are connected with the religion of the people who built them.

Passage graves often occur in groups and those found in the Boyne valley are superb: Newgrange, Knowth and Dowth. Newgrange is a vast earthen

Dolmen near Ardara, Co. Donegal

mound penetrated by a long narrow passage. The tumulus is surrounded by a ditch with a number of the original pillar stones in place. A kerb of 97 huge stones (many with spiral motifs) supports a dry wall. The threshold stone is carved with a triple spiral, circles and diamonds about whose meaning we can only speculate.

The passageway is narrow and low and the central chamber artificially lit. However, on one day of the year, the Winter Solstice (21 December), a shaft of light enters the passage at dawn and for a few minutes strikes the centre of the floor illuminating the chamber. It is by all accounts an extraordinary experience.

Stone circles (cromlechs) are quite rare but can be visited at Lough Gur, Co Limerick, whose shores have a large number of ancient monuments including forts and tiny remains of stone-age dwellings.

Pillar stones (gallans) can often be seen in fields alongside the road. The most interesting are indicated by a signpost. Some have tracks of carving and many have inscriptions in ogham writing. The letters consist of up to five lines cut above, below or across the stem line and may record a name or event in Irish. They date from about AD 300 and are the earliest form of writing known in Ireland. While it is easy enough to transliterate ogham the meaning is often unclear because the Irish use is very obscure. Dunloe, Co Kerry, has a number of ogham stones in good condition. One inscription reads 'Cunacena' – probably someone's name. There are many more in Kerry and Cork.

Crannògs are lake dwelling built on a small island, sometime reached by a causeway. There are crannògs at Fair Head, Co Antrin and a splendid reconstruction a Quin, near Shannon Airport in Co Clare. There, the Craggaunowen Project has recreated a number o ancient dwellings and ring fort which vividly show the lifestyle o people in Ireland 3,000 years ago

Clochàns are the distinctive beehive huts built of stone which were used as monk's cells. Man are on offshore islands such a Bishop's Island, Co Clare, High Island, Co Galway, Inishmurray, Co Sligo, and the breathtakingl beautiful Skellig Michael, Co Kerry There are many more accessible ones on the Dingle peninsula including the delightful Gallaru Oratory.

Round towers are spread

evenly across the country, with about 65 examples to be seen. Many are still intact with the distinctive conical cap. They were used as places of refuge and as belfries, usually with the entrance high off the ground. Once the occupants were inside the ladder was drawn up. It is worth climbing at least one round tower just for the view of the surrounding countryside. Among the best are those at Glendalough, Co Wicklow, Ardmore, Co Waterford, Devenish, Co Fermanagh, Clonmacnois, Co Offaly and that beside St Canice's Cathedral, Kilkenny town.

High crosses vary from small inscribed stones to massive free-standing sculptures with beautifully detailed carvings and a celtic circle around the head of the cross. Good examples are Muiredach's Cross at Monasterboice, Co Louth and Clonmacnois, where a number of inscribed crosses are individually displayed. Both sites have round towers and extensive monastic remains. Another high cross and the stump of a round tower are located at Drumcliff, Co Sligo, the burial place of the poet William Butler Yeats.

ARCHITECTURE

The Rock of Cashel, once the palace of the kings of Munster, dominates the surrounding plain

and has a fine collection of early Irish buildings. The 13th-century cathedral, although a ruin, is a most impressive edifice. Nearby there is a round tower and the delightful 11th-century Cormac's Chapel built in Irish-Romanesque style. It is similar to Clonfert Cathedral with its ornate yet delicate doorway.

Gothic architecture was brought to Ireland by the Normans and the expanding monastic orders. The ruined Mellifont Abbey which still has part of its cloister and octagonal lavabo is an early example. Boyle Abbey, also built around 1200, retains its solid arcade but St Patrick's Cathedral, Dublin, and St Canice's, Kilkenny, are perhaps the finest examples of gothic architecture intact today. Also worth a visit is Jerpoint Abbey which has a 15th-century tower and an elaborately decorated cloister. Nearby is the restored Duiske Abbey at Graiguenamanagh with its outstanding processional doorway and delightful medieval tiles (ask to see them).

Castles or fortified houses are found in great numbers in Ireland. One of the largest is Trim Castle, whose extensive ruins cover several acres. It was built in 1170 by Hugh de Lacy. Reginald's Tower in Waterford pre-dates Trim by nearly two centuries and is a circular building with a conical roof and walls 3 m (10 ft) thick. Once used as a prison, it now houses a small museum. Blarney Castle is a large tower with a parapet 25 m (83 ft) from the ground and houses the famous Blarney Stone, which promises eloquence to all who kiss it. The 15th-century Bunratty Castle near Shannon Airport has been carefully restored and holds a good collection of old Irish furniture and tapestries. In the grounds is the Folk Park where typical

thatched farmhouses, fishermen's and labourers' cottages have been reconstructed. The park also includes shops and workshops.

Kilkenny city has a number of first rate buildings. The medieval castle of the Dukes of Ormonde stands on a commanding site above the River Nore. Rothe House dates from the 16th-century and is built around a cobbled courtyard. Other noteworthy buildings are the Black Abbey, the Tholsel and St Canice's Cathedral.

Among other superb castles worth visiting are Carrickfergus, Cahir, Malahide, Dunguaire, Thoor Ballylee (once home of W.B. Yeats) and Dublin Castle. An outstanding unfortified 16th-century house is that of the Ormondes at Carrick-on-Suir. Town walls have survived in part at Limerick, Dublin, Clonmel, Fethard (near Clonmel), Youghal, Wexford and Kilmallock. The walls of Derry are complete and give an excellent view over the whole city.

Dating from the late 17th-century is one of Ireland's prize buildings, the Royal Hospital, Kilmainham. Originally an old soldiers' home, it is in the form of an arcaded quadrangle with dormer windows on its two stories. It also has a spacious hall and a beautiful clock tower. The Irish Museum of Modern Art has been added.

Classical architecture came to Ireland in the early 18th-century when Castletown House was built for William Conolly, speaker of the Irish House of Commons. Many of Dublin's finest buildings, including Trinity College, the Bank of Ireland (old Parliament House), Leinster House, the Rotunda, the Custom House, Powerscourt House, the Four Courts, the Marino Casino, Carton House, the King's Inns and the City Hall were built in the Palladian style. They are

the supreme jewels of Irish archi-tecture. This was also the period when the gracious Georgian squares of Dublin were laid out – Merrion Square, Fitzwilliam Square, Parnell Square, Mountjoy Square and St Stephen's Green. The interior of many of these buildings are equally beautiful. Visit Russborough House, Castle-town, Powerscourt Town House, Newman House, St Stephen's Green, and you will appreciate the exquisite plasterwork, carving and decor of these magnificent houses. Outside Dublin several towns were built along classical lines, for example Tyrellspass, Hillsborough, Birr, Armagh, Portarlington and Westport.

The 19th-century saw an upsurge in church building. Noted examples are Killarney and Enniscorthy cathedrals both by Pugin the gothic revivalist – St Finbarre's, Cork and St Saviour's, Dublin. The railway companies have also left a valuable heritage in the large number of elegant stations. In Dublin the terminals of Heuston, Connolly, the Broad-stone and Harcourt Street are gracious buildings. When travel-ling by train it is also worth noting the many excellent country stations, especially en route to Galway/Sligo and Kilkenny. Their structure has, for the most part, scarcely altered since the day they opened. From the same period are the sturdy coastal forts known as Martello towers, built to counter the threat of a French invasion. The best known is probably James Joyce's tower at Sandycove, south of Dublin.

Not all interesting buildings were designed for the wealthy. All over Ireland the traditional thatched cottage may be seen, especially in the west and in Adare.

Kilcooley Abbey, Co. Tipperary

There are also elaborate, brightly painted shop fronts in every town along with neat little churches and simple public houses that have escaped 'modernisation'. The local Protestant church is usually older, and of more interest, than its Catholic counterpart, but, except for Sunday services, they are normally closed to the public.

Twentieth-century architecture is the subject of some controversy. Most towns have undergone ribbon housing development, and modern rural bungalows some-times show a depressing sameness with unimaginative siting. The population of inner cities has fallen as people move to the suburbs, and a number of archi-tectural horrors have been inflicted on Dublin – notably O'Connell Bridge House and the ESB headquarters in Lower Fitzwilliam Street. However, some new buildings blend happily into their background, such as the Irish Life Centre in Abbey Street and the corporation housing schemes in Ringsend, the Coombe and along the south quays of the Liffey. A great addition to the Smithfield area is the attractive Irish Distillers' building, while the Central Bank, the Arts Block in Trinity College and the Abbey Theatre with its fine new façade, deserve favourable mention.

From the 6th to the 17th century most literature was composed in Irish. Some has been lost but a good deal is still available in the original and in translation. The early monks produced a large body of poetry, much of it religious, but they also recorded a great deal of pre-Christian material. Perhaps the best known of these is *The Táin Bó Cuailnge* (The Cattle Raid of Cooley). This is the epic account of the raid of the men of Connaught led by Queen Maeve to capture the marvellous bull owned by the men of Ulster. It has been beautifully translated by Thomas Kinsella, among others. The *Navigatio Brendani* (Voyage of St Brendan) is another example of this type of writing.

Later classics include *The Book of the Dun Cow* and *The Book of Leinster* which date from the 12th-century and feature the adventures of Cuchulain, Finn McCool, Oisin, the Fianna and other legendary heroes who succumbed to Patrick's crozier. These works provided great inspiration for writers such as W.B. Yeats and James Stephens.

Also dating from this period are the *Annals of the Four Masters*, a magnificent historical record of events in Ireland from the earliest times. Much of our knowledge of

Irish history comes from the work of these Donegal scholars. In the 18th-century a schoolmaster from Clare, Brian Merriman, composed *The Midnight Court* (Cuirt an Mhean Oiche), a witty satire on the reluctance of Irishmen to marry. Writing later in the same century Jonathan Swift was the first Irish author to win international acclaim. He lampooned social and political mores at the time and the English attitude to Ireland in *A Tale of a Tub, A Modest Proposal* and *Gulliver's Travels*. Contemporary with him was George Berkeley, the noted philosopher and author of *Principles of Human Knowledge*.

Other outstanding figures of this period are Edmund Burke, the philosopher and orator whose statue stands outside Trinity College and Oliver Goldsmith, the gentle author of *The Vicar of Wakefield, The Deserted Village* and *She Stoops to Conquer*. Richard Brinsley Sheridan is remembered for his dramatic works including *The Rivals* and *The School for Scandal* while Thomas Moore gained a reputation as a poet, author and musician. The brilliant wit and bohemian lifestyle of Oscar Wilde, coupled with his novel *The Picture of Dorian Gray* and comic plays such as *Lady Windermere's Fan* and *The Importance of Being Earnest*, have made his name immortal. George Bernard Shaw had no doubt of his ability and compared his best works, *Arms and the Man, Saint Joan* and *Candida*, to those of Shakespeare; his play *Pygmalion* was the basis for the musical *My Fair Lady*. In 1925 he won the Nobel Prize for literature.

William Butler Yeats is probably Ireland's best known poet and has had an immense influence on Irish letters. He won the Nobel Prize in 1923. Collections of his poetry and plays are now available in many languages. In celebration of life on the western seaboard J.M. Synge wrote *Riders to the Sea* and *The Playboy of the Western World*. The Irish-speaking Blasket Islands off the Kerry coast have produced three great writers: Peig Sayers (*An Old Woman's Reflections*) Tomas O Criomhtain (*An tOileanach*) and Muiris O Suilleabhain (*Fiche Blian ag Fas*). They lyrically portrayed the hard but contented life of the islanders at the turn of the century. *Irish Fairy Tales* and the exquisitely written *The Crock of Gold* are the fanciful work of James Stephens while Sean O'Casey is remembered for his tragicomedies *The Shadow of a Gunman, Juno and the Paycock* and *The Plough and the Stars*. James Joyce, the author of *Ulysses* and *Dubliners*, now has a worldwide following. Samuel Beckett (another Nobel Prize winner), was a magnificent novelist as well as playwright, who first achieved fame with his play *Waiting for Godot*.

Among the leading contemporary poets are Patrick Kavanagh, Louis MacNeice, Thomas Kinsella, Seamus Heaney, John Montague, Richard Murphy and Derek Mahon. Prominent prose writers include masters of the short story such as Sean O'Faolain, Frank O'Connor, Liam O'Flaherty, Bryan McMahon, Benedict Kiely, Mary Lavin and James Plunkett. While Brian Moore, Francis Stuart, Flann O'Brien and Edna O'Brien have also been widely praised for their fiction. Of the major living Irish playwrights mention must be made of Brian Friel, Tom Murphy, M.J. Molloy and Hugh Leonard.

The founding of the Abbey Theatre in 1904 by Lady Gregory, Edward Martyn and W.B. Yeats marks a turning point for Irish drama. The early years of the Abbey were marked by great controversy. One of the first productions was *The Playboy of the Western World* and it caused a small riot when members of the audience disrupted the performance, saying it was an attack on rural life. This was the occasion on which Yeats delivered his famous rebuttal of the audience's narrowmindedness. Such protests occurred from time to time when any works considered remotely salacious or critical of the old Gaelic-Catholic way of life were performed. Indeed at one point such a disrupted performance became the guarantee of a work's success.

These events marked the growing pains of the literary movement as Irish writers fought to free themselves from the suffocating constraints of a narrow nationalist philosophy. It was a time when any foreign work of art was considered suspect and led to the vicious and absurd censorship laws which plagued Irish writing for half a century, driving many of the finest authors into exile. Happily times have changed and there is now a diverse richness in the literary and theatrical diet which is unsurpassed. Modern farce, Shakespeare, classical pieces and modern Irish plays can now be seen happily coexisting. Every large town has its own amateur drama group which puts on at least one production a year. Ask at the tourist office for details of amateur dramatics in your area.

As the national theatre, The Abbey is dedicated to producing the best works of Irish and international playwrights. Michael MacLiammoir and Hilton Edwards set up the Gate Theatre in 1928 to produce a broad range of plays, while the Project Arts Centre is an experimental theatre. In addition there are a large number of repertory groups, amateur enthusiasts, lunchtime plays and pub theatres offering a rich programme of drama throughout Ireland. Among them is Siamsa Tíre, the national folk theatre established in Tralee, which presents authentic folk productions in the Kerry area.

FOLKLORE

Ireland has a vast heritage of folklore going back to pre-Christian times. The sagas, epics, legends, stories, poems, proverbs, riddles, sayings, curses and prayers are all part of that tradition. Much of it comes by way of the *seanachie*, the storyteller who sat beside the fire and enchanted his audience with tales of times past. Often he was a nomad and moved from house to house earning his bed and board by storytelling.

The Department of Irish Folklore at University College, Dublin, has recorded and preserved a great part of the country's heritage, and almost every sizeable town in Ireland has a small museum where the life and history of the local community is documented in antiquities and relics of the past. A good place to start is the National Museum in Dublin which has a large collection dating from pre-history. Also in Dublin are the Civic Museum for items relating to the capital, the Heraldic Museum where you can trace your ancestors, the Guinness Museum, dedicated to Dublin's famous brew, and the Royal Hospital, Kilmainham, which has a superb array of folklore items gathered over many years. Other recommended museums are the Ulster Museum in Belfast, the Ulster Folk and Transport Museum, Co Down, Rothe House in Kilkenny, the James Joyce Museum at Sandycove, Enniscorthy Museum, Co Wexford, Limerick and Galway Museums, and Kinsale Museum, Co Cork, which displays mementoes of the ill-fated Lusitania sunk off Kinsale in 1915. A number of towns have developed heritage centres and folk parks where the richness of local life is displayed in a less formal setting. Fine examples are located at Damer House, Roscrea (Co Tipperary), Glencolumbkille (Co Donegal), Bunratty (Co Clare), Cultra (Co Down) and the Ulster American Folk Park near Omagh (Co Tyrone).

A delightful way to see a collection of old furniture, farming implements and kitchenware is to visit one of the many pubs displaying such items and imbibe a pint and some culture at the same time. Among them are The Seanachie (Dungarvan, Co Waterford), Durty Nelly's (Bunratty, Co Clare), The Asgard (Westport, Co Mayo) and The Hideout (Kilcullen, Co Kildare).

Craftworkers now produce a wide range of first-class products such as pottery, ceramics, leatherwork, wood carving, jewellery, weaving, basketry, linen, lace, crystal, tweed, pewter and other quality souvenirs. Almost everywhere you will find a shop selling the products of local craftworkers, many of whom employ techniques handed from one generation to the next. Craft centres where these skills can be seen in practice will be found at Marlay Grange and Powerscourt Town House in Dublin and at Muckross House, Killarney (see also 'Shopping').

FESTIVALS

Wherever you go in Ireland you can't avoid coming across a festival. Some of the best known are the Rose of Tralee Festival, a week-long Irish beauty contest which draws the comely daughters of exiles from as far afield as Australia and the USA. The Galway Oyster Festival offers the chance of sampling delicious Irish shellfish washed down with Guinness of course, while the Yeats Summer School in Sligo is a gathering of the followers of Ireland's foremost poet. The Wexford Opera Festival has international status and attracts world stars but you need to book months in advance. There are many more which take in dancing, traditional music, drama, boating, agricultural shows and sports of all kinds. In fact there are very few you need to book beforehand so look through the list and plan your vacation to take in those that interest you most. Dates and venues may change so check with the tourist office on arrival.

CALENDAR OF EVENTS

January

National Crafts Trade Fair, Royal Dublin Society (RDS), Ballsbridge, Dublin.
Aer Lingus Young Scientist Exhibition, RDS, Dublin.

February

Cavan International Song Contest.
Dublin Film Festival.
Kate O'Brien Weekend, Limerick.

March

St Patrick's Day, 17 March: national holiday with parades in Dublin and many other centres.
Arklow Music Festival, Arklow, Co Wicklow
Traditional Irish Music Festival. Dublin.
Western Drama Festival, Tubbercurry, Co Sligo.
West Cork Drama Festival, Clonakilty, Co Cork.
Church Music International Choral Festival, Limerick.
Galway International Band Festival, Salthill, Co Galway.
Limerick International Marching Band Parade, Limerick.
Guinness Roaring '20s Festival, Killarney.

April

Spring Season of Opera, Dublin Grand Opera Society.
Killarney Easter Folk Festival.
Cork International Choral and Folk Dance Festival, City Hall, Cork.
Sligo Feis Ceoil, Sligo.
West of Ireland Golf Championships, Rosses Point, Co Sligo.
World Championships in Irish Dancing, Dublin.
Pan Celtic Festival, Galway.
International Motor Rally, South Kerry and West Cork.

May

All-Ireland Amateur Drama Festival, Athlone. Co Westmeath.
Dublin International Piano Competition.
Dundalk International Maytime and Drama Festival, Dundalk.
Birr Castle Exhibition, Birr, Co Offaly.
Belfast Civic Festival.
Dublin Grand Opera season, Dublin and Cork.
International 3-day event, Punchestown Racecourse.
Sligo School of Landscape Painting.
Royal Ulster Agricultural Show, Belfast.
Listowel Writers Week.
Belfast City Marathon.
Eigse, Carlow Arts Festival.

June

Kinsale Arts Week.
Ardara Weavers' Fair, Co Donegal.
Kenmare Walking Festival, Co Kerry.
Dublin International Organ Festival.
Walter Raleigh potato festival, Youghal, Co Cork.

Murphy's Irish Open Golf Championship.
Music Festival in Great Irish Houses: recitals by world famous artists in lovely 18th century mansions.
Glengarriff Festival.
Spancilhill Horse Fair, Ennis.
Ballybunion Bachelor Festival.
Wexford Strawberry Fair, Enniscorthy.
Goldsmith Summer School, Longford.
International Cartoon Festival, Rathdrum, Co Wicklow.
An Tostal Traditional Pageant, Drumshanbo, Co Leitrim.
Donegal Car Rally.
Budweiser Irish Derby, The Curragh.

July

Dun Laoghaire Summer Festival .
Clones Agricultural Show, Co Monaghan.
West Cork Festival, Clonakilty.
Festival of the Erne, Co Cavan.
North of Ireland Amateur Golf Championship, Portrush.
Willie Clancy Summer School, Miltown Malbay.
Drimoleague Festival.
Schull Festival.
Cobh International Folk Dance Festival.
Kerry Summer Painting School, Cahirsiveen.
Glens of Antrim Feis, Glenariff: music, dancing, sports.
Bandon Week.
Skibbereen Annual Show.
Orangeman's Day, 12th July: parades throughout Ulster.
Mary from Dungloe Festival, Dungloe.
Sham Fight, Scarva, Co Down: re-enacts Battle of the Boyne.
Ulster Steam Traction Rally, Shane's Castle. Antrim.
South Sligo Summer School of Traditional Irish Music, Song and Dance.
Mullingar Festival.
Ballina Salmon Festival.
Galway Arts Festival Race Week.
French Festival, Portarlington.
Ballyshannon International Folk Festival, Co Donegal.
Rosc of Arranmore Festival, Co Donegal.
O'Carolan Harp and Traditional Irish Music Festival, Keadue, Co Roscommon.

August

Gorey Arts Week.
Stradbally Steam Rally.
Claddagh Festival, Galway.
Sligo School of Landscape Painting.
Yeats International Summer School, Sligo.
Irish Antique Dealers' Fair, Dublin.
Kerrygold Horse Show, RDS, Dublin.
Granard Harp Festival.
John Millington Synge Summer School, Co Wicklow.
Puck Fair, Killorglin.
Percy French Festival, Newcastle, Co Down.

Oul' Lammas Fair, Ballycastle: one of the oldest fairs in Ireland.
Connemara Pony Show, Clifden.
Ulster Grand Prix (motorcycling), Belfast.
Schull Regatta.
Birr Vintage Week.
Merriman Summer School, Lahinch.
Limerick Show.
Carlingford Oyster Festival.
Letterkenny International Folk Festival.
Fleadh Cheoil na hEireann: top festival for traditional music, song, dance; location changes each year.
Kilkenny Arts Week.
Galway Races: more than just horse racing.
Rose of Tralee Festival.
Wexford Mussel Festival.
All-Ireland Road Bowls Final, Armagh.
Abbeyshrule Fly-in Festival (Air Show), Co Longford.
Moynalty Steam Threshing, Co Meath.
Parnell Summer School, Avondale.
Rathdrum, Co Wicklow.

September

Autumn Fair, RDS, Dublin.
Clifden Arts Week, Co Galway.
Cork Folk Festival.
Waterford International Festival of Light Opera.
Listowel Harvest Festival and Races.
Lisdoonvarna Folk Festival.
All-Ireland Hurling and Football Finals, Dublin.
Galway Oyster Festival.
Clarinbridge Oyster Festival, Co Galway.

October

Kinsale Gourmet Festival.
Flower Festival, St Nicholas, Galway.
Ballinasloe October Horse Fair.
Cork Film Festival.
Wexford Opera Festival.
Guinness Jazz Festival, Cork.
Queen of the Burren Autumn Festival, Lisdoonvarna.
Dublin Theatre Festival.
Monaghan County Arts Festival.
Dublin City Marathon.

November

Belfast Festival at Queen's.
Dublin Indoor International Showjumping. RDS, Dublin.
Sligo International Choral Festival.
Allingham Arts Festival, Ballyshannon, Co Donegal.

December

Grand Opera International Season, Dublin.
Irish Craft Fair, Arnotts, Dublin.
Christmas Crafts Fair, Mansion House, Dublin.
Moving Crib, Dublin.
Christmas Races, Leopardstown.
New Year's Eve Celebrations, Dublin and regional centres.

MUSIC

Like the seanachie, the music teacher of old once wandered the country, playing an instrument and teaching music and dance to his pupils. The best known is probably Turlough O'Carolan, the blind harpist and composer of the late 1600s. His beautiful lilting airs are now available on record. Two 19th century composers are particularly outstanding: John Field, the inventor of the nocturne, and Thomas Moore, whose famous *Irish Melodies* includes the "Last Rose of Summer" and "The Vale of Avoca". There is a monument to Moore at the Meeting of the Waters near Avoca, Co Wicklow, where he is said to have composed the song, and it is a magical spot. Notable among modern composers are A.J. Potter, Gerard Victory, Seoirse Bodley and Sean O Riada, who wrote the haunting "Mise Eire".

Traditional music and dance is jealously guarded by Comhaltas Ceoltóirí Éireann which organises music festivals all over the country and has regular sessions at its Monkstown headquarters in south Dublin. Many pubs also hold impromptu ballad evenings. In Dublin they occur regularly at O'Donoghue's, The Abbey Tavern, The Chariot Inn, Slattery's, The Stag's Head, and The Old Shieling. Irish cabaret can be seen at Jury's,

the Burlington and Clontarf Castle. There are nightly sessions also at the Granary in Limerick, McCann's and O'Connor's in Doolin, near Ennis, Co Clare, Duchas in Tralee, Teach Beg in Cork and O'Flaherty's in Dingle, but every town has at least one pub with music. All you have to do is stroll around until you hear singing or the sound of an accordion, tin whistle or the wail of uileann pipes.

The National Concert Hall in Dublin has become the centre for music in Ireland. There is a musical event there every day of the year ranging from classical to jazz, traditional, folk music, piano recitals and pop concerts. There are two principal orchestras, the National Symphony Orchestra in the Republic and the Ulster Orchestra in Northern Ireland. Both can be heard throughout the year at the National Concert Hall in Dublin and the Ulster Hall in Belfast respectively, with occasional performances in other centres. The Dublin Grand Opera Society has one or two seasons in the Gaiety Theatre, Dublin and at the Opera House, Cork. In Dublin, other concerts and recitals take place in the Royal Dublin Society, Ballsbridge, the National Stadium and the Examination Hall of Trinity College. In Belfast the recently refurbished Opera House provides an impressive venue for concerts, plays and musicals. During the winter months musicals and light opera are performed in many provincial towns by amateur groups, culminating in the Waterford Festival of Light Opera.

Discos and night clubs will be found in the major cities, sometimes attached to hotels. In Dublin the area around Leeson Street and Baggot Street has a number of such places, while in Belfast try the famous "Golden Mile" – a mile long strip of pubs, clubs and restaurants.

SPORT & RECREATION

The traditional Irish games are known as gaelic games and include the ancient game of hurling, plus football, handball and camogie. The Gaelic Athletic Association (GAA) organises hundreds of local clubs, and county teams compete in hurling and gaelic football at the All-Ireland finals each year in Croke Park, Dublin. Hurling is a fast game played with wooden hurley sticks while gaelic football resembles Australian rules football.

Ireland offers many opportunities for recreational sport, in unspoiled landscapes and waters. Angling is a popular visitors' pastime. Coarse fishing, for such species as beam, carp, dace, eel, pike, perch and rudd, is abundant in the Grand and Royal Canal systems and in the Shannon system. In the North, the River Erne and its tributaries are good coarse fishing grounds, while the lakes of counties Cavan, Meath and Monaghan are excellent for such species as pike.

Ireland is often described as the best game fishing location in Europe, with brown trout widely distributed in parts of the north, the midlands and the south-east. The north-west, west and the south-west are salmon territory. Controversy rages over the extent to which fish farming may have

At the Dublin Horse Show

affected salmon fishing in the west. Sea-angling, too, is good, with many fine catches possible from beaches and boats. Species range from the mundane to the exotic, cod to shark, the latter caught off the south coast.

Ireland has innumerable locations for water sports in their many facets, canoeing, cruising, rowing, sailing and windsurfing.

Golf is the most popular sport for visitors to Ireland, with most clubs welcoming guests for modest entrance fees. In Ireland as a whole there are over 300 courses. The North has some truly spectacular courses, like those at Newcastle and Portrush and some old established clubs within the city itself. In the south, many of the most prestigious courses, the likes of Portmarnock, Co Dublin, Lahinch, Co Clare and Waterville,

Co Kerry are long established. Numerous new courses are equally spectacular in their settings and their golfing challenges. The Dublin area has some magnificent new courses, including the Kildare Country Club at Straffan, St Margaret's near Dublin Airport and Luttrellstown, just west of the city. Some of the finest new courses are located by the coast, including the Carn course at Belmullet, Co Mayo, St Helen's Bay near Rosslare and Charlesland near Greystones, Co Wicklow.

The horse, that quintessential animal in Ireland, provides many sporting opportunities including trail riding and hunting. Ireland, north and south has an excellent selection of racecourses, the most prestigious of which include the Curragh, Leopardstown, Down Royal and Downpatrick. The Irish

Grand National is run at Fairyhouse on Easter Monday and the Irish Sweeps Derby at the Curragh in June. At certain races, as with the Galway Races at the end of July and again in September, the social content is every bit as important as the racing.

The hills, mountains and uplands of Ireland give ample opportunity to those in search of physical exercise, whether hill walking, orienteering or mountain climbing. Walking has been developed substantially over the last few years, with over thirty long distance walking ways provided throughout Ireland, including the Ulster Way in Northern Ireland, Western Way, Dingle Way, Kerry Way and the Wicklow Way. The towpaths of the Grand Canal and Royal Canal have been developed into long distance walking ways.

FOOD & EATING OUT

Four thousand years ago the Irish cooked enormous joints of meat by filling a ditch with water and dropping in heating stones to keep the water boiling. Recent duplicate experiments proved that this method works perfectly although it seems rather troublesome! In pre-Christian times the feasts at Tara and other royal palaces were known to go on for several weeks without a break. Since then the Irish have lost little of their enthusiasm for food although appetites are now more moderate!

A unique pleasure of a stay in Ireland is enjoying the unpretentious but delicious cooking. Fresh ingredients simply prepared and served without fuss make eating in Ireland a real pleasure. The rich pastures produce meat of the highest quality, so that beef, lamb and dairy products, like cream, cheese and butter, are second to none. Among the tempting dishes on offer are Limerick ham, Irish stew, bacon and cabbage, Galway oysters, sirloin steak and onions, game of all sorts, smoked salmon, Dublin Bay prawns, spring lamb, grilled trout, fresh farm eggs and delicious wheaten bread.

In Irish cooking the basic ingredients are so good that elaborate sauces are unnecessary to bring out the flavour of the food. The humble potato is appreciated as nowhere else and a plate of steaming, floury 'spuds' with butter, salt and a glass of milk is a meal in itself. Indeed potatoes are the principal ingredients of several dishes which once formed the bulk of the countryman's diet: colcannon is mashed potato with butter and onions; boxty is grated potato fried in bacon fat while potato cakes are often served at breakfast but are delicious anytime.

It is difficult to suggest food items to take home, as dairy products and the like do not travel well. However no-one should leave Ireland without at least one side of smoked salmon which keeps fresh for up to ten days. Whiskey cake, wheaten and soda bread can also be carried easily.

An Irish breakfast is a substantial affair: fruit juice, cereals, bacon, egg, sausage, tomato, mushrooms, (plus soda farls and potato bread in the North!), wheaten bread, toast, tea or coffee. Many pubs serve tasty lunches ranging from a simple sandwich to a full meal and this is a pleasant way to break up a day's sightseeing. Visit Bewley's in Grafton St or Westmoreland St, if in Dublin, for excellent tea, coffee and cakes, or one of the tea rooms attached to many of the stately homes. For dinner eat in your hotel or choose a restaurant to suit your taste and pocket from the list provided by the tourist board or from the booklet of the Irish Country Houses and Restaurants Association. Some people prefer to go out to a hotel to eat and this is quite acceptable.

International cooking is available in Ireland and includes Italian, French, Spanish, Indian, Chinese, Greek, Russian and Japanese. There is also a wide price range from a simple one-course meal to haute cuisine. It is worth looking for restaurants which have the Bord Fáilte award for excellence, an independent commendation of good and reasonable value. In addition to table d'hôte and à la carte menus many restaurants also participate in the special value tourist menu scheme. This involves offering a three-course meal at a fixed price and is usually excellent value. Look for the symbol or ask Bord Fáilte for a list of participating restaurants. In Northern Ireland the Tourist Board publishes a useful book *Let's Eat Out*.

Recommending restaurants is a highly risky business, however the following Dublin restaurants have been highly praised. For a tasty lunch try the Kilkenny Shop (Nassau St), the National Gallery (Merrion Square), the Municipal Gallery (Parnell Square), or any of the very pleasant Bewley's cafés in Grafton St, Westmoreland St and South Great George's St. You could also drop into one of the many pubs serving lunch such as the Stag's Head (Dame Court), Henry Grattan (Lr Baggot St), Kitty O'Shea's (Upr Grand Canal St), Foley's (Merrion Row). For dinner try Restaurant Na Mara (Dun Laoghaire), Le Coq Hardi (Pembroke Rd), Patrick Guilbaud (James Place), King Sitric (Howth), Le Coquillage (Blackrock), Locks (Portobello), Nico's (Dame St), Trocadero (Andrews St). The Powerscourt Town House Centre (South William St) also has several excellent restaurants and coffee bars. Outside Dublin the Cork/ Kerry region is excellent for eating out, with Kinsale the gourmet capital of Ireland.

Other recommended restaurants include Ballymaloe House (near Cork), the Arbutus Lodge (Cork City), Aherne's (Youghal), Doyle's Seafood Bar (Dingle), the Park Hotel (Kenmare), Ballylickey

Pub, Ennistymon, Co. Clare

House (Bantry), Renvyle House Hotel (Connemara), the Galley Floating Restaurant (New Ross), Durty Nelly's (Bunratty), Restaurant St John's (Fahan), and Dunraven Arms Hotel (Adare). In Northern Ireland try Balloo House (Killinchy, Co Down), The Nutgrove (Downpatrick), Nick's (Belfast), Roscoff (Belfast), The Grange (Waringstown), The Ramore (Portrush) and Portaferry Hotel (Portaferry).

PUBS & DRINK

The Irish have always had a close relationship with drink. Public houses began as illicit drink shops or *shebeens* where people met to exchange news and drink the raw fiery spirit, poteen. Pubs are still very much a social centre and a convivial meeting place where you can chat to local people in informal surroundings.

Opening hours are 11am–11pm/11.30pm on weekdays and 12.30pm–2pm and 4pm–10pm on Sundays. In Northern Ireland most pubs are open between 11am and 11pm on weekdays and between 12.30pm–2.30pm and 7pm–10pm on Sundays.

Many pubs have preserved their original decor with features such as solid mahogany bar furniture, brass lamps, lovely old mirrors and stained glass. To experience a traditional Irish session it is best to head for one of these pubs and avoid the more modern places. There are some 900 pubs in Dublin alone and many are excellent. The following is just a representative sample of the best but there are lots more worth exploring.

Doheny and Nesbitt's (Lr Baggot St) has kept the original interior and has a delightful little snug. This is a small enclosed room with a hatch opening directly on to the bar for discreet imbibing and is found in many pubs. Toner's (Lr Baggot St) has lots of atmosphere and traditional music and so has O'Donoghue's nearby. Neary's (Chatham St) is a pleasant watering hole with an attractive old bar while the Stag's Head (Dame Court) is noted for its beautiful stained glass and highly ornate snug. There is a fine collection of cartoons, photographs and drawings of noted customers in the Palace Bar (Fleet St) and Mulligan's (Poolbeg St) has a low beam inscribed 'John Mulligan estd. 1782'. Ryan's (Parkgate St) is perfectly preserved and has lovely old bar furniture.

Other traditional pubs worth visiting on a pub crawl are McDaid's, Bowe's, Davy Byrne's, the Long Hall, the Auld Dubliner, Kitty O'Shea's, Conway's, Keogh's, Mulligan's (Stoneybatter), The Brazen Head, O'Brien's and the International. Outside the capital you will find every Irish town is well endowed with pubs. You should have no trouble finding a welcoming hearth, a blazing turf fire and a cheering glass. But just in case you're stuck head for one of the following: Kate O'Brien's (Fermoy), The Breffni Inn (Dromod), Dan Lowry's, Teach Beag and The Vineyard (Cork) the Seanachie, Dungarvan and Kate Kearney's (Killarney), Taylor's (Moyasta), O'Shea's (Borris), The Thatch (Ballysodare), Crown Liquor Saloon (Belfast), The Spaniard (Kinsale), Durty Nelly's (Bunratty), The Abbey Tavern (Howth), Morrissey's (Abbeyleix), The Granary, South's and Hogan's (Limerick), and O'Flaherty's (Dingle).

When someone asks for a pint they usually mean Guinness, the dark stout with a white head which is synonymous with Ireland. There is hardly a pub in the country that does not stock Guinness on draught or in bottles. Try it on its own or with some oysters. Other top quality beers are Murphy's, Macardle's, Smithwick's, Bass, Harp and Beamish.

Visitors are welcome at the Guinness brewery in Dublin, Smithwick's in Kilkenny, Beamish in Cork and Harp and Macardle's in Dundalk and will be invited to taste the product. Guinness is the oldest brewery; Arthur Guinness (Uncle Arthur as he is affectionately known) began brewing at St James's Gate in 1759.

Equally famous is Irish whiskey (spelt with an 'e'). The word comes from the Irish *uisce beatha* meaning water of life and there is an old saying "There's more friendship in a glass of spirit than in a barrel of buttermilk!" The whiskey is matured for 7 to 12 years and has a mellow distinct flavour. It is made from malted and unmalted barley, yeast and pure spring water. The oldest (legal) distillery is at Bushmill's near the Giant's Causeway, dating from 1609, and it welcomes visitors by appointment. At the Irish Distillers' head office in Smithfield, Dublin, there is an excellent display of models, kits and tools showing the history of whiskey and how it is made. Midleton, Co Cork has a fine new whiskey heritage centre, so has Kilbeggan, Co Westmeath. A comparatively recent development is the number of cream liqueurs which are made from a blend of whiskey and cream. These include Bailey's, Carolans and Waterford Cream.

Irish people often drink their whiskey diluted with water. So if you order "a ball of malt" you will usually get a jug of water with it. Try it on its own first. Some of the 12-year-old whiskeys are like nectar and are as good as a fine brandy.

Irish Coffee is now world famous and often drunk at the end of a meal or on a cold day. Another warming drink is a hot whiskey which is simply whiskey with hot water, sugar, lemon and cloves. Black Velvet is a potent mixture of Guinness and champagne.

GENEALOGY

Many people visiting Ireland would like to find out more about their family history. What makes ancestor research so fascinating is that it increases your knowledge of yourself; who you are and where you come from. You would expect to find Christian names recurring in a family but you might be surprised to see the same occupation held by members of the family over several generations or even spot similarities between your handwriting and theirs! You can engage a professional to do the research work or you can have a go yourself. There are many sources of information although some records have been lost in the various upheavals of Irish history.

It will make things much easier if you do some simple research before you leave home. Try to find out: the full name of your emigrant ancestor; where he came from in Ireland; dates of birth, marriage and death; occupation and background (rich, poor, farmer, tradesman, professional, etc.); religion; date of emigration from Ireland. The more details you have the greater the chance of success. Sources are old letters and diaries, family bibles, military service records, emigrant ship lists, newspapers, local church and state records. Ask the oldest member of your family about their earliest memories too.

Armed with as much information as you can muster, you can then visit the following places in Ireland: The Registrar General in Joyce House, 8–11 Lombard Street East, Dublin 2 holds the general civil registration of births, marriages and deaths from 1864. Non-catholic marriages are listed from 1845. You can make the search yourself or have it done for you. A small fee is payable.

The Public Record Office, Four Courts, Dublin 7, although badly damaged in 1922, has many valuable records including tithes dating from 1800 (the first valuation records), wills and extracts of wills and marriage licences for some families. The returns for the extensive 1901 census may be seen here. The National Archives, Bishop Street, Dublin 8, tel (01) 478 3711, also have many relevant documents.

The Registry of Deeds, Henrietta Street, Dublin 2 has documents from 1708 relating to property such as leases, mortgages and settlements. You make the search yourself and a small fee is due.

The National Library, Kildare Street, Dublin 2 has an enormous collection of useful sources including historical journals, directories, topographical works, private papers and letters and local and national newspapers from the earliest times. It is necessary to contact the Library for a reader's ticket in advance. Catholic Parish Records can now be consulted in the National Library on microfilm. The staff are helpful and there is no charge.

The Genealogical Office, Kildare Street, Dublin 2 records official pedigrees, coats of arms and will extracts of the more well-to-do families. Staff will conduct a search on your behalf for a fee.

The detailed full-colour brochure published by Bord Fáilte, *Tracing Your Ancestors*, has useful information on the subject, including a full listing of all heritage centres now in operation throughout the Republic. Information on the 243 Irish clans researched to date from the Clans of Ireland Office, c/o Genealogical Office, 2 Kildare Street, Dublin 2, tel. (01) 661 8811.

The Public Record Office, Four Courts, Dublin 1 has the excellent and comprehensive Griffith's Valuation. This was a national survey of land ownership and leases made in the 1850s. There is an immense amount of detail in it. The Valuation Office, 6 Ely Place, Dublin 2 has records of subsequent alterations in land ownership.

If your ancestors came from Northern Ireland the Public Record Office of Northern Ireland at 66 Balmoral Avenue, Belfast BT9 6NY will help. It has tithe appointment books and other valuable sources. Linked to it is the Ulster Historical Foundation which will carry out a search for you.

The Presbyterian Historical Society at Church House, Fisherwick Place, Belfast 1 also has various records of its members. You might also contact the Registrar General's Office, Oxford House, 49 Chichester Street, Belfast BT1 4HL.

If you know the parish where your ancestor came from, then start there. Every parish keeps records of the baptisms performed in it giving details of the child's parents and sometimes their date of birth and domicile. Many go back 150 years and some Church of Ireland registers go back to the 1700s. To see them apply to the parish priest or minister. Study the baptismal and marriage registers for five years before and after the date you have. Jot down each name that seems likely. Remember too that there is another useful source nearby – the graveyard. Note the details of each gravestone bearing your family name, rubbing away the moss and using a piece of chalk to bring up faint lettering.

Contact the local historical society. Their journal may well have interesting information and perhaps articles on the history of the parish. They will put you in touch with any genealogist specialising in the families of the at district. If there is a parish newsletter ask the editor if he would insert an item on your search: 'Information sought about Sean Murphy, believed born in this parish about 18–, emigrated 18–. Please contact …' A similar letter should be sent to the local newspaper; every county has at least one. Lastly, before you leave the area ask to speak to the person who knows most about local history. Even if he or she can't shed light on your elusive ancestor you will learn a great deal about the place where your family originated and that alone should make the trip worthwhile. If you are unsuccessful or don't want to do a search you can employ a professional to do it for you. Results cannot be guaranteed but for a modest sum they will complete an initial search and let you know the likelihood of success. Try one of the following: Irish Genealogical Office, Kildare Street, Dublin 2; Heraldic Artists, 3 Nassau Street, Dublin 2: Hibernian Research, Windsor Road, Dublin 6. For coats of arms, plaques, parchments and the full range of heraldic goods visit Mullins, 36 Upr O'Connell Street, Heraldic Artists (see above) or Historic Families, 8 Fleet Street, Dublin 2.

SHOPPING

Shopping in Ireland is leisurely and while the choice may not be as wide as London or New York you will discover lots which cannot be found elsewhere. Opening hours are usually 9am–5.30pm Monday to Saturday. Most shops close on Sunday and in smaller towns many close for lunch and on one afternoon a week. The larger shops will change currency and traveller's cheques but you will get a better rate in a bank. There is a value added tax (VAT) refund scheme for goods taken out of the Republic. You must have the invoice stamped by customs at the exit point before returning it to the shop for refund. Ask Bord Fáilte or the Tourist Information office for a leaflet explaining how the system works and the allowances.

Visitors to Ireland will want to take home some gifts or memen-

toes of their stay and there is a wide choice of quality Irish-made goods available. Avoid those displaying an excessive amount of shamrocks, leprechauns, etc. they probably came from the Far East! If it is not marked ask the assistant where the item was made and look for the 'Guaranteed Irish' symbol, an assurance that the product is quality Irish-made. Many of the larger shops will pack, insure and mail goods home for you and don't forget to visit the enormous duty-free shop if passing through Shannon Airport where you can save a lot of money on the full price.

In Dublin the main shopping areas are all within easy walking distance: Grafton Street, Wicklow Street, O'Connell Street and Henry Street. The Powerscourt Town House in South William Street has a large assortment of shops, boutiques, restaurants and a craft centre all housed within a carefully restored 18th-century mansion. There are more shopping complexes in the ILAC Centre off Henry Street, St Stephen's Green Centre, Grafton Street, and the Irish Life Centre, Talbot Street. The principal department stores are Clery's (O'Connell St), Brown Thomas's (Grafton St), Arnott's, Dunne's and Roche's (Henry St). Not to be missed at any cost is the Kilkenny Shop in Nassau Street which displays and sells only the best designed Irish goods such as clothing, pottery, jewellery, glass and furniture. It is also a pleasant spot for lunch or afternoon tea.

In Belfast the principal shops are located in Donegall Place and Royal Avenue and the streets nearby. Cork, the Munster capital, has Patrick Street and Grand Parade as the main shopping thoroughfare. In Galway the aptly named Shop Street has a good selection of stores, especially for

clothes and crafts. In fact every town, no matter how small, is usually amply catered for by its retail trade. Watch out for the combined grocery shop and bar where you can order your rashers and have a pint under the same roof.

What to buy

Waterford is almost synonymous with crystal and the factory just outside the city welcomes visitors by appointment. There you can see the ancient skill of moulding, blowing and cutting glass. The factory does not sell direct to the public but the glass is available in outlets everywhere. Less well-known but equally beautiful crystal is made in Tyrone, Galway, Dublin, Cavan, Kilkenny, Tipperary, Cork and Sligo, and many have shops attached where you can pick up first-rate bargains.

Tweed is a strong woollen fabric used in making suits, skirts, curtains, jackets, ties, hats and carpets. It comes in many beautiful designs, much of it from Donegal and Connemara where the rugged landscape provides the colour and texture of this versatile cloth. You can buy tweed garments made up or choose a pattern and order a length of fabric to be made up at home. A tweed hat or cap is a useful precaution against unpredictable Irish weather.

Aran sweaters have been worn by west coast fishermen for generations. The patterns are so varied and intricate that it is said a drowned man could be recognised by his pullover alone. The báinin or undyed wool came originally from the Aran Islands and makes the garment warm and rain resistant. You can buy sweaters, cardigans, dresses, caps and mitts in Aran patterns. Ask for a card explaining the meaning of the pattern. A hand-knitted Aran sweater (more expensive than handloomed) will last for more than 15 years if looked after.

The north has a long tradition of weaving linen for tablecloths, sheets, handkerchiefs and garments, and Irish poplin is now woven in Cork. Locally-made pottery is on sale in most towns although Kilkenny is now the mecca for potters (and most other crafts). The tiny village of Belleek in Fermanagh is the home of delicate, almost transparent porcelain. Other well-known potteries are Noritake (Arklow), Stephen Pearce (Shanagarry, Co Cork) and Royal Tara. In these you can buy anything from an egg cup to a full dinner service.

Claddagh rings, celtic design plaques and jewellery in gold and silver are popular souvenirs and you can have a pendant engraved with your name in ogham (ancient Irish lettering). Every record shop stocks a selection of traditional Irish music. Among the well-known performers are the Chieftains, Clannad, The Dubliners, Paddy Reilly, the Furey Brothers and the Clancy Brothers. Irish publishers produce an enormous range of books on every aspect of Irish life and there are bookshops in every large town.

Rail

All train services in the Republic are operated by Iarnród Éireann-Irish Rail. Fast trains operate from Dublin to the main centres of population, namely Cork, Belfast, Sligo, Westport, Ballina, Galway, Limerick, Tralee, Waterford and Wexford. There are two main-line stations in Dublin: Connolly Station (Amiens St) runs services to Belfast, Sligo and Wexford/Rosslare. All other long distance trains depart from Heuston (Kingsbridge). The number 90 bus runs at regular intervals between the two stations.

Train frequency varies according to the route and time of year but there are at least three or four trains in each direction daily, and more to Cork and Belfast. The service is sparse on Sundays and public holidays.

The suburban rail lines in Dublin stretch from Drogheda to Greystones and westwards to Maynooth. There is also a new fast commuter train service on the east coast line between Dundalk and Arklow, and from Dublin to Maynooth and Kildare. The three city centre stations are Connolly, Tara Street and Pearse. The DART (Dublin Area Rapid Transit) electric service is a marvellous way

to get about on the 32 km (20 mile) coastal line. Trains run from early morning to late at night at 5 minute intervals during peak hours and every 15 minutes at other times.

There are many kinds of tickets available for use on Dublin public transport. Weekly and monthly commuter tickets are valid on suburban rail and all city bus services. Ten journey tickets can be bought for a specific journey and used without a time limit. Reduced fares at off-peak periods apply for journeys within the city centre.

Northern Ireland Railways (NIR) operate trains within Northern Ireland and run the Belfast–Dublin service jointly with Iarnród Éireann. From Belfast Central Station, trains run to Derry, Portrush, Bangor and Dublin. York Street (connecting bus from Central via the city centre) is the station for the ferryport of Larne. Local trains to Bangor, Portadown, Ballymena and Larne are frequent, with fare reductions for travel at certain times.

When travelling by train at peak times it may be worthwhile reserving a seat for a small charge. In addition, restaurant and buffet cars are provided on the main services where you can enjoy a drink, a snack or a full meal (served at your seat in first class). The food is in the main excellent and the service courteous. It is a very pleasant way to travel. Check that the train you are aiming for has a restaurant car.

Bus

Dublin has an extensive bus network, operated by Bus Átha Cliath/Dublin Bus. On weekdays,

The Antrim Coast Road near Larne, Co. Antrim

main services start just after 7am and run until just before midnight. Some all-night services run from the city centre to certain suburbs. An extensive feeder service links in to stations on the DART line, while Imp services and CitySwift services are new variations designed to be quicker. CitySwift services have a very limited number of stops. All main bus routes either traverse the city centre, going through O'Connell Street, or have their termini in the city centre, either along the quays or in adjacent streets, especially College Street, Fleet Street and Middle Abbey Street.

A regular express bus service connects Dublin airport, Heuston station, Connolly station and Bus Áras, the main provincial bus station. For the Stena Sealink ferry terminal at Dun Laoghaire, the 46A bus from Fleet Street has its Dun Laoghaire terminus near the ferry terminal. A special bus service connects the ferry terminal and Heuston station. For the Irish Ferries ferry terminal in Dublin, a bus service runs from Bus Áras, the city centre bus station in Store Street. The 53 and 53A bus routes can also be used.

A wide variety of commuter tickets is available, for different periods of bus use, from one day to one month, or even a year if you wish. Some tickets combine DART and suburban rail travel. These tickets offer reasonable savings, of about 10 per cent, on the cash price of bus tickets. These pre-paid tickets can be bought either at Dublin Bus headquarters, 59 Upper O'Connell Street, Dublin 1 or at a wide variety of shops in the greater Dublin area. They can also be bought at the CIE desk in Dublin airport. For full details of timetables, fares, etc. call Dublin Bus at 873 4222, Monday to Saturday, 9am–7pm.

Cash fares range from about 60 pence for the shortest distance, to about IR£1.20 for the longest. Fares are subject to price increases.

The only privately-owned, scheduled bus service in the greater Dublin area is the St Kevin's service, which starts outside the College of Surgeons at St Stephens Green, Dublin, and runs regular daily services to and from Glendalough, Co Wicklow. Telephone 281 8119 for details.

Belfast bus routes radiate out from the city centre and operate from about 6am until just before midnight. Buses from the city centre depart mostly from the City Hall area and pick up and set down passengers from clearly marked stops along the route.

You can either pay the driver upon boarding or present a 4-journey ticket. The latter may be purchased from the Citybus kiosks at Donegall Square West or Castle Place and at a wide variety of shops throughout the city, and represent a saving of about 20 per cent on the cash fare. A number of other discounted tickets are available. For full details of these and other bus information, telephone 246485.

Ulsterbus (out of town) scheduled services will pick up and set down passengers within the city on Sundays only (on Lisburn and Falls Road every day).

· The Rail-Link bus (No. 100), a regular bus service connecting the city's two train stations and the city centre, departs approximately every 15 minutes between 7.18am and 8.25pm (Monday to Saturday, no Sunday service) from both stations with stops at Royal Avenue, Donegall Place and Chichester Street in the city centre.

The airport bus runs every half hour from Monday – Saturday, from the Europa Bus Centre in

Glengall Street to Belfast International Airport and approximately every 45 minutes on Sundays, between 6am and 9.30pm.

The provincial bus network in Ireland is extensive; there is hardly a village in the country that does not have a bus passing through at some time or another. Some operate in conjunction with trains so that on arrival at the station you can continue your journey without delay. For example, buses to Dingle and Clifden connect with the Tralee and Galway trains respectively. Full details are available in the bus and train timetables. Expressway buses run between the major towns and cities on a number of routes not served by the railways. These include cross-border routes and services to Britain. Many buses start from Bus Áras, the Central (Provincial) Bus Station in Store Street, Dublin. This is also the starting point for the airport coach and Bus Éireann coach tours which can be booked for a half day or up to two weeks with accommodation and guides included.

Ulsterbus has a similar itinerary of provincial routes and express buses. These normally depart from two points in Belfast, the Europa Bus Centre in Glengall Street and the Oxford Street Bus Station. Tourist excursions run during the summer to the main beauty spots of Ulster. If you plan to use public transport a lot enquire about Rambler and Overlander tickets. These are valid for 8 or 15 days and give unlimited travel by rail or rail and bus. For a supplement you can include both Northern Ireland and the Republic in your itinerary. They are very good value indeed and cost no more than the price of two or three ordinary return tickets.

While timetables are issued for all services, it is worth enquiring ocally before setting out, specially in rural areas. xpressway buses are usually eliable but in remote areas the ocal bus may not adhere so ainstakingly to the schedule.

WHERE TO STAY

efore departure contact Bord áilte or the NITB in your own ountry for full information on the ange of accommodation available n Ireland. You can stay in anything om a hostel to a luxurious castle. n tourist board approved remises the rates are fixed and if ou wish you can make your ooking through the tourist office ee Useful Addresses). During the ummer it is advisable to book well n advance and remember that ome places close for part of the inter. Tourist staff will help you hoose accommodation and give dvice on eating out, excursions, ightseeing, shopping, public ansport, etc.

Each year Bord Fáilte and the ITB assess and grade hotels and uesthouses listed in their rochures, based on the overall tandard of accommodation and ervice. Grading also establishes ne maximum price which may be harged:

Hotels

Five star. Ireland's most luxurious hotels, with high international standards. These hotels have some of the country's finest restaurants.

Four star. Contemporary hotels of excellent quality and charming period houses renovated to high standards. Excellent restaurant cuisine.

Three star. These range from small, family operated premises to larger, modern hotels. All rooms have private bathroom. Restaurants offer high standards of cuisine.

Two star. Usually family operated premises, with all guest rooms having a telephone and most with a private bathroom. Dining facilities offer wholesome food.

One star. Simple hotels where mandatory services are to a satisfactory standard. Some guest rooms have a private bathroom.

Guesthouses

Four star. Accommodation includes half suites and all guest rooms have private bathroom and direct dial telephone. Many provide dinner.

Three star. All guest rooms have private bathrooms and direct dial telephones. Restaurant facilities in some guesthouses.

Two star. Half or more of the guest rooms have private bathrooms. Facilities include reading/writing room or lounge area. Some have restaurant facilities.

One star. These premises meet the mandatory requirements for guesthouses and offer simple accommodation. Some have restaurant facilities.

Town and Country Homes

A large number of houses in urban and rural areas ranging from period style houses to modern bungalows; evening meals by appointment.

Farmhouses

Many farming families offer accommodation in a unique rural setting where fresh farm produce and tranquillity are guaranteed. Ideal for children; evening meals by arrangement.

Self-Catering

Houses, cottages and apartments can be rented at numerous locations across the country with sleeping accommodation for up to 10 people. These are very popular and should be booked well in advance. Contact the Regional Tourism Organisation in the area of your choice for a list of such places (see Useful Addresses).

Camping and Caravanning

With quiet country roads and approved sites this can be a perfect holiday for those who don't want to rush. Many sites have shops, laundry, cafés and play areas for children.

Boating

Ireland's waterways are beautiful, uncrowded and clean and you can hire a fully equipped 2–8 berth cruiser. Cruisers are fitted with a fridge, cooker, central heating, hot water, shower, charts, dinghy, bed linen, crockery, etc. They are easy to handle and the inexperienced sailor can receive instruction before casting off. The River Shannon is the most popular cruising waterway but equally attractive are the Grand Canal, the River Barrow, the River Erne and the new Shannon–Erne Link. Hire companies are located at Carrick-on-Shannon, Co Leitrim; Whitegate, Co Clare; Portumna, Co Galway; Tullamore, Co Offaly; Athlone, Co Westmeath; Belturbet, Co Cavan; Kesh, Enniskillen, Killadeas, Lisbellaw, Bellanaleck, Co Fermanagh.

Rates

The current brochures from Bord Fáilte and the NITB contain the rates for all approved accommodation in Ireland. Check that these apply when booking. Reductions are usually available for children under 12 and those under 4 are free if they share their parents' bedroom. Special rates apply for full board and a stay for a week or longer; ask for details. Generally you will pay less and have greater choice outside the high season (July and August).

Please contact the tourist boards if you are particularly pleased with your accommodation. Likewise any complaints should be taken up with the manager in the first instance. Failing satisfaction, contact the Regional Tourism Organisation who will investigate the matter and if appropriate refer it to Bord Fáilte or the NITB. Every effort will be made to satisfy the complainant.

USEFUL INFORMATION

Tourist Information Offices

Bord Fáilte – Irish Tourist Board, PO Box 273, Dublin 8 (postal enquiries).
The following offices are open all year round or for most of the year. About fifty others are open only in summer (details from Bord Fáilte).
Athlone, The Castle, tel. (0902) 96430/92856.
Belfast, 53 Castle Street, Belfast BT1 1GH, tel. (01232) 327888, fax (01232) 240201.
Cashel, Town Hall, tel. (062) 61333.
Cork, Tourist House, Grand Parade, tel. (021) 273251, fax (021) 273504.
Derry, Foyle Street, tel./fax (01504) 369501.
Dublin, 14 Upper O'Connell Street, tel. (01) 284 4768, fax (01) 284 1751. St Andrews church, St Andrew Street, due to open 1995.
Dundalk, Market Square, tel. (042) 35484, fax (042) 38070.
Dun Laoghaire, St Michael's Wharf, tel. (01) 284 4768, fax (01) 284 1751.
Ennis, Bank Place, tel. (065) 28366.
Galway, Eyre Square, tel. (091) 583081, fax (091) 585201.
Kilkenny, Rose Inn Street, tel. (056) 51500, fax (056) 63955.

Killarney, Town Hall, tel. (064) 31633, fax (064) 34506.
Letterkenny, Derry Road, tel. (074) 21160, fax (074) 25180.
Limerick, Arthur's Quay, tel. (061) 317522, fax (061) 317939.
Mullingar, Dublin Road, tel. (044) 48650, fax (044) 40413.
Nenagh, Kickham Road, tel. (067) 31610.
Rosslare Harbour, tel. (053) 33622, fax, (053) 33421.
Shannon Airport, tel. (061) 471664.
Skibbereen, North Street, tel. (028) 21766, fax (028) 21353.
Sligo, Temple Street, tel. (071) 61201, fax (071) 60360.
Tralee, Godfrey Place, tel. (066) 21288.
Waterford, 41 The Quay, tel. (051) 75788, fax (051) 77388.
Westport, The Mall, tel. (098) 25711, fax (098) 26709.
Wexford, Crescent Quay, tel. (053) 23111, fax (053) 41743.
Wicklow Town, Fitzwilliam Square, tel. (0404) 69117.

Regional Tourism Organisation
Cork/Kerry, Tourist House, Grand Parade, Cork, tel. (021) 273251, fax (021) 273504.
Donegal/Leitrim/Sligo, Temple Street, Sligo, tel. (071) 61201, fax (071) 60360.
Dublin, 1 Clarinda Park East, Dun Laoghaire, Co Dublin, tel. (01) 280 8571, fax (01) 280 2641.
Midland East Tourism (Kildare, Louth, Wicklow, Meath, Cavan, Laois, Longford, Monaghan, Offaly, Roscommon, Westmeath) Dublin Road, Mullingar, tel. (044) 48650, fax (044) 40413.
Shannon Development (Clare, Limerick, North Tipperary, South East Offaly, North Kerry), Shannon, Co Clare, tel. (061) 361555, fax (061) 361903.
South-Eastern (Carlow, Kilkenny, South Tipperary, Waterford,

exford), 41 The Quay,
aterford, tel. (051) 75788, fax
)51) 77388.
eland West (Galway, Mayo),
ctoria Place, Eyre Square,
alway, tel. (091) 583081, fax
)91) 585201.

.I. Tourist Offices (all year)

number of offices open summer
ıly; details from NITB.
rmagh, 40 English Street, tel.
)1861) 527808.
allycastle, 7 Mary Street, tel.
)12657) 62024.
anbridge, Newry Road, tel.
)18206) 23322.
angor, 34 Quay Street, tel.
)1247) 270069.
elfast, 59 North Street, tel.
)1232) 246609.
ookstown, 48 Molesworth
reet, tel. (016487) 66727.
erry, 8 Bishop Street, tel.
)1504) 267284.
nniskillen, Wellington Road, tel.
)1365) 323110.
ungannon, Ballygawley Road,
l. (01868) 767259/725311.
rne, Narrow Gauge Road, tel.
)1574) 260088.
rne Harbour, tel. (01574)
70517.
mavady, Benevenagh Drive, tel.
)15047) 22226.
magh, l Market Street, tel.
)1662) 247831/2.

avel

ır

elfast City Airport, tel. (01232)
57745.
elfast International Airport, tel.
)18494) 22888.
ork Airport, tel. (021) 313131.
erry Airport, tel. (01504)
l0784.
ublin Airport, tel. (01) 844
)00.
ıannon Airport, tel. (061)
71444.

Rail

Connolly Station, Amiens Street,
Dublin, tel. (01) 836 3333.
Heuston Station, Dublin, tel.
(01) 836 3333. Passenger
enquiries, Dublin, tel. (01) 836
6222.
Belfast Central Station, tel.
(01232) 899400.
Yorkgate Station, Belfast, tel.
(01232) 899400. Passenger
enquiries, Belfast, tel. (01232)
230310.

Bus

Bus Éireann, Bus Áras central bus
station, Dublin, tel. (01) 836 6111.
Dublin Bus, Dublin, tel. (01) 873
4222.
CIE Tours International, Lower
Abbey Street, Dublin 1, tel. (01)
677 1871.
Citybus, Belfast, tel. (01232)
246485.
Ulsterbus, Belfast, tel. (01232)
333000.
Europa Bus Station, Glengall
Street, Belfast, tel. (01232)
320574.
Oxford Street Bus Station,
Belfast, tel. (01232) 232356.

Embassies

Australia, 6th floor, Fitzwilton
House, Wilton Terrace, Dublin 2,
tel. (01) 676 1517.
Belgium, 2 Shrewsbury Road,
Dublin 4, tel. (01) 269 2082.
Canada, 65 St Stephen's Green,
Dublin 2, tel. (01) 478 1988.
France, 36 Ailesbury Road,
Dublin 4, tel. (01) 260 1666.
Germany, 31 Trimleston Avenue,
Booterstown, Co Dublin, tel.
(01) 269 3011.
Italy, 63 Northumberland Road,
Dublin 4, tel. (01) 660 1744.
Netherlands, 160 Merrion Road,
Dublin 4, tel. (01) 269 3444.
Spain, 17a Merlyn Park, Dublin 4,
tel. (01) 269 1640.

Switzerland, 6 Ailesbury Road,
Dublin 4, tel. (01) 269 2515.
United Kingdom, 33 Merrion
Road, Dublin 4, tel. (01) 269
5211.
United States of America, 42
Elgin Road, Dublin 4, tel. (01)
668 8777.

Cultural Institutes

Goethe Institut, 37 Merrion
Square, Dublin 2, tel. (01) 676
6451.
Alliance Française, 1 Kildare
Street, Dublin 2, tel. (01) 676
1732.
Instituto Italiano di Cultura, 11
Fitzwilliam Square, Dublin, 2, tel.
(01) 676 6662.
Instituto Cervantes (Spanish), 58
Northumberland Road, Dublin 4,
tel. (01) 668 2024.

Government Offices

Department of Foreign Affairs, 80
St Stephen's Green, Dublin 2,
tel. (01) 478 0822.
Government Information
Services, Upper Merrion Street,
Dublin 2, tel. (01) 660 7555.
European Commission Press &
Information Office, 39
Molesworth Street, tel. (01) 671
2244.
National Library, Kildare Street,
Dublin 2, tel. (01) 661 8811.
National Museum, Kildare Street,
Dublin 2, tel. (01) 661 8811.
Northern Ireland Information
Office, Stormont Castle, Belfast,
BT4 3ST, tel. (01232) 763255.

If you plan a touring holiday it is worth contacting your local automobile association and the tourist board beforehand. They will supply you with full details of the rules of the road, insurance, breakdown services, petrol, road signs, etc. Most of this information can be had in Ireland but it is better to find out before you arrive. Bring your driving licence and insurance certificate, and display a nationality plate if bringing your car into Ireland.

There are lots of sea routes to choose from. Irish Ferries operate car ferries from Holyhead-Dublin, Pembroke-Rosslare; Sealink: Holyhead-Dun Laoghaire, Fishguard-Rosslare; Stranraer-Larne; Norse Irish Car Ferries: Liverpool-Belfast; Townsend Thoresen: Cairnryan-Larne; Irish Ferries: Le Havre-Rosslare, Le Havre-Cork; Cherbourg–Rosslare; Brest–Rosslare; Brittany Ferries: Roscoff-Cork; Swansea-Cork; Seacat: Stranraer-Belfast. There are also regular summer sailings from the Isle of Man to Belfast and Dublin.

Cars can be hired from a number of companies in Ireland. Bord Fáilte and the NITB will supply you with a list of authorised car hire firms and you can pick up your chauffeured or self-drive car at the port or airport. If you plan

to cross the border check with the hire company that your insurance is valid north and south. Rates vary according to the model, time of year and hire period. Weekend rates are good value especially in the off-season. Make sure you know whether the rate is for limited or unlimited mileage. You can also save money by transferring your own insurance to the hire car.

You can avail of numerous packages involving travel by sea or air and a self-drive car for the duration of your holiday. Hotel or farmhouse accommodation can be included. If you choose to stay in one area you can arrange your holiday through CIE, travelling by train to Galway or Killarney, for example, and picking up a car at the station. For full details of all these combinations and special offers contact your local tourist board, Aer Lingus, Irish Ferries or CIE (see Useful Addresses).

Ireland has the lowest population density in Europe so there is lots of room on the roads, which makes driving a pleasure. The speed limit is 112 kmph (70 mph) on motorways, 96 kmph (60 mph) outside towns and 48 kmph (30 mph) in towns. On motorways and dual carriageways in Northern Ireland the speed limit is 112 kmph (70 mph); otherwise the limits are as in the Republic. In the Republic roads are classed as motorway (M7), national primary (N5), secondary (N71) and regional (R691). In the north you will find motorways (M1), class A (A5) and class B (B52) roads. However, when seeking directions it is more common to refer to "the Longford Road" than "the N4". The road network is very extensive and while the principal highways are good those in more remote areas will vary. In the country watch out for cows, sheep and other animals being herded along the road.

You will find most routes we signposted although there may n be much advance warning. It hard to get really lost and in a case it is a pleasure to drift along country road admiring th countryside. Ask someone on th road or stop at a country pub shop and you'll get all th directions you need and a gre deal more besides. Placenames a written in Irish and English in th Republic and signposts increasin ly give distances in kilometre Motorists should take care whe reading roadsigns since at prese some distances are given in mil and some in kilometres.

In Ireland drive on the left ar yield to traffic from the right. drivers and front-seat passenge must wear a seat belt at all time the gardai (police) are likely stop you for not wearing on Children under twelve are n allowed on front seats. While Dublin you would be advised park your car in an attended c park, place all valuables in the bo and lock the car securely. Illegal parked cars in Dublin are liable be towed away by the Gard Parking is unrestricted in count towns and there are many lay-by picnic sites and beauty spots whe you can pull in to take a break fro driving. You must not park in tow centres in Northern Ireland. F security reasons these are class as control zones and unattende cars will be removed. Watch o also for ramps and be prepared stop for security checks.

Roadsigns of various kinds a in operation. Hazards are inc cated by black and yellow symbc on a diamond shaped boar Speed limits and parki restrictions are shown by bla spots which are clearly marke These often indicate dangero junctions or very sharp bends ar can be deceptive, especially night. An unbroken white line in the centre of the road indicates that overtaking is forbidden.

Parking meters are common in cities although you can park at one after 6pm without charge. The meter works by clocking up one or two hours according to the number of coins inserted. A single yellow line next to the kerb allows parking for a short period only. A double yellow line forbids parking at any time. In Cork and parts of other cities, including Dublin, you must display a parking disc inside the car indicating the time of day. These may be bought from newsagents and tobacconists. Bus lanes operate in cities and are reserved for buses and cyclists at certain times of the day. Watch out for the signs. Although some leniency is extended to visitors it is worthwhile observing the traffic regulations otherwise you risk being fined or having your car towed away!

TEN TOURING IDEAS

These ten scenic tours are designed to help you get the most from your motoring holiday in Ireland – to show you the most beautiful scenery, and to introduce you to Ireland's many interesting cities and towns. As all ten tours are circular you can commence at any point of the given routes. The daily distance covered is shown with each tour, in kilometres and miles. Included are maps of the ten tours, with alternative routes indicated by broken lines.

TOUR OF IRELAND

A ten-day tour over 1,600 kilometres (1,000 miles), suggested starting point – Dublin.

Tour of Ireland

Day 1: Dublin–Tramore 190 km (118 miles).

Having seen Dublin's historic buildings and Georgian squares and having sampled its lively cosmopolitan atmosphere, you're on your way to Enniskerry, a pretty hillside village just 19 km (12 miles) south of the city. Nearby you can visit the splendid Powerscourt Estate, with its gardens, deer herd and waterfall. Continue on through Roundwood to Glendalough and see the ruins of an early-Christian settlement in a beautiful wild setting of mountains and lakes. Your next stop, via Rathdrum, is Avoca, made famous by Thomas Moore's song "The Meeting of the Waters". Southwards is the prominent holiday resort of Arklow, overlooking the sea. Onwards to Enniscorthy, with its old-world charm – just 53 km (33 miles) from the car ferry port of Rosslare Harbour – and then by New Ross, with its twisting lanes and Dutch-type houses, to Waterford. Or visit Wexford and on to Waterford by the Ballyhack-Passage East car ferry. Spend your first night at Tramore, a family resort with 4 km (3 miles) of sandy beaches.

Day 2: Tramore–Cork 117 km (73 miles).

After lunch leave for Cork, via

Dungarvan and Youghal, a popular holiday resort. Continue through the market town of Midleton to Cork. Enjoy the friendly atmosphere of Cork, built on the banks of the River Lee. Visit St Mary's Shandon, where the famous Shandon Bells can be played by visitors, and admire the many fine public buildings.

Day 3: Cork–Killarney 151 km (94 miles).

Leaving Cork on the third day your first stop is Blarney Castle with its famous stone, said to impart the gift of eloquence to all who kiss it! Continue through Macroom, Ballingeary, Pass of Keimaneigh – 3 km (2 miles) from Gougane Barra Forest Park, Ballylickey, and into the beautiful holiday resort of Glengarriff. Then in a northerly direction you drive through Kenmare into Killarney, enjoying one of the finest scenic drives on the way. You'll find plenty to do in Killarney – pony riding, boating and visiting islands and ancient abbeys. Drive around the 'Ring of Kerry', a brilliant 174 km (109 mile) scenic drive bringing you to Killorglin, Cahirsiveen, Waterville, Sneem, Parknasilla, Kenmare and back to Killarney.

Day 4: Killarney

It's worth spending a day in Killarney, setting out the next day for Galway.

Day 5: Killarney–Galway 251 km (156 miles).

On the fifth day your drive takes you through Abbeyfeale, Newcastle West, the lovely village of Adare, and into Limerick, 25 km (16 miles) from Shannon Airport on the River Shannon, a graceful and historic city, featuring King John's Castle, the Treaty Stone and

Glencolumbkille, near Ardara, Co. Donegal

St Mary's Cathedral. Traditional medieval banquets can be enjoyed at Bunratty Castle, 13 km (8 miles) from Limerick, and Knappogue Castle, 13 km (8 miles) from Ennis. Continuing on you reach Ennis with its old abbey and the seaside resort of Lahinch, featuring excellent golf courses. You should make your next stop by the breathtaking Cliffs of Moher, before driving to Lisdoonvarna, Ireland's premier spa. Drive through the bare limestone hills of the Burren to Ballyvaughan, to Kinvarra (medieval banquets at Dunguaire Castle), Clarinbridge and into Galway. Galway is the capital of the 'Western World' with its famous Spanish Arch and Church of St Nicholas, where, tradition holds, Columbus prayed before sailing to America.

Day 6: Galway–Westport 138 km (86 miles).

The next day your route through Connemara takes you to Moycullen, Oughterard, Recess, Clifden (capital of Connemara), Leenane and Westport on Clew Bay, with over 100 islands.

Day 7: Westport–Bundoran 154 km (96 miles).

Head north next day to Castlebar, Pontoon, Ballina and the family resort of Enniscrone. Enjoy a swim before driving on to Sligo, where you can look around the 13th c. Franciscan Friary and the museum, situated in the county library. Head on to Drumcliff (burial place of W.B. Yeats) to complete your day's driving at Bundoran.

Day 8: Bundoran–Dunfanaghy 193 km (120 miles).

On the following day head further up the Atlantic Coast through Ballyshannon to Donegal town, visiting the Franciscan Friary and castle. Drive through Dunkineely,

Ardara, Glenties, Maas and Kinscasslagh noted for their cottage industries and Donegal tweed. Then by Annagry, Crolly, Bunbeg, Bloody Foreland, Gortahork into Dunfanaghy, nestling in the cosy inlet of Sheephaven Bay.

Day 9: Dunfanaghy–Carrick-on-Shannon 177 km (110 miles).

Next day your tour takes you south via Portnablagh to Letterkenny – Donegal's chief town. This is an excellent point from which to extend your drive, by taking the 'Inishowen 100' an extremely scenic trip around the Inishowen Peninsula, to Buncrana, Malin Head and Moville. Return to Letterkenny by Bloody Foreland and Manorcunningham. Total mileage for the trip is 193 km (120 miles). Continue south through the picturesque Finn Valley to the twin towns of Stranorlar and Ballybofey, completing your round trip of County Donegal in Donegal town. The next stage takes you to Ballyshannon and Bundoran in a southerly direction to Manorhamilton. Overlooking the town you'll see the picturesque ruin of Sir Frederick Hamilton's castle – built in 1638. Continue south through Drumkeeran along the beautiful shores of Lough Allen into Drumshanbo. Drive on through Leitrim into Carrick-on-Shannon, an important cruising and angling centre.

Day 10: Carrick-on-Shannon–Dublin 240 km (150 miles).

On the final day head for Cavan, travelling by Mohill, Carrigallen, Killeshandra and Crossdoney, enjoying the lake scenery on the way. Continue to Bailieborough – 14 km (9 miles) from the important angling centre of Virginia and into the attractive town of Carrickmacross. The last stage of your trip takes you to Drogheda –

Sunset over Lough Key, Co. Roscommon

a historic town in Co. Louth. From Drogheda visit the prehistoric tombs at Newgrange, Knowth and Dowth. Drive on by Slane into Navan. 10 km (6 miles) from here see the Hill of Tara, a former residence of Irish High Kings. Complete your tour of the Boyne Valley in Trim, rich in historical associations and ancient monuments, before returning to Dublin, via Black Bull, Clonee, Blanchardstown and the Phoenix Park.

The following alternative two-day route from Dunfanaghy to Dublin takes in the Antrim Coast and the Mourne Mountains.

Day 9: Dunfanaghy–Belfast 240 km (150 miles).
Take the road from Dunfanaghy to Letterkenny, travelling north-east from here to Londonderry (you will cross the border into Northern Ireland at Bridgend). Stop to explore this historic city on the banks of the River Foyle, whose walls (the only remaining unbroken fortifications in either Britain or Ireland) afford superb views of the surrounding countryside and of the city itself. Continue north-east to Limavady, Downhill, Castlerock and Coleraine and on to the bracing seaside resort of Portrush. Then follow the coastal road eastwards to see the famous Giant's Causeway, the beautiful beaches at White Park Bay and the Carrick-a-Rede Rope Bridge (not for the faint-hearted). The steep, winding road around Torr Head and down to picturesque Cushendun is worth the slight detour – views are breathtaking. From Cushendun head for Larne, departure point for ferries to Scotland. The final stage of your journey takes you to Belfast via Carrickfergus, where you can visit the country's best-preserved Norman castle.

Day 10: Belfast–Dublin 192 km (120 miles)
The last day of your tour takes you south out of Belfast through the heart of County Down towards the spectacular Mourne Mountains. Stop at Downpatrick en route to see Down Cathedral, in whose churchyard you will find St Patrick's grave marked by a crude slab. Continue towards Newcastle, County Down's most popular holiday resort, where, in the words of the song, "The Mountains of Mourne sweep down to the sea." Stroll along the beach at Dundrum or, if you're feeling energetic, make an assault on Slieve Donard (the

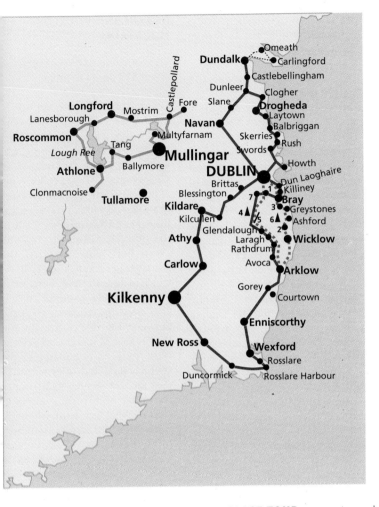

East Coast Tour

Dublin and Wicklow Mountains

Lakeland Tour

1 Enniskerry
2 Delgany
3 Kilmacanogue
4 *Kippure*
5 *Sally Gap*
6 *Djouce*
7 *Glencree*

Kilometres
0   40

Miles
0   20

Mournes' highest peak), which can be reached either through Donard Park or from Bloody Bridge (just outside Newcastle). Follow the road from Newcastle via Kilkeel and Warrenpoint to Newry, cross the border into the Republic, then continue to Dundalk whose surrounding hills and forests are full of history and charm. Then make your way south to Drogheda (stopping at Monasterboice on the way to admire one of the most magnificent High Crosses in the country). From Drogheda, the mysterious passage tomb of Newgrange is easily accessible and well worth a visit. The last stretch of road takes you south into Dublin city.

EAST COAST TOUR

Two circular tours – one north, the other south of Dublin.

Day 1: Northern tour 306 km (190 miles).
Take the Navan road out of Dublin to Tara site of a former royal acropolis, situated in an area rich in ancient monuments and historical associations. Continue north to Navan, Donaghmore and Slane. Visit the Bronze Age cemeteries at Brugh na Boinne, King William's Glen, Mellifont Abbey and Monasterboice, before heading for Dunleer, Castlebellingham and Dundalk – an ideal base for explor-

ing the surrounding countryside. If you wish you can travel further north to see the delightfully rugged Carlingford Peninsula, taking you through Ballymascanlon, Carlingford, Omeath and back into Dundalk.

Heading south you reach Castlebellingham, Clogher, Termonfeckin, Baltray, with its fine beach and golf course and on into Drogheda, on the River Boyne. In Bettystown, further south, there's a long sandy beach linking up with Laytown, while further on is Julianstown. Following the coast enjoy a pleasant drive through Balbriggan, Skerries, Rush, Lusk, Swords and Howth, stopping to admire the magnificent views from the rocky Hill of Howth. Return to Dublin via Sutton.

Day 2: Southern Tour 467 km (290 miles).

Next day the southern tour takes you through Dun Laoghaire, Dalkey and Killiney – with its magnificent view over the bay from the Vico Road – into Bray, one of Ireland's premier seaside resorts. Continuing on you reach Enniskerry, a pretty village beneath the Sugarloaf Mountain and near the beautiful Powerscourt Estate. The scenic mountain drive takes you to Glendalough, with its ancient ruins and picturesque lakes, passing through Glencree, Glenmacnass and Laragh. If you wish you can return to Dublin by Blessington, making a short but enjoyable trip – or keep south to Rathdrum, Avoca and Woodenbridge into Arklow, where you can enjoy a swim or go sea fishing. Driving on through County Wexford takes you to Gorey, Courtown Harbour (seaside resort), Ferns, Enniscorthy and Wexford, which is within easy reach of Rosslare Harbour. These charming old towns are well worth a visit. Follow the coast through Rosslare, Duncormick, Arthurstown and into New Ross. From here take the road to Kilkenny, a cheerful city steeped in history. Visit the Kilkenny Design Workshops, Rothe House and Kilkenny Castle. Return to Dublin through Carlow and County Kildare towns of Athy, Kildare, Kilcullen, and Ballymore Eustace, taking in the lake drive near Blessington and reaching the city via Brittas.

LAKELAND TOUR

This is a two-day circular drive of about 240 km (150 miles). This tour of Ireland's quiet heart offers a charm of a different kind from the coastal tours.

Day 1: Athlone–Mullingar 135 km (84 miles).

The starting point is Athlone – capital of the midlands. From here drive to Roscommon visiting Hodson Bay and Rinndown Castle en route. Have a look around Roscommon Abbey. North-east of Roscommon is Lanesborough, a popular angling centre at the head of Lough Ree. Then visit the busy market town of Longford with its nineteenth-century cathedral. Move on to Edgeworthstown, which gets its name from the remarkable literary family. Continue to Castlepollard, a good angling centre near Lough Derravaragh which is featured in the tragic myth "The Children of Lir". See nearby Tullynally Castle. Drive to Fore, with its ancient crosses and Benedictine Abbey, returning to Castlepollard and south via Multyfarnham to Mullingar – an important town and noted angling centre. Spend the night there.

Day 2: Mullingar–Athlone 105 km (65 miles).

Next day a westward drive takes you to Ballymore and to the Goldsmith country via Tang. Visit Lissoy and The Pigeons on the road to the pretty village of Glasson, passing the tower-like structure marking the geographical centre of Ireland. Return to Athlone.

From Athlone make an excursion to Coosan Point for a good view of Lough Ree, one of the largest Shannon lakes. Going downriver it's worth a visit to Clonmacnois, one of the country's most celebrated holy places, completing your tour in Athlone.

DUBLIN AND WICKLOW MOUNTAINS

This is a one-day scenic tour of about 177 km (110 miles).

Leave Dublin by the suburb of Rathfarnham, 6 km (4 miles) south of the city. The ruined building known as "The Hell Fire Club" forms a prominent landmark to the summit of Mount Pelier, 6 km (4 miles) south of Rathfarnham. Drive via Glencullen, Kilternan and the Scalp into Enniskerry – one of the prettiest villages in Ireland. From here you can visit the Powerscourt Estate and Gardens, which include the highest waterfall in these islands. Continue to Sally Gap, a notable crossroads situated between Kippure Mountain and the Djouce Mountain, where the road leads to Glendalough, by Glenmacnass and Laragh. Have a look around Glendalough – one of the most picturesque glens of County Wicklow with extensive ruins of the 6th c. Irish monastery of St. Kevin. Drive on through Laragh by the Military Road to Rathdrum. Head south by the Vale of Avoca into Arklow, a popular holiday centre. From Arklow drive north to Wicklow where you can admire the view over the bay. Ashford is the next village on your route close by the beautiful Mount Usher Gardens with countless varieties of trees, plants and shrubs. Move on through the rugged Devil's Glen to Newtownmountkennedy, Delgany and into the attractive resort of Greystones, which retains the atmosphere of the former quiet fishing village. Head back through Delgany to the Glen of the Downs, Kilmacanogue (from where you can climb the great Sugar Loaf) into Bray. From this fine resort at the base of Bray Head take the route to Killiney and the Vico Road to Dalkey, enjoying

Kate Kearney's cottage, Co. Kerry

the superb views of Killiney Bay. Follow the coast road to Dun Laoghaire into Dublin.

SOUTH-WEST TOUR

This is a two-day circular tour of about 700 km (440 miles) on main route.

Day 1: Cork–Killarney 359 km (223 miles).

The suggested starting point is Cork – a charming city on the River Lee, excellent for shopping and offering first-class pubs and restaurants with entertainment for every member of the family. Blarney Castle, with its famous Stone of Eloquence is 8 km (5 miles) away. Visit there to kiss the stone, before continuing to the old-world town of Kinsale. Drive on to Timoleague – where you'll see the remains of the once largest friary in Ireland – to Clonakilty, Rosscarbery, Glandore, Union Hall and Skibbereen. Continue this exceptionally beautiful drive through Ballydehob, Schull, Toormore, Durrus and Bantry into Glengarriff – visiting the Forest Park and Garinish Island, with its ornate gardens. Afterwards take the "Tunnel Road" to Kenmare or head west over the Healy Pass.

Some of the finest sea and mountain scenery in Ireland can be enjoyed on the next stage of the tour, around the 'Ring of Kerry' through Sneem, Castlegrove, Derrynane, Waterville, Cahirciveen, Glenbeigh and Killorglin into Killarney. There are some lovely quiet beaches in this region for example Rossbeigh near Glenbeigh. Spend the night in Killarney.

Day 2: Killarney–Cork 352 km (220 miles).

From Killarney drive direct to Tralee or alternatively explore the Dingle Peninsula, the heart of *Ryan's Daughter* country. Places along the route are: Inch, Anascaul, Dingle, Ventry, Slea Head, Dunquin, Ballyferriter, Murreagh, back to Dingle and on through Stradbally and Camp to Tralee. An unforgettable drive of breathtaking beauty. Follow the coast from Tralee to Ardfert, Ballyheigue, Causeway, Ballyduff, Lisselton Cross Roads, Ballylongford, and Tarbert, where a car ferry operates to Killimer, Co Clare. Drive through Foynes along the Shannon Estuary via Askeaton to Limerick – an old and historic city, not far from Bunratty Castle, with its medieval-style banquets.

Having spent some time look-

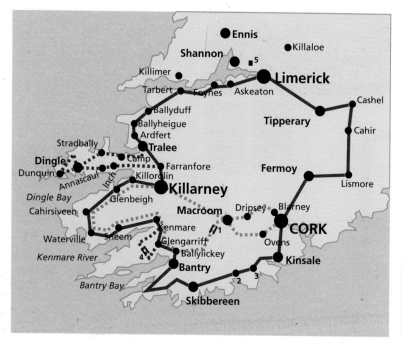

South-West Tour

Cork and "Ring of Kerry"

1 *Keimanagh Pass*
2 *Clonakilty*
3 *Timoleague*
4 *Healy Pass*
5 *Bunratty*

Kilometres
0   40

Miles
0   20

ing around Limerick, head back to Cork through Tipperary and Cashel, visiting the magnificent ruins of the Rock of Cashel – including a cathedral, castle, chapel and round tower. Enjoy the mountain views on the way to historic Cahir and into Cork by Clogheen, Lismore and Fermoy, providing a splendid trip through the Knockmealdown Mountains.

CORK AND 'RING OF KERRY'

A one-day tour about 354 km (220 miles).

Travel west from Cork via Ovens to Macroom. Turn off for Toon Bridge and Inchigeelagh through the wild mountain scenery of the Pass of Keimaneigh into Bally-lickey. Along the way you could visit Gougane Barra Forest Park which is just north of your route.
From Ballylickey enjoy the superb views of Bantry Bay en route to Glengarriff, from where you can visit the beautiful Italian

gardens of Garinish Island. Head north to Kenmare through rugged mountains. Here your trip around the 'Ring of Kerry' begins encircling the Iveragh Peninsula, which features Ireland's highest mountains, the Macgillycuddy's Reeks. Excellent views are provided over Dingle Bay to the north and the estuary of the Kenmare River to the south. Travel south-west through Parknasilla and Sneem, into Caherdaniel, where you'll find excellent swimming and diving along the fine beach. Go north to the well-known resort of Waterville, continuing your tour by Cahirsiveen, Glenbeigh and Killorglin, completing this excep-tionally scenic trip to Killarney.
Your route back to Cork takes you through the Derrynasaggart Mountains to Macroom, turning off the main road for Dripsey and Blarney Castle, where you can stop to kiss the famous Blarney Stone.

WEST COAST TOUR

This is a four-day circular tour of about 842 km (523 miles).

Day 1: Athlone–Limerick 151 km (94 miles).
Athlone is the suggested starting point for a tour of this richly varied region. From this impressive town south of Lough Ree you pass the early-Christian site of Clonmacnois to the south and on to Birr, where the gardens of Birr Castle are open to visitors. Driving in a southerly direction you come to Nenagh with its fine castle, built about 1200. Continue via Portroe with fine views over Lough Derg into Killaloe, a popular water-skiing centre. From here drive to O'Brien's Bridge, Ardnacrusha and on to Limerick for the night.

Day 2: Limerick–Galway 232 km (144 miles).
Having seen the sights of Limerick head for Bunratty Castle where medieval banquets are held, and

visit the Bunratty Folk Park. Drive south-west from Ennis to the resorts of Kilrush and Kilkee, going north to Lahinch and around Liscannor Bay to the magnificent ruggedness of the Cliffs of Moher, reaching up to 213 m (700 ft). Move on to Ireland's premier spa, Lisdoonvarna, enjoying the remarkable "Burren Country", consisting of a desert of bare limestone hills which are a botanist's paradise in the spring. Take the road from Lisdoonvarna through Black Head, Ballyvaughan, Kinvarra and Clarinbridge into Galway. Discover Galway for your-self – its Church of St Nicholas, the Spanish Arch and the gathering of salmon (in season) under the Salmon Weir Bridge.

Day 3: Galway–Westport 196 km (122 miles).

Next day start your tour of Connemara by Spiddal, Costelloe, Screeb, Gortmore, Carna, Toombeola, Ballynahinch and Glendalough. From Clifden you head northwards to Tullycross and on to Leenane, on the corner of picturesque Killary Harbour. Drive northwards through the mountains to Louisburgh, in the shadow of Croagh Patrick. Stop in Westport, an important sea angling centre. Alternatively you can get from Leenane to Westport through Joyce Country, talking you to Maam, Cong, Ballinrobe, Partry Mountains, Ballintubber with its famous abbey and into Westport.

Day 4: Westport–Athlone 262 km (163 miles).

The following day explore the beauties of Achill Island, taking the road to Newport, Mulrany, through Curraun Peninsula, Achill Sound and on to Keel and Dooagh. Return via Newport to Castlebar,

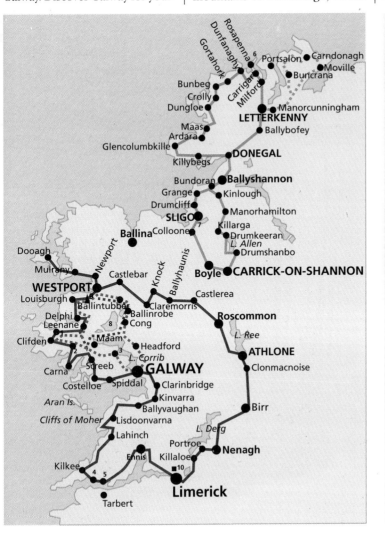

West Coast Tour

Galway and Connemara

Donegal and Yeats Country

1 Letterfrack
2 Recess
3 Oughterard
4 Kilrush
5 Killimer
6 *Rosguill Peninsula*
7 *L. Glencar*
8 *L. Mask*
9 *Croagh Patrick*
10 *Bunratty*

Kilometres
0   40

Miles
0   20

visiting Clonalis House. Then on to Claremorris, Ballyhaunis, Castlerea, Roscommon and back to Athlone.

GALWAY AND CONNEMARA

This is a one-day tour of about 257 km (160 miles)

Travel north-west of Galway to the pretty village of Oughterard, with views of Lough Corrib along the way. Continue through the rugged countryside of Connemara, dominated by the craggy peaks of the Twelve Bens, via Maam Cross and Recess into Clifden – the capital of Connemara.

From Clifden drive to Letterfrack and on to Leenane, at the head of picturesque Killary Harbour. Along the way you'll see the magnificent Kylemore Abbey. Having left Leenane, turn off the main road and head for Louisburgh and Westport, passing Doo Lough and the lofty Croagh Patrick. The town of Westport was designed by James Wyatt – an architect of the Georgian period. Castlebar, principal town of County Mayo, is the next on your route offering you a charming old-world atmosphere. Of particular note is the pleasant tree-lined Mall. Return to Galway by Ballintubber with its impressive abbey, Ballinrobe and Headford.

DONEGAL AND YEATS COUNTRY

This is a two-day circular tour over 515 km (320 miles) on main route.

Day 1: Carrick-on-Shannon–Carrigart 322 km (200 miles).
The popular centre of Carrick-on-Shannon well known for cruising

Near Recess, Co. Galway

and coarse fishing is the starting point for this tour. The first town on this route is Boyle – 3 km (2 miles) from Lough Key Forest Park, with its numerous facilities, from boating to nature trails. Your drive will continue to Collooney, entering the magical country of Yeats. Share his experiences as you drive through Ballisodare, Kilmacowen and Strandhill on your way to Sligo, a beautifully situated town, surrounded by mountains. Pay a visit to Sligo Abbey and the museum, situated in the county library. Follow the road through Drumcliff (Yeats' burial place) to Grange and Cliffoney into Bundoran – a resort where you'll find enjoyment for all the family.

Begin your tour of Donegal from Ballyshannon, heading north to Donegal town and on to Killybegs by way of Mountcharles, Inver and Dunkineely. Following the coast to Glencolumbkille, a popular holiday centre, you are now in a part of Ireland's 'Gaeltacht' or Irish speaking region. This area of Donegal is noted for its excellent crafts and the production of handmade Donegal tweed. From Glencolumbkille head east to Ardara, Maas and Dungloe – a remarkable tract of rocky lakeland. Drive north from Crolly to the lovely fishing village of Bunbeg, along the coast to Gortahork and Dunfanaghy, with its lovely beaches and superb cliff scenery. Turn off at Creeslough for Carrigart beautifully situated on Mulroy Bay. Spend the night here.

Day 2: Carrigart–Carrick-on-Shannon 193 km (120 miles).
From Carrigart there is a charming 19 km (12 miles) trip around the little Rosguill Peninsula, taking in Tranarossan Bay and Rosapenna. Continue south to Letterkenny via Milford. Before driving south for Donegal town again you could

take a trip around the Inishowen Peninsula, an extra 192 km (129 miles) in all, giving unrivalled views, a top class resort at Buncrana and some very interesting antiquities, such as the cross of Carndonagh. Complete your tour from Donegal by Ballyshannon, Bundoran, Kinlough, Manorhamilton, Killarga, Drumkeeran and along the shores of Lough Allen by Drumshanbo into Carrick-on-Shannon.

NORTH-EAST TOUR

Two circular tours – one north, the other south of Belfast.

Day 1: North Coast Tour 288 km (180 miles).
Travel north out of Belfast through Carrickfergus to the car ferry port of Larne. Continue along the scenic route to Cushendall and Ballycastle, enjoying the gently scooped-out contours of the Antrim Glens to your left. (You can turn inland to visit Glenariff Forest Park, where wooded paths lead to superb viewpoints.) Continue to the popular town of Ballycastle famous for its Ould Lammas Fair – before following the road to Portrush via the Giant's Causeway. (Bushmills, home of the world's oldest distillery, is only 5 km (3 miles) away, and can be visited.) Pass through Portrush and Coleraine towards Downhill and Limavady, taking in the view from the Binevenagh plateau on the way. Then head for Derry, whose historic features deserve to be explored. When you are ready to leave, turn south-east towards Dungiven and cross the Glenshane Pass into Castledawson. From here you can go on to Antrim town and back to Belfast.

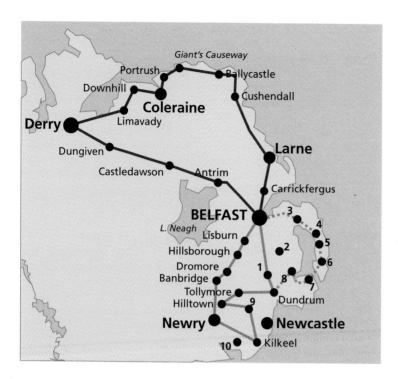

North Coast Tour

Mourne Country

1 Ballynahinch
2 Saintfield
3 Newtownards
4 Greyabbey
5 Kircubbin
6 Portaferry
7 Strangford
8 Downpatrick
9 *Silent Valley*
10 Warrenpoint

Kilometres
0   40

Miles
0   20

Day 2: Mourne Country 166 km (104 miles).

Leave Belfast on the south side and drive via Lisburn to Hillsborough, a remarkably pretty small town with adjacent fort, park and lake – ideal for a quiet stroll. Continue through Dromore and Banbridge to Newry, where you can turn eastwards along the shores of Carlingford Lough to the picturesque fishing port of Kilkeel. Take a walk down by the harbour to admire the fleet – and perhaps buy some freshly-landed fish – before heading north and inland towards the Silent Valley, in the heart of the beautiful Mourne Mountains (follow Hilltown directions). It is worth stopping the car for a breath of the clear mountain air and the chance to enjoy the wonderful views. Then proceed via Tollymore (with its forest park) to Dundrum, whose long, unspoilt beach is always inviting. From here you can head straight back to Belfast through Ballynahinch, or travel to Downpatrick and Strangford, visiting Castleward before taking the ferry across Strangford Lough to Portaferry. Drive up the Ards Peninsula via Kircubbin and Greyabbey (interesting ruins) to Newtownards, overlooked by Scrabo Tower. From here it's only a short drive back to your Belfast base.

Dublin and the East

Dublin has all the attractions of any major European city. The Phoenix Park is Europe's largest, while the city gives on to the sea at the great beaches of Sandymount and Dollymount, and the fishing village of Howth. There are many cultural attractions, among them the National Gallery, National Library, National Museum and the Chester Beatty Library and Gallery of Oriental Art, together with many smaller galleries, museums, eighteenth-century houses and three cathedrals. North of Dublin, seaside towns like Skerries lead on to the great historic sites: Drogheda, Trim and the Boyne Valley with prehistoric Newgrange. To the south, Killiney Bay is positively Italianate in its coastal vista, while Powerscourt Gardens are also Italian in style. The Wicklow mountains, with the medieval ecclesiastical centre of Glendalough, have some of Ireland's finest uplands.

Dublin and the Liffey Valley

Dublin

Pop. 1 million. TIOs 14 Upper O'Connell Street; Arrivals Hall, Dublin Airport; Baggot Street Bridge, tel. (01) 284 4768, all year. St Andrew's Church should be open in 1995.

Few European capitals have a more natural setting, with the sea bordering the city, countryside within a few minutes drive and to the immediate south of the city a great range of hills, unspoiled and unpolluted.

Dublin is nearly 2,000 years old, and has been in turn a Viking, a Norman and an English city. World renowned for its writers, artists and musicians, the city has always been proud of its culture which in recent years has flourished. The city has numerous venues for traditional music, the visual arts and classical music, particularly since the advent of the National Concert Hall.

Since 1922, it has been the capital of an independent state, made up of 26 of the 32 counties in Ireland. The setting up of the new state was financially draining and the city experienced 40 years of economic hardship before it once again began to flourish. Unfortunately, in their eagerness to encourage new business, developers in the 1960s destroyed much Georgian 18th c. architecture in favour of modern commercial office blocks. Despite the developers' ravages, many parts of the city, such as the Liberties, retain their inherent interest.

People who enjoy the "buzz" of great cities and those who like open-air splendours and delights will find everything they wish in and around this lively and very human city, where strangers and visitors are made welcome.

Major festivals and events include: St Patrick's Week festivities (starting Mar 17); Festival of Classical Music in Great Irish Houses (June); Kerrygold/Dublin Horse Show (July or Aug); Irish Antique Dealers' Fair (Aug); Dublin Grand Opera Society winter season (Nov/Dec).

CATHEDRALS & CHURCHES

Christ Church Cathedral (CI)
Christchurch Place. Open daily, all year.
Founded 1038 and rebuilt by the Normans in 1169. Magnificent stonework in aisles and naves. Alleged tomb of Strongbow. Visits to the Norman crypt.

St Patrick's Cathedral (CI)
St Patrick's Close. Open daily, all year.
Founded 1190, extensively restored with Guinness money about 1860. Jonathan Swift, Dean from 1713 to 1745, is buried in the south aisle, 'where savage indignation can no longer rend his heart'. Monument to Turlough O'Carolan, last of the Irish bards.

St Michan's Church (CI)
Church Street, near the Four Courts. Open 10am-4.45pm Mon-Fri, 10am-12.45pm Sat, Apr-Oct, 10am-12.45pm Mon-Sat, Nov-Mar. Tel. (01) 872 4154.
Dates from the 17th c. and is famous for the bodies in its vaults – the dry atmosphere has helped prevent their decomposition. Handel is said to have played the 18th c. organ.

Pro-Cathedral (C)
Marlborough Street, near O'Connell Street.
Built in the early 19th c. as an imitation of St Philippe du Roule Church in Paris. Its famous Palestrina choir sings mass in Latin on Sundays. Creepy crypt is often open to inspection by visitors.

The Abbey Presbyterian Church
Parnell Square. Open daily during the summer.
Dates from 1864 and was funded by Alex Findlater, a noted Dublin grocer. Fine interior.

St Audeon's Church (CI), *High Street*, dates back in part to the 12th c., while the nearby **St Werburgh's Church (CI)**, *High Street*, has foundations from the same period, although the present building is 18th c.

GALLERIES

National Gallery
Merrion Square West. Open 10am-5.30pm Mon-Wed, Fri and Sat, 10am-8.30pm Thurs, 2pm-5pm Sun, all year. Tel. (01) 661 5133.
Has some 2,000 paintings from all major European schools, including works by Goya, Gainsborough and Poussin. In the Irish Rooms, outstanding works by Jack B. Yeats, together with Hone, Osborne, Lavery and Orpen. Turner watercolours only on show in weak light of January. The building has been extensively renovated. Frequent exhibitions. Reference library by arr. Restaurant.

Hugh Lane Municipal Gallery
Parnell Square. Open 9.30am-6pm Tues-Fri, 9.30am-5pm Sat, 11am-5pm Sun. Tel. (01) 874 1903.
Fine collection of Irish Impressionists, Lane Collection of paintings, sculpture, stained-glass. Restaurant.

RHA Gallagher Gallery
Ely Place. Open 11am-5pm Mon-Wed, Fri, Sat, 11am-5pm Thurs, 2pm-9pm Sun. Tel. (01) 661 2558.
A vast new gallery, ideal for contemporary art.

Irish Museum of Modern Art
Royal Hospital, Kilmainham. Open 10am-5.30pm Tues-Sat, 12 noon-5.30pm Sun. Tel. (01) 671 8666.
Another fine collection of 20th c. Irish and international art, including the Gordon Lambert and Sidney Nolan collections. Frequent exhibitions.

Douglas Hyde Gallery, *Trinity College. Open 11am-6pm Mon-Fri, 11am-7pm Thurs, 11am-4.45pm Sat. Tel. (01) 677 2941.* Contemporary art exhibitions. **Solomon Gallery**, *Powerscourt Townhouse Centre. Open 10am-5.30pm Mon-Sat, 12 noon-5.30pm Sun. Tel. (01) 679 4237.* Contemporary art. **Kerlin Gallery**, *Anne's Lane, off South Anne Street. Open 10am-5.45pm Mon-*

O'Connell Street, Dublin

Fri, 11am-4.30pm Sat. Tel. (01) 677 0179. Contemporary paintings and sculpture. **Davis Gallery**, *11 Capel Street. Tel. (01) 872 6969.* Regular contemporary exhibitions. **Oriel Gallery**, *17 Clare Street. Open 10am-5.30pm Mon-Fri, 10am-1pm Sat. Tel. (01) 676 3410.* Regular exhibitions of mainly 20th c. Irish paintings. **Gallery of Photography**, *33/34 Essex Street. Open 11am-6pm Mon-Sat, 12 noon-5pm Sun. Tel. (01) 671 4654.* Regular photographic exhibitions, Irish and international. **Project Arts Centre**, *Temple Bar. Open 11am-6pm Mon-Sat. Tel. (01) 671 2321.* Contemporary artwork. **City Arts Centre**, *Moss Street, opposite Custom House. Open 11am-5.30 pm Mon-Fri, 11.30am-5.30pm Sat. Tel. (01) 677 0643.* Contemporary work. **Guinness Hop Store**, *Crane Street, Dublin 8. Open 10am-4.30pm Mon-Fri. Tel. (01) 453 6700.* Regular exhibitions. **Bank of Ireland Arts Centre**, *Foster Place. Tel. (01) 661 5933.* Regular exhibitions. **United Arts Club**, *3 Upper Fitzwilliam Street. Tel.*

(01) 661 1411. Exhibitions of members' work. **Alliance Française**, *1 Kildare Street. Tel. (01) 676 1732.* Exhibitions on French themes and artists.

LIBRARIES

National Library
Kildare Street. Open 10am-9pm Mon, 2pm-9pm Tues and Wed, 10am-5pm Thurs and Fri, 10am-1pm Sat, all year. Tel. (01) 661 8811.
Vast repository of information about Ireland with copies of virtually every book, magazine or newspaper ever published in Ireland. More recent newspapers are on microfilm. Frequent exhibitions.

Marsh's Library
St Patrick's Close, behind St Patrick's Cathedral. Open 10am-5pm Mon, Wed-Fri, 10.30am-12.30pm Sat. Tel. (01) 454 3511.
Early 18th c. library with some 25,000 volumes. Interior has great atmos-

phere, complete with cages where readers are locked in with rare books. Library has own bindery and restoration section. Exhibitions.

Royal Irish Academy
Dawson Street. Open 9.30am-5.30pm Mon-Fri, Sept-July. Tel. (01) 676 2570.
Has one of Ireland's largest collections of ancient Irish manuscripts.

National Archive
Bishop Street. Open 10am-5pm Mon-Fri, all year. Tel. (01) 478 3711.
Old State papers, up to 1960, can be read in elegant, comfortable surroundings.

Chester Beatty Library and Gallery of Oriental Art
20 Shrewbury Road, Dublin 4. Open 10am-5pm Tues-Fri, 2pm-5pm Sat, all year. Guided tours at 2.30pm on Wed and Sat. Tel. (01) 269 2386.
Books, paintings, papyri, clay tablets and bindings from 2700 BC to present day. Also visual arts, including vast array

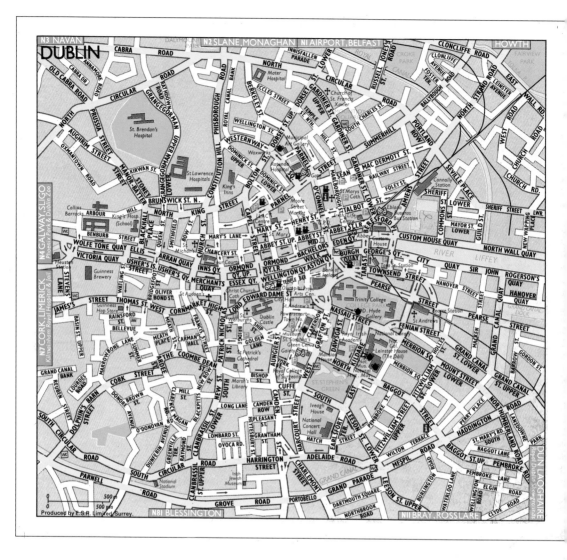

of Japanese prints. One of the world's main collections representing Islamic culture. Due to move to new premises at Dublin Castle.

Trinity College Old Library
Open 9.30am-5pm Mon-Sat, 12 noon-5pm Sun, all year. Tel. (01) 677 2941. Many rare manuscripts and books. Its main treasure, The Book of Kells, is in the new Colonnades Gallery.

The Central Catholic Library.
74 Merrion Square. Reading room open 12 noon-7pm Mon-Fri, 12 noon-6pm Sat, all year. Tel. (01) 676 1264. Has about 80,000 volumes of general,

religious and Irish interest.

Irish Architectural Archive
73 Merrion Square. Open Mon-Fri, all year. Tel. (01) 676 3430. Reference material on historic buildings in Ireland. Reading room.

Pearse Street Library. *Tel. (01) 677 2764.* Material on Dublin history. **ILAC Centre Library**, *off Henry Street. Tel. (01) 873 4333.* High-tech with extensive reference and music sections. **Goethe Institut**, *37 Merrion Square. Tel. (01) 661 1155.* German reference material. **Dublin Diocesan Library**, *Clonliffe Road, Dublin 3. Tel. (01) 874*

1680. Extensive reference facilities. **Genealogical Office**, *Kildare Street. Tel. (01) 661 8811.*

NOTABLE BUILDINGS

Ashtown Castle
Phoenix Park. Open 9.30am-5pm daily, Mar, Apr and Oct, 9.30am-5.30pm daily, May, 9.30am-6.30pm daily, June-Sept, 9.30am-4.30pm daily, Nov-Feb. Tel. (01) 677 0095. Tower house, probably 17th c., has adjoining visitor centre detailing park's history, its flora and fauna. Exhibitions, audio-visual presentations, restaurant.

Ayesha Castle
Killiney, Co Dublin. Open 10am-2pm Tues-Thur, Mar, 2pm-5pm Tues-Thur, Apr-May, 11am-3pm Sat-Sun, Jun-Jul. Tel. (01) 285 2323.
Early-Victorian, with a round tower and turrets, gardens with exotic species, woodland.

Casino
Off Malahide Road, Marino, Dublin 3. Open 9.30am-6.30pm daily, mid-June-Sept. Tel. (01) 833 1618.
One of Ireland's finest 18th c. classical buildings. Includes four state rooms.

City Hall
Dame Street, facing top of Parliament Street. Open 9am-5pm Mon-Fri, all year. Tel. (01) 679 6111.
Late 18th c., with impressive entrance hall.

Custom House
Custom House Quay
Designed by James Gandon and completed in 1791, it is one of Dublin's most impressive buildings, recently restored and gleaming white. Exterior only.

Drimnagh Castle
Long Mile Road, Dublin 12. Open 12 noon-5pm Wed, Sat and Sun, Apr-Oct, or by arr. Tel. (01) 450 2530.
Dublin's only authentic medieval castle, incongruous amid a bleak industrial landscape. Recently restored Great Hall and medieval gardens with moat.

Dublin Castle
Open 10am-5pm Mon-Fri, 2pm-5pm, Sat and Sun, all year. Tel. (01) 677 7129.
An elaborate restoration programme has now been completed and the State apartments have been returned to their former glory. St Patrick's Hall was built as a ballroom in the mid-18th c. Church of the Most Holy Trinity in lower yard was designed in early 19th c. by Francis Johnston of GPO fame and has elaborate interior decorations. Restaurant. Also, home to the records of the Company of Goldsmiths.

Four Courts
Tel. (01) 872 5555.
At the heart of Ireland's legal system, the building dates from 1785, restored with some incongruities after the civil war. Central hall can be inspected, while the dome affords good views over the city.

GPO
O'Connell Street. Open daily, all year.
Early 19th c., much restored after 1916. Central hall and portico has been refurbished recently. Statue of Cuchulainn.

Kilmainham Jail
Dublin 8. Open 1pm-4pm Mon-Fri, 1pm-6pm Sun, Oct-Apr, 11am-6pm daily, May-Sept. Tel. (01) 453 5984.
Many of Ireland's political leaders were held captive here and their stories are told in audio-visual presentations, mementoes and tours of the cells.

Newman House
85-86 St Stephen's Green. Open 10am-4.30pm Tues-Fri, 2pm-4.30pm Sat, 11am-2pm Sun. Tel. (01) 475 7255.
Two finely restored Georgian houses where the Catholic University of Ireland began in 1850. Exquisite plasterwork and other interior features.

Number 29 Lower Fitzwilliam Street
Open 10am-5pm Tues-Sat, 2pm-5pm Sun, all year. Tel. (01) 676 5831.
This corner house, owned by the Electricity Supply Board, has been totally and authentically restored to show lifestyle of a typical Dublin middle-class household c.1790-1820.

Powerscourt House
South William Street. Open daily.
Late 18th c. town house has been elaborately restored, now a fashionable shopping centre with Craft Council gallery, craft shops, restaurants.

Rathfarnham Castle.
Open 10am-6pm daily, Apr-Oct. Tel. (01) 493 9462.
Parts are now open to visitors, although restoration work is continuing and is unlikely to be finished until 1995.

Royal Hospital
Kilmainham. Open 10am-6pm Tues-Sat, 12 noon-5.30pm Sun, all year. Tel. (01) 671 8666.
This late 17th c. structure, replicating Les Invalides in Paris, has been finely restored in recent years. Great hall and chapel.

Shaw House
33 Synge Street, off South Circular Road, Dublin 8. Open 10am-5pm Mon-Sat, 2pm-6pm Sun and bank holidays, May-Sept. Tel. (01) 475 0854.
The house where George Bernard Shaw was born and lived until he was 10 years old, has been totally restored to 19th c. ambiance.

St Mary's Abbey
Off Capel Street. Open 10am-5pm Wed, June-Sept. Tel. (01) 872 1490.
12th c. Benedictine abbey. Historical exhibitions.

Tailors' Hall
Back Lane, near Christchurch Cathedral. Tel. (01) 454 4794.
Early 18th c., last surviving Dublin Guild Hall, now An Taisce (National Trust for Ireland) headquarters.

Trinity College.
Tel. (01) 677 2941.
Founded in 1592, though nothing remains of original college. The buildings around the great central square, including the marvellous chapel, date from 18th c. Various historical and cultural events on campus.

MUSEUMS

National Museum
Kildare Street. Open 10am-5pm Tues-Sat, 2pm-5pm Sun, all year. Tel. (01) 661 8811.
Many fascinating relics from prehistoric to modern times, giving a good overview of prehistoric, early Christian and medieval Ireland. From more recent times, much material on Ireland's struggle for independence. Highlights of the museum include the Treasury Room, while its antiquities include the Ardagh Chalice, the Cross of Cong and the Tara Brooch. Frequent exhibitions. The extension in Merrion Row is used mainly for exhibitions. Many sections of the museum are due to move to a new location, the former Collins Barracks, near Heuston station.

Bewleys
Grafton Street. Open daily. Tel. (01) 677 6761.
Museum of family and company history gives insight into Dublin café society.

Childhood Museum
20 Palmerstown Park, Dublin 6. Open 2pm-5.30pm Wed and Sun, July-Aug, 2pm-5.30pm Sun, Sept-June. Tel. (01) 497 3223.
Wonderful collection of dolls and other childrens' playthings.

Dublin Civic Museum
South William Street. Open 10am-6pm Tues-Sat, 11am-2pm Sun, all year. Tel. (01) 679 4260.
Material on Dublin history, frequent exhibitions. Also Dublin Corporation city archive.

Dublin Writers Museum
Parnell Square. Open 10am-5pm Mon-Sat, 1pm-5pm Sun and bank holidays, all year. Tel. (01) 872 2077.
Memorabilia on Ireland's most famous writers. Exhibitions. Café, restaurant.

Education Museum
Church of Ireland College of Education, 94 Upper Rathmines Road, Dublin 6. Open 2.30pm-5.30pm Wed, all year. Tel. (01) 497 0033.
The story of Ireland's schools, told through interactive displays. A 19th c. classroom has been recreated.

Findlater's Museum
Harcourt Street Vaults, 10 Upper Hatch Street. Open 10am-6pm, Mon-Sat, all year. Tel. (01) 475 1699.
Fascinating wine cellars, beneath old Harcourt Street railway station have much memorabilia on the Findlater family and the chain of wine and grocery shops it owned until the 1960s. A veritable social history of Dublin over the last 150 years.

Freemason's Hall
Molesworth Street. Tel. (01) 679 9799/ 679 5465.
This 18th c. building with fine portico is headquarters of Masonic Order in Ireland. Interior and historical contents can be seen by arr.

Fry Model Railway Museum
Malahide Castle. Tel. (01) 845 2337. Open 10am-5pm Mon-Fri, 11am-5pm Sat and Sun, bank holidays, all year.
Vast working model railway display shows how transport has evolved in Ireland over the past 150 years.

Kilmainham Jail, Dublin

Garda Siochana Museum
Garda headquarters, Phoenix Park. By arr, tel. (01) 677 1156.
Fine collection of material on Irish police history.

Guinness Museum
Hop Store, Crane Street. Open 10am-4.30pm Mon-Fri. Tel. (01) 453 6700.
A 19th c. hop store has been skilfully converted into a museum and exhibition centre. An elaborate and fascinating audio-visual presentation details the history of the brewery since 1759. Free product sampling in ground floor bar. Adjacent secure car park.

Heraldic Museum
Kildare Street. Open 10am-4.30pm Mon-Fri. Tel. (01) 661 4877.
Collection of family coats of arms.

Irish Jewish Museum
3-4 Walworth Road, off South Circular Road. Open 11am-3.30pm Tues, Thurs, Sun, May-Sept, 10.30am-2.30pm Oct-Apr. Tel. (01) 453 1797.
Memorabilia of the Jewish community in Ireland over the past 150 years.

Irish Railway Records Society
Heuston Station. Open 8pm-10pm, Tues, all year.
Printed and photographic material on Ireland's railway history.

Irish Whiskey Corner
Bow Street, Dublin 7. Tours 3.30pm Mon-Fri, all year. Tel. (01) 872 5566.
Fine recreation of whiskey history, audio-visual presentation, product sampling.

James Joyce Museum
Sandycove. Open 10am-5pm Mon-Sat, 2pm-6pm Sun, bank holidays, Apr-Oct, or by arr. Tel. (01) 872 2077.
This Martello Tower contains a fine museum devoted to one of the most outstanding 20th c. writers.

National Maritime Museum
Haigh Terrace, Dun Laoghaire. Open 2.30pm-5.30pm Tues-Sun, May-Sept, Sat and Sun, Oct-Apr. Tel. (01) 280 0969.
Old church has been converted to house extensive collection, including models of ships and working optic formerly used in the Baily lighthouse at Howth.

National Wax Museum
Granby Row, off Parnell Square. Open 10am-5.30pm Mon-Sat, 12 noon-5.30pm Sun, all year. Tel. (01) 872 6340.
Chamber of Horrors. Children's world of fantasy and fairytales. Many Irish stars and personalities in wax.

Natural History Museum
Merrion Square. Open 10am-5pm Tues-Sat, 2pm-5pm Sun. Tel. (01) 661 8811.
All kinds of preserved birds, fish and mammals, including a whale's skeleton.

Pearse Museum
St Enda's, Grange Road, Rathfarnham, Dublin 16. Open 10am-4pm daily, Nov-Jan, 10am-5pm daily, Feb-Apr, Sept, Oct, 10am-5.30pm daily, May-Aug. Tel. (01) 493 4208.
School formerly run by Patrick Pearse, leader of 1916 Easter Rising. Exhibitions, audio-visual presentation, tea room.

Printing Museum
Beggar's Bush, Dublin 4. Tel. (01) 874 3662.
Former military garrison chapel being converted into elaborate printing museum, should be ready 1995.

Steam Museum
Straffan, Co Kildare. Open 2.30pm-5.30pm Sun, bank holidays, Easter-May, Sept, 2pm-6pm daily, except Mon, June-Aug. Tel. (01) 627 3155.
Exhibition of models, also working stationary steam engines. Garden, Steaming Kettle tea house.

Transport Museum
Howth. Open 12 noon-5pm Sat, 2pm-5pm Sun, all year. Tel. (01) 848 0831.
Exhibits include restored trams and wide variety of other transport vehicles, some horse-drawn. Photographs and other memorabilia.

PARKS & GARDENS

Beech Park
Clonsilla, Dublin 15. Open 2pm-6pm first weekend every month, Mar-Oct, also Sun, bank holidays, July, Aug. Tel. (01) 821 2216.
Large walled garden with some 10,000 species.

The Grand Canal, Dublin

Fernhill Gardens
Sandyford, Co Dublin. Open 11am-5pm Tues-Sat, 2pm-6pm Sun, Mar-Nov. Tel. (01) 295 6000.
On slopes of Three Rock Mountain, with specimen trees, rhododendrons, rock and water gardens. Nursery.

Garden of Remembrance
Parnell Square. Open daily, all year.
Tribute to Ireland's historic dead, including 1916 and War of Independence.

Arbour Hill Cemetery
Dublin 7. Open 9am-4.30pm Mon-Sat, 9.30am-12 noon Sun.
Burial place of the leaders of the 1916 uprising.

Herbert Park
Ballsbridge.
Delightful park, with tennis courts, bowling, pond, music in summer, flower displays, built on site of 1907 International Exhibition.

Iveagh Gardens
Rear St Stephen's Green South.
Delightful but little-known city centre park with fountains, water cascades and statue-lined walks.

Marley Park
Rathfarnham.
Extensive parkland, model steam railway, craft courtyard with interesting workshops.

Merrion Square
City centre.
Plans to build a new Catholic cathedral here never came to fruition, but a new outdoor Museum of Public Lighting is planned.

National Botanic Gardens
Glasnevin. Open 9am-6pm Mon-Sat, 11am-6pm Sun, summer, 10am-4.30pm.
Dating back to 1795, the gardens contain about 20,000 plant species and cultivars, a rose garden and a vegetable garden. Strolls beside the River Tolka. The main attraction, the mid-19th c.

Turner Palm House, is being restored a vast undertaking that should be completed for 1995. *Tel. (01) 837 4388*

North Bull Island
5 km (3 miles) long island created by the action of the tides in the last century. Vast beach and dunes, nature conservancy area.

Phoenix Park
Open 9.30am-sunset, daily, all year. Tel. (01) 677 0095.
Europe's largest public park, extending to 709 ha (1752 acres), with numerous tree-lined roads, several lakes, deer herds. Furry Glen nature trail in NW of park has many trees and plants. Dublin Zoo dates back to 1830s and has many exotic species, including lions and monkeys. Children's corner. Major expansion plans. Café, restaurant.

St Anne's Park Rose Garden
Mount Prospect Park, Clontarf. Open daily all year.
Magnificent rose displays.

t Catherine's Park
ff Thomas Street.
mall secluded inner city oasis created
·om old graveyard.

t Enda's Park
athfarnham, Dublin 16. Open daily,
ll year.
:harming park near the Pearse
Iuseum, with riverside walks, water-
ill, walled garden.

t Stephen's Green
)pen daily.
·robably Ireland's oldest public park,
.n oasis of lakes and walks, surrounded
·y flowers, shrubs. Lunchtime concerts
1 the summer.

Var Memorial Gardens
slandbridge, Dublin 8. Open daily, all
ear.
)edicated to the memory of the Irish
oldiers who were killed in World War
, the gardens were designed by Sir
:dwin Lutyens. They have been well
estored in recent years.

·UBS

tyans
.arkgate Street, near Heuston Station.
uperb traditional bar, with snugs and
·ld-fashioned lamps.

·he Brazen Head
·ridge Street.
.eckoned to be Dublin's oldest pub,
lating back to at least late 17th c.

tag's Head
)ff Dame Street.
·ounded in 1770, remodelled late
·9th c.

·alace Bar
·leet Street.
:enuine, old-time Dublin pub, dark
·anelling and mirrors.

·owes
·leet Street
mall pub that is popular with
·urnalists.

·1ulligan's
·oolbeg Street.
)ark, ancient, noisy, another place for
·urnalists.

Long Hall
South Great George's Street.
The city's most ornate traditional pub,
with interior woodwork, mirrors,
chandeliers.

McDaid's
Harry Street, Off Grafton Street.
Literary and theatrical pub.

Waterloo House
Upper Baggot Street.
Agreeable Victorian-style pub that dates
back nearly a century and hasn't been
spoiled by the tide of pub modernisation that's swept the city. An interesting arty set frequents here.

Davy Byrnes
Duke Street.
Famous meeting place.

Toner's
Lower Baggot Street.
Old-style pub, as is **Doheny &
Nesbitt's**, nearby.

ROUND & ABOUT

The Royal Dublin Society (RDS)
*Ballsbridge, Dublin 4. Tel. (01) 668
0645.*
Many exhibitions, concerts and
lectures.

National Concert Hall
Earlsfort Terrace. Tel. (01) 671 1888.
Has frequent musical events, at lunch-
time and in the evenings.

Dublin Experience
*Trinity College. Open 10am-5pm daily,
May-Sept. Tel. (01) 677 2941.*
Elaborate audio-visual presentation on
the city's history.

James Joyce Cultural Centre
*35 North Great George's Street. Details,
tel. (01) 873 1984.*
Has frequent Joyce-related cultural
events.

Waterways Visitor Centre
*Ringsend, Dublin 4. Open 9.30am-
6.30pm daily, June-Sept, 12.30pm-
5pm, Wed-Sun, Oct-May. Tel. (01) 677
7510.*
Futuristic-looking building which
details the history and development of
Ireland's inland waterways. Audio-

visual presentation, working models.

Bewley's Cafés
*Westmoreland Street, South Great
George's Street and Grafton Street.*
City centre cafés that have great atmosphere, while the latter also has some
fine Harry Clarke stained glass
windows.

Geological Survey of Ireland
*Beggar's Bush, Dublin 4. Tel. (01) 666
0951.*
Exhibitions related to geology.

Sandymount Strand
South Dublin's answer to North Bull
Island, a vast stretch of sand that is
enlarged greatly at low tide. Walk along
the South Wall, past the electricity
generating station; this wall matches
the Bull Wall on the north side of the
estuary.

Dublinia
*Beside Christchurch Cathedral. Open
10am-5pm daily, Apr-Sept, 11am-4pm
Mon-Sat, 10 am-4.30-pm, Sun, Oct-
Mar. Tel. (01) 679 4611.*
Everyday life in medieval Dublin is
recreated by high tech audio-visual and
computer techniques. Scale model of
what Dublin looked like in 1500.
Medieval maze.

Traditional Markets
For abundant bargains and banter, try
one of the city's markets: Iveagh
Market, Francis Street; Liberty Market,
Meath Street; Mother Redcap's Market,
Back Lane; Moore Street Vegetable
Market, off Henry Street; St Michan's
Street, behind Four Courts; Rathmines
and Blackrock weekend markets.

Temple Bar
The Temple Bar district stretches from
Westmoreland Street to Parliament
Street and from Dame Street to the
south quays. A new curved bridge, to
be called the **Poddle Bridge**, is
planned to extend the area further and
to connect it with the north quays. The
entire area is undergoing a total
transformation and has been described
as Dublin's answer to the Left Bank in
Paris. An impressive variety of facilities
are opening.
 A new curved street will have a
centre for the visual arts, while Eustace
Street has **The Ark Children's Arts**

20
BOXTY
GALLAGHER'S
HOUSE
GBH
Traditional Irish Restaurant & Wine Bar
Sandwich Menu
Haymaker
Turfcutter
Cattle Drover
Ploughman
Fisherman
Poacher
An bhfuil tú ag dul?

entre. The **DESIGNyard** is an
plied arts centre, while **The
ommissioning Gallery** has contem-
orary applied art. The well-
tablished **Gallery of Photography**
s a new base at 33/34 East Essex
reet. **Project Arts Centre**, *East Essex
reet*, is also well-founded for theatre
d exhibitions, while the Irish Film
entre is based in Eustace Street.

Temple Bar has several new hotels,
any restaurants and some lively pubs,
cluding **Bad Bob's Backstage Bar**,
st Essex Street, described as Dublin's
st-known late-night music venue.
he **Rock Garden**, *Crown Alley*, is
other noted rock venue. **The Music
entre** has various musical facilities,
cluding the **Temple Lane Studios**.

If you prefer something a little more
storic try **Thomas Read & Co's**
tlery shop at Parliament Street –
ublin's oldest shop, it dates back to
70. Fishamble Street is the site of the
eatre where Handel's "Messiah" had
s first performance in 1742. **The
king Museum** is due to open in
95 in the 1815 Gothic church of St
ichael & St John.

For further details contact the
mple Bar Information Centre, *18
ustace Street. Open daily. Tel. (01)
71 5717.*

HEATRES & CINEMAS

ate Theatre
avendish Row. Tel. (01) 874 4045.
evivals and contemporary work in
ublin's best-regarded theatre.

bbey and Peacock Theatres
ower Abbey Street. Tel. (01) 8/8 7222.
ish and international plays at the
bbey, more experimental work at the
eacock.

ndrew's Lane Theatre
ff Dame Street. Tel. (01) 679 5720.
ontemporary work in intimate
eatre.

aiety Theatre, *South King Street. Tel.
1) 677 1717* – variety shows and
lays; **Lambert Puppet Theatre**,
*onkstown, Co Dublin. Tel. (01) 280
974* – puppet theatre; **Olympia**

mple Bar, Dublin

Theatre, *Dame Street. Tel. (01) 677
7744* – variety, drama; **Point Theatre**,
East Link Bridge. Tel. (01) 836 3633 –
the place for the spectacular/large-scale
shows and concerts; **Tivoli Theatre**,
Francis Street. Tel. (01) 453 5998 –
popular drama.

Dublin has three city centre
cinemas showing commercial releases,
while the **Light House**, *Middle Abbey
Street, tel. (01) 873 0438*, has
contemporary and archive art films.
The Irish Film Centre, *Eustace Street,
tel. (01) 677 8788*, is the other centre
specialising in art films.

Out of town multiplexes offer good
cinematic variety, the **UCI Multiplex,
Tallaght**, *tel. (01) 452 2611*, has 12
screens while the **UCI Multiplex,
Malahide Road**, *tel. (01) 848 5133* and
the **Omniplex, Santry**, *tel. (01) 842
8844* have 10 screens each.

SPORT

Croke Park
Dublin 3. Tel. (01) 836 3222.
Dublin's major venue for Gaelic
Athletic Association games.

Lansdowne Road
Tel. (01) 668 4601
The main stadium for international
rugby and soccer matches.

Ardgillan Demesne
*3 km (2 miles) W of Skerries. Open
from 10am daily, all year. Tel. (01) 849
2212.*
Extensive house dating from early 18th
c. Demesne, rose and herb gardens.

Blackrock
South Dublin.
Walk along the sea front terrace.
Dublin Crystal Glass, *off Caryfort
Avenue. Open daily, all year. Tel. (01)
288 7932/288 8627.* Traditional
glassmaking.

Carton House
E end of Maynooth. Tel. (01) 628 6250.
Classical house built about 1740, with
Shell House in gardens, made entirely
of sea-shells. The house has been
acquired by the Office of Public Works
and is being refurbished.

Castletown House
*24 km (15 miles) W of Dublin. Open
10am-6pm Mon-Fri, 11am-6pm Sat,
2pm-6pm Sun, Apr-Oct, 2pm-6pm Sun,
bank holidays, Nov-Mar. Tel. (01) 628
8252.*
Beside Celbridge village, the Palladian
style house is one of Ireland's most
superb pieces of 18th c. architecture.
Among the interior highlights are the
plasterwork, the long gallery, the
downstairs nursery room and kitchen.
Formal gardens.

Celbridge Abbey
*24 km (15 miles) W of Dublin. Open
12 noon-6 pm Tues-Sun, bank
holidays, Mar-Oct. Tel. (01) 628 8350.*
The abbey itself was built around 1697,
while the grounds, beside the River
Liffey, have been developed by the
religious order of St John of God.
Vanessa's Bower is where Jonathan
Swift and his beloved Stella viewed the
weir. Oldest stone bridge over the
Liffey.

Dalkey
Near Dun Laoghaire.
Delightful seaside village with medieval
castle. Two small harbours, trips to
Dalkey island during the summer.

Dun Laoghaire
*11 km (7 miles) S of Dublin. TIO St
Michael's Wharf, tel. (01) 284 4768, all
year.*
Major ferryport. Walks along the east
and west piers. Site of the **National
Maritime Museum**.

Howth
16 km (10 miles) N of Dublin.
Attractive seaside village, with walks
around two piers, trips to Ireland's Eye,
an offshore island, walks around
Howth Head and Howth Castle rhododendron gardens. Also transport
museum and Abbey Tavern, the ruins
of old abbey.

Kilcock
35 km (22 miles) W of Dublin.
Village set beside Royal canal, which
provides extensive towpath walks.
Bridestown Rare Breeds Farm. *Open
12 noon-5.30pm daily.* Includes Kerry
cows, four horned Manx sheep and a
horse museum.

Malahide
14 km (9 miles) N of Dublin.
Impressive new marina development.
Malahide Castle dates from 12th c.
and features include Great Hall, library,
drawing room, National Portrait
Gallery, botanic garden, parkland. **Fry
Model Railway Museum.** *Open 10am-
5pm Mon-Fri, 11am-5pm Sat, Sun,
bank holidays, all year. Tel. (01) 845
2655.*

Maynooth
28 km (18 miles) W of Dublin.
University town. **Maynooth Castle,**
open 3pm-6pm daily, June-Sept. At the
entrance to the campus, the castle
dates in part from 13th c. **Maynooth
Museum.** *Open 2pm-4pm Tues, Thurs,
2pm-5pm Sun, summer. Tel. (01) 628
5222.* Ecclesiastical relics, 19th c. elec-
trical equipment, including batteries,
invented by Rev Nicholas Callan,
professor of natural philosophy at St
Patrick's College, Maynooth, between
1826 and 1864.

Monkstown
South Dublin suburb.
Comhaltas Ceoltóirí Éireann, *32
Belgrave Square. Tel. (01) 280 0295.* An
Irish cultural institute, which provides
summer entertainment in its tradi-
tional Irish country kitchen.

Newbridge House
*18 km (11 miles) N of Dublin. Open
10am-5pm Mon-Sat, 2pm-6pm Sun,
bank holidays, Apr-Oct, 2pm-5pm Sun,
bank holidays, Nov-Mar. Tel. (01) 843
6534.*
18th c. mansion with old kitchen, craft
workshops, walled garden, farm animals, parkland. Nearby **Lusk Heritage
Centre,** *open 10am-6pm daily, mid-
June – mid-Sept. Tel. (01) 843 7683.* Has
many local historical items, in old
church adjoining round tower.

Skerries
30 km (19 miles) N of Dublin.
Attractive seaside town with busy
fishing pier and seafront walks. A few
cottages still have old-style thatched
roofs.

Straffan
13 km (8 miles) S of Maynooth.
Pleasantly situated village on banks of
River Liffey. **Butterfly Farm,** *open
10am-6pm daily, May-Aug. Tel. (01)*

627 1109. Also **Steam Museum**.

Swords
5 km (3 miles) W of Malahide.
Church of Ireland church on west side
of town, with round tower, dating from
6th c. monastery. **Swords Castle** dates
from 13th c. **Town Museum,** *Carnegie
Library Building, open 2.30pm-
5.30pm, Sun, all year,* has fascinating
details on the way the townsfolk used
to live.

Boyne Valley and Co Louth

Annagassan
5 km (3 miles) SE of Castlebellingham.
Walk along shores of Dundalk Bay to
Salterstown, a secluded bathing place.

Ardee
20 km (13 miles) SW of Dundalk.
St Mary's Church **(CI)** has part of
13th c. Carmelite church. Also 13 c.
Castle keep, in Main Street.

Ballymascanlon
7 km (4 miles) NE of Dundalk.
Proleek dolmen, one of the largest in
Ireland, with huge capstone, is near the
Ballymascanlon Hotel.

Baltray
8 km (5 miles) E of Drogheda.
Small village has one of Ireland's finest
links golf courses and along the
seashore, one of longest beaches on
the east coast.

Bective Abbey
8 km (5 miles) S of Navan.
Founded as a Cistercian House in
12th c. There are ruins of the original
chapter house and church, plus

remnants of the fortified house in
which the abbey was converted afte
the Dissolution.

Bettystown
8 km (5 miles) E of Drogheda.
Sandy strand runs for 9 km (6 miles
ideal for walking at low tide. Hors
races here for one day in Augus
Neptune Hotel has many histor
photographs of locality. Amuseme
park during the summer.

Carlingford
20 km (13 miles) NE of Dundalk.
Much of this medieval town has bee
restored, including the town wall
Ruins of **King John's Castle,** 13th
Also 16th c. **Taaffes Castle,** 15th c. mi
and 14th c. Dominican Abbey. **Hol
Trinity Heritage Centre,** *open 9an
5pm daily, all year. Tel. (041) 7345*
Details of the town's history from i
Anglo-Norman foundation to Thoma
D'Arcy McGee, 19th c. poet and Can
dian statesman, who was born in th
town. **Oyster Festival** held in Augus

Clogherhead
14 km (9 miles) NE of Drogheda.
Short walk from village to Port Ori
fishing harbour and the headlan
which gives fine views of Dundalk Ba
north to Mountains of Mourne.

Cooley Peninsula
Begins 8 km (5 miles) NE of Dundal
A drive round the peninsula fro
Dundalk is approximately a 40 km (2
miles) round trip. It offers many fir
scenic views and small, seclude
bathing places, such as **Gyles Qua**
and pleasant resorts like **Omeat**
Riverstown Old Corn Mill Craf
Centre, *open daily, tel. (042) 76157*
a restored 18th c. mill.

Drogheda
48 km (30 miles) N of Dublin. Po
24,000. TIO tel. (041) 37070, June-Au
Hilly, medieval town set on slope
rising from the River Boyne. The riv
is spanned by a spectacular mid-19t
c. railway viaduct. Not far from th
quays, the old laneways and war
houses retain the atmosphere of
19th c. port town.
   St Peter's Church (C), *West Stree*
houses the shrine of St Oliver Plunke

Proleek dolmen, Co. Louth

Laytown, near Drogheda, Co. Meath

which contains the martyr's head. **St Peter's Church (CI)**, *top of Peter Street*, affords fine town views from the surrounding graveyard. **The Siena Convent**, *Chord Road*, decorated with 19th c. mosaics, is a haven of calm after the town's bustle. **St Lawrence's Gate** is only one of ten to survive from medieval times.

Millmount Museum, *open 10am-5pm daily, summer, Wed, Sat, Sun, 3pm-5pm during winter. Tel. (041) 33097/36391*. Craft workshops include **Boyne Pottery**. Also, restored **Governor's House**. Buttergate restaurant offers fine river town views from its conservatory. Fridays and Saturdays are Drogheda's liveliest days, with town markets in West Street where fish merchants sell their wares. Walks along the quays.

Dundalk

84 km (52 miles) N of Dublin. Pop. 26,000. TIO tel. (042) 35484, all year. The town fell in 1177 to the Anglo-Normans and for the next 300 years it was repeatedly attacked as a frontier town of the English Pale. Most of its fortifications were removed during the 18th c. and little of Dundalk's historic past is to be seen today, nevertheless parts of the town are interesting, particularly the area around the Courthouse.

New **Industrial Heritage Centre**, *Jocelyn Street. Open Tues-Sun, all year. Tel. (042) 27056/35457*. Details of the town's manufacturing traditions, including brewing, shoe-making, cigarette manufacture, railway engineering and many other aspects of the town's history, including its role as a frontier town of the Pale. Situated in a converted 18th c. distillery warehouse, with adjacent library. **Graveyard of St Nicholas (CI)**, *Clanbrassil Street* has tomb of Agnes Galt, sister of Robert Burns, the 18th c. Scottish poet. The nearby **St Patrick's Cathedral (C)**, built in the mid-19th c., was modelled on King's College, Cambridge. **Seatown Castle**, on eastern outskirts of the town, has the ruins of a 13th c. Franciscan monastery. **Carroll's** cigarette factory, *tel. (042)*

36501, visits by arr. **Harp Lag** **Brewery**, *tel. (042) 34793, visits by a* Also horse and greyhound racing.

Dunleer

8 km (5 miles) N of Drogheda. **White River Mills**, *open Mon-Fri, year. Tel. (041) 51141.* A restored wat powered flour mill; the waterwhee over three centuries old. Stonegrou wholemeal flour continues to produced. **Monasterboice Hi Cross**, 5.4 metres (17' 8") tall, one Ireland's best preserved crosses.

Faughart

6 km (4 miles) N of Dundalk. Robert the Bruce's brother is buri here. Outstanding scenic views fro the graveyard.

Inniskeen

14 km (9 miles) W of Dundalk. The poet Patrick Kavanagh was bo here and is commemorated in the **f museum**, *tel. (042) 78109*, which a has local railway artefacts. The poe specifically remembered in the n

atrick Kavanagh Literary Resource
entre, *open daily, tel. (042) 78560.*

ells
km (10 miles) NW of Navan.
ncient town in the Blackwater Valley,
e site of a 6th c. monastic settlement
unded by St Colmcille, where the
ook of Kells (now in Trinity College,
ublin) was written.

ellifont Abbey
*km (6 miles) W of Drogheda. Open
30am-5.30pm Tues-Sat, May mid-
ne; 9.30am-6.30pm daily, mid-June
mid-Sept, 10am-5pm daily, mid-Sept
end Oct. Tel. (041) 26459.*
eland's first Cistercian monastery,
unded in 1142. The octagonal
vabo, built around 1200, is its most
nusual feature.

ornington
km (3 miles) E of Drogheda.
easant village beside Boyne estuary.
oran's pub with its wooden interior
nd shelves for groceries has changed
tle since the 19th c.

osney
km (5 miles) S of Drogheda.
nis holiday centre has many attrac-
ons, including a water-based leisure
ntre, pets corner, nature walks and
ru na Boinne. Audio-visual
esentation of Boyne valley history.

avan
km (17 miles) W of Drogheda.
nis hilly town set at the confluence
the Boyne and Blackwater, was once
walled and fortified outpost of the
le. **Athlumney House**, *3 km (2
iles) from the town centre*, by the
ver Boyne, contains impressive
mains of the original four-storey, 15th
castle.

ewgrange
*km (7 miles) W of Drogheda. TIO
r-Oct, tel. (041) 24274. Open 10am-
30pm daily, Nov-Feb, 10am-5pm
ily, Mar-Apr, 9.30am-6pm daily,
ay, 9.30am-7pm daily, Jun-Sept,
am-5pm daily, Oct. Tel. (041) 24488.*
ting from about 2,500 BC, New-
ange is one of the finest prehistoric
ssage graves in Europe, built with
0,000 tonnes of stones. The site also
s considerable astronomical signifi-
nce; on the day of the winter solstice,

the sun shines straight down the
passageway – an effect which is
recreated for visitors using electric
light. Frequent guided tours.

Knowth, *open 10am-5pm daily,
May – mid-June, 9.30am-6.30pm daily,
mid-June – mid-Sept, 10am-5pm daily,
mid-Sept – end Oct. Tel. (041) 24824.*
Has the greatest collection of prehistoric tomb art ever found in western
Europe. Beneath its great mound,
there are two passage tombs and
around it, 17 satellite tombs. Frequent
guided tours. The third tomb, at
Dowth, is still closed.

In nearby **King William's Glen**, the
site of the Battle of the Boyne (1690)
is marked. Also nearby is **Newgrange
Farm**, *open 10am-5.30pm daily, Apr-
Sept, tel. (041) 24119.* Animals, birds,
vintage farm machinery, rural life
museum, farm tours, gift shop, coffee
shop. **Óengus Lodge**, *open 10am-6pm
Mon-Sat, Apr-Oct. Tel. (041) 24150.*
Next to Newgrange Farm, the lodge has
farm machinery, a cooper's workshop
and a blacksmith's forge. High quality
fabrics are woven on hand looms. **Ledwidge Museum**, *Slane, open 10am-
6pm Mon-Wed, Mar-Oct, or by arr. Tel.
(041) 25201.* Once the home of Francis
Ledwidge, a noted poet killed in the
First World War. **Slane Hill**, where St
Patrick proclaimed Christianity in 433,
gives spectacular views (in clear
weather) of the Boyne Valley, from
Drogheda to Trim.

Trim
16 km (10 miles) S of Navan.
Trim Castle, in the centre of the town,
is the largest Anglo-Norman castle in
Ireland, and well worth a visit, especially for its massive keep. Across the
river from this is **Talbot's Castle**, an
impressive fortified manor house. **Trim
Heritage Centre**, *tel. (046) 37227.*

The Midlands

Ardagh
11 km (7 miles) SE of Longford.
Small, well-kept village has new **Heritage Centre**, *open 10am-6pm Mon-Fri,
10am-9pm Sun, summer, also open in
winter by arr. Tel. (043) 75277.* Displays and audio-visual presentations on
local history.

Athy
*19 km (12 miles) N of Carlow. TIO tel.
(0507) 31859, July, Aug.*
Modern Dominican church has
stained-glass windows and Stations of
the Cross by George Campbell, a noted
20th c. Northern Irish artist. **Heritage
Centre** *open daily in the summer, tel.
(0507) 31424.* Riverside walks beside
the River Barrow begin at Emily Square.

Ballaghmore Castle
*Near Borris-in-Ossory. Open daily, all
year. Tel. (0505) 21453.*
Built in late 15th c. and rising five
storeys high, the castle has been
superbly restored in recent times.

Birr
*37 km (23 miles) SW of Tullamore. TIO
tel. (0509) 20110. May-Sept.*
A fine heritage town, full of Georgian
features, well worth a day spent in
exploration. **Birr Vintage Festival** has
a lot to offer in August. **Birr Castle**,
home of Earl and Countess of Rosse,
has demesne and gardens open to the
public. Features include an ornamental
lake, trees, shrubs, flowers and 200
year-old box hedges, claimed to be the
oldest in the world. Theme exhibitions
in the castle. In the demesne, see the
walls and tube of the huge telescope
that remained the largest in the world
for 75 years after it was built in 1845.
Open 9am-6pm Apr-Oct, 9am-5pm

Nov-Mar. Tel. (0509) 20056. A historic science centre is planned for Birr, detailing scientific development in Ireland.

Birr's new **Heritage Centre**, *John's Hall, open 2.30pm-5.30pm daily, Apr-Sept,* built in the fashion of a miniature Greek temple, details town history. **Slieve Bloom display centre**, *Railway Road, open 10am-6pm Mon-Fri, 2.30pm-6pm Sat, Sun, July-Sept. Tel. (0509) 20029.* Includes details on wildlife of Slieve Bloom mountains.

Carrickmacross
24 km (15 miles) W of Dundalk.
Carrickmacross Lace Gallery, *Market Square, open 9.30am-5.30pm Mon-Tues, Thurs-Sat, May-Oct. Tel. (042) 62506.* Displays of locally-made lace, which is offered for sale.

Carrigglas Manor
5 km (3 miles) NE of Longford. Open 1pm-5.30pm Mon, Thurs-Sat, 2pm-6pm Sun. Tel. (043) 45165.
Gothic house built in 1837 retains much of its original furnishings. The stable block dates from 1790 and was built on the site of an earlier house. Small costume museum. Woodlands, garden, tearoom.

Castleblayney
19 km (12 miles) SE of Monaghan.
Small inlet town on shores of Lough Muckno. The **Regional Park** is *open daily, tel. (042) 46356,* and is ideal for water sports, boats, coarse fishing. The surrounding wooded park offers nature trails, orienteering and golf. Bar, restaurant.

Cavan
30 km (19 miles) SW of Clones. TIO tel. (049) 31942, June-Sept.
Small town set amid low hills with excellent coarse fishing in nearby lakes. See glass being blown and cut at **Cavan Crystal factory**, *Dublin Road, open 9.30am-5.30pm Mon-Fri, 10am-5pm for factory tours. Tel. (049) 31800.* The shop and video presentation suite are open the same hours. Shop also open 2pm-5pm, Sat-Sun. **Lifeforce Mill**, *open daily,* is a restoration of an 1840s water-powered flour mill which has been fully refurbished as a visitor centre.

Clones
21 km (13 miles) SW of Monaghan.
Ancient Celtic Cross in Diamond, 22 m (75 ft) high round tower in graveyard near the Cavan road and early bronze age court cairn. Sarcophagus dates back to early Christian times. Exact origins unknown but worth a close look. **Clones Lace Guild**, *open daily, tel. (047) 51051/51729,* has displays of locally made lace, some items are also for sale. Coffee shop.

Corlea Centre
13 km (8 miles) S of Longford. Open 9.30am-6.30pm, daily, June-Sept, tel. (043) 22386.
A timber trackway found here was dated to 147 BC, well preserved by the bog. This unique example of Irish prehistory is documented in the new **Corlea Trackway Exhibition Centre**.

Dún A' Rí Forest Park
34 km (21 miles) W of Dundalk. Open daily all year. Tel. (042) 67320.
Set beside the Cabra River, some of the many highlights include walks, nature trails, red deer enclosure, wishing well, ruins of flax mill and an old ice-house.

Emo
9 km (6 miles) S of Portlaoise. Gardens open 10.30am-5.30pm daily, all year. House open 2pm-6pm Mon, mid-Mar – mid-Oct. Tel. (0502) 26110.
Wonderful gardens with ornamental lake, fine trees and statuary complementing the 1790 house designed by James Gandon. The front of the house is approached by a 1.6 km (1 mile) long avenue of Wellingtonias.

Fore
5 km (3 miles) E of Castlepollard.
The **Seven Wonders of Fore** include water that never boils and a mill without a race. Ask for details at Abbey pub in Fore.

Heywood Gardens
6 km (4 miles) SE of Abbeyleix. Open daily, all year. Tel. (0502) 33334.
The formal gardens, completed in 1912, were designed by Sir Edwin Lutyens and landscaped by Gertrude Jekyll. They include formal Italianate gardens, lakes and woodlands.

Kilbeggan
11 km (7 miles) N of Tullamore.
Locke's Distillery, *open 9am-6p daily, Apr-Oct, 10am-4pm Nov-Ma Tel. (0506) 32134.* Founded in 17 and closed down in 1954, has bee restored as a fascinating industri museum, complete with beam engin waterwheel and old stills. Fo museum, shop, restaurant.

Kildare
13 km (8 miles) SE of Naas. TIO, te (045) 22696, June-Aug.
St Brigid's Cathedral (CI) is 19th restoration of a 13th c. buildin Visitors can climb to top of adjace round tower.

National Stud, *open 10am-6p* where breeding stallions are stable now includes new visitor centre. **Iri Horse Museum**, *open 10am-6pm, t (045) 21617,* explains history of t horse in Ireland and includes t skeleton of Arkle, the Irish racehor who won numerous races in Irela and England in the late 1960s.

The **Japanese Gardens**, *op 10am-6pm,* are considered the fine in Europe. They were laid out in t first decade of this century a symbolise man's passage through li Bridges, trees and flowers make t gardens an earthly paradise. Gard centre with bonsai trees, tea room.

Longford
44 km (27 miles) NW of Mullingar. T Main Street, tel. (043) 46566, June-Au
St Mel's Cathedral (C), was design in 1840 in the Italianate style. **Di cesan Museum**, in the right transe of the cathedral, *open 11am-1pm Mo Wed, 1pm-3pm Sat, 4pm-6pm Su June-Sept.* Has many interesting item including the 10th c. St Mel's Crozie The **Town Museum** in the old po office, *open 2pm-6pm daily, summ tel. (043) 45052,* has many interesti items of local folk and social histor

Monaghan
22 km (14 miles) NE of Castleblayne TIO Market House, tel. (047) 811. June-Sept.
St Macartan's Cathedral (C) on t Dublin Road was built between 18 and 1892 in the French Gothic sty and is one of a number of interesti public buildings in the town. T **County Museum**, *Hill Street, op 11am-5pm Tues-Sat, all year. Tel. (04 82928.* Has many prehistoric item

·gether with more recent material, cluding the 14th c. **Cross of Clogher**. ·cal lacemaking, canals and railways ·e well represented. Also has an art ·llery.

St Louis Convent, *open 10am-4pm ·on, Tues, Thurs and Fri, 2pm-4pm Sat ·d Sun, all year. Tel. (047) 82928.* ·rmerly a brewery, the convent has a ·ritage centre tracing the history of ·e order in Monaghan and Ireland.

Rossmore Forest Park, 3.5 km (2 ·iles) has lakeside and forest walks, ·ature trails, rhododendron arbours ·d fishing. Panoramic views from the ·e of **Rossmore Castle**.

Castle Leslie, *Glaslough, 11 km (7 ·iles) NE of Monaghan, open 12 noon- ·m daily, June-Aug, 12 noon-7pm Sat ·d Sun, Easter-Oct. Tel. (047) 88109.* · late 17th c. edifice, the castle was ·ce a favourite haunt of W.B. Yeats.

·ountmellick

·km (6 miles) N of Portlaoise.
·sitor Centre, Irishtown, *open ·30am-5pm Mon-Fri, 2pm-6pm Sat ·d Sun, all year. Tel. (0502) 24525.*

Has details of Quaker history in the town, the local industrial heritage and Mountmellick lace.

Mullagh
9 km (6 miles) E of Virginia.
Small, attractive village planning a heritage centre to one of Ireland's first Christians, St Kilian, who was born here.

Mullingar
51 km (32 miles) SE of Longford. TIO Dublin Road, tel. (044) 48650, all year.
Cathedral of Christ the King (C) is a striking structure, built in 1936. The mosaics in the chapels near the high altar were executed by Russian artist, Boris Anrep. **Cathedral Museum**, *open by arr., tel. (044) 48333*, includes a letter written by St Oliver Plunkett, together with his vestments.

Town Museum, *open 2pm-5.30pm Mon-Fri, June-Sept.* Located in 18th c. Market House, the museum has many local history relics. **Military Museum**, *Columb Barracks, open by arr., tel. (044) 48391*, has mementoes of the

Army in Mullingar and on UN service.
Midlands Arts Resource Centre, *Austin Friar Street, open daily, tel. (044) 43308.* Contemporary Irish art exhibitions. **Mullingar Pewter**, *46 Dominick Street*, renowned pewter maker. *Open 9am-5.30pm Mon-Fri, all year. Tel. (044) 48791.* **Canton Casey's pub**, town centre, dates back 200 years and has suitably historic interior.

Belvedere House Gardens, *5 km (3 miles) S of Mullingar. Open 12 noon-6pm daily, May-Sept, tel. (044) 40861.* Terraced gardens descend in three levels to shores of Lough Ennell. Also walled gardens, landscaped parkland.

Newbridge
11 km (7 miles) W of Naas. TIO tel. (045) 33835, July-Aug.
Newbridge Cutlery makes attractive tableware. **Visitor Centre** *open daily, all year. Tel. (045) 31301.*

Peatland World, Lullymore
24 km (15 miles) N of Kildare. Open 10am-6pm Mon-Fri, 2pm-6pm Sat, Sun, all year. Tel. (045) 60353.

·cke's distillery, Kilbeggan, Co. Westmeath

The interpretative centre highlights the history and development of the bogs that cover much of the flat central plain of Ireland, as well as their flora and fauna. Nearby **Lullymore Heritage Park** recreates times past.

Portarlington
27 km (17 miles) SW of Tullamore.
Once home to a strong French-speaking Huguenot community, who built the French church in 1696 (it was rebuilt in 1853). Many of the French settlers are buried in the graveyard. **Town Museum**, *Main Street, open 2pm-5pm Sun, all year.* Details some French history relating to the town, besides Bronze Age artefacts and an 1866 pillar box, one of the oldest in Ireland.

Rathdowney
14 km (9 miles) W of Durrow.
Donaghmore Museum, *open 2pm-5pm daily, summer. Tel. Portlaoise TIO on (0502) 21178.* Once a workhouse, the museum now has collection of antique farm machinery, kitchen implements. Matron's room has been reconstructed, as has the dairy house.

Rock of Dunamase
6 km (4 miles) E of Portlaoise.
This rock, rising from the plain, is capped by a ruined fortress. Excellent views of the surrounding countryside from the 60 m (200 ft) high summit.

Slieve Bloom Environment Park, Kinnity
18 km (11 miles) E of Birr.
Forest walks on slopes of Slieve Bloom mountains. Waterfalls and wildlife.

Stradbally
11 km (7 miles) E of Portlaoise.
Most attractive main street, steeply sloping and flower lined. The **Steam Museum**, *open 10am-4pm Tues-Sat, Easter-Oct, tel. (0502) 25444,* has a collection of old steam powered machinery, including threshing machines. Narrow gauge railway runs for 1. 6 km (1 mile) through adjacent woods. **Vintage steam rally** held on August bank holiday. **Steam train trips**, *tel. (0502) 60609/46535.*

Timahoe
8 km (5 miles) S of Stradbally.
Attractive village set around an extensive green, with 12th c. round tower

in good condition. A memorial on the green marks the visit here by a former President of Ireland, Erskine Childers, in 1974. The late Richard Nixon, US President 1969–1974, came here in 1970 in search of his family's ancestral links.

Tullamore
40 km (25 miles) SE of Athlone. TIO tel. (0506) 52617, June-Aug.
Attractive heritage town that owed much of its earlier development to the opening of the Grand Canal in 1798. **Charleville Forest Castle**, *open 2pm-5pm Sat, Sun and bank holidays, Apr-May, 11am-5pm Wed-Sun, June-Sept. Tel. (0506) 21279.* Just outside the town on the Birr road, this magnificent Gothic revival building dates from 1812 and was designed by Francis Johnston, who was also the architect of Dublin's GPO. With 56 rooms, the castle has been extensively renovated in recent years. Set in fine woodland grounds.

Tullynally Castle
2 km (1 mile) W of Castlepollard. Open 2pm-6pm daily, July-Aug and by arr. Gardens open 10am-5pm daily, May-Oct. Tel. (044) 61159.
The castle, built in the 18th c. and extended in the 19th c., is the largest castellated house in Ireland, the seat of the Earls of Longford and the Irish base of the Pakenham literary family. Portraits, furnishings, library, large kitchen worth seeing, also landscaped park, flower and kitchen gardens.

Tyrellspass
24 km (15 miles) SW of Kinnegad.
Village set around an impressive green. **Tyrellspass Castle**, *open 10am-6pm Mon-Sat, 12.30pm-6pm Sun, all year. Tel. (044) 23105.* This 15th c. castle has a museum, antiques and books.

Virginia
83 km (52 miles) NW of Dublin.
Charming village in South Cavan. Main street leads to yew-tree lined grounds of Church of Ireland church. Walks to shores of Lough Ramor.

Carlow & Kilkenny

Abbeyleix
35 km (22 miles) N of Kilkenny.
Attractive town with a broad ma[...] street and interesting parish chur[...] (C). A **heritage centre**, detailing t[...] history of the town and its defun[...] textile manufacturing tradition[...] should be completed in 1995. In t[...] meantime, **Morrissey's pub** is [...] perfect heritage place, preserving [...] turn of the century style, complete wi[...] photographs, old bottles and other o[...] packaging. You can buy everythi[...] here – drinks, groceries and new[...] papers. The **de Vesci demesne**, *op[...] daily in summer,* is worth seeing, as [...] the CI church adjoining the estate, [...] it's open.

Altamont Gardens
9 km (5 miles) SE of Tullow. Open 2p[...] 6pm Sun and bank holidays, Apr-O[...] or by arr. Tel. (0503) 57128.
Fine gardens on the banks of the Riv[...] Slaney, with views of the Wickl[...] Mountains. Ornamental lakes, wa[...] and nature paths.

Ballitore
4 km (3 miles) N of Moone.
The **Quaker Museum**, *open 11a[...] 6pm Tues-Sat, 2pm-5pm Sun, duri[...] the summer. Tel. (01) 668 3684.* T[...] museum is housed in an 18th c. scho[...] house, and has a great deal of mater[...] on the Quakers who lived in the ar[...] **Crookstown Mill**, *open daily, all ye[...] tel. (0507) 23222,* has many fascinati[...] artefacts from the old milling indus[...] and records social order.

Callan
16 km (10 miles) SW of Kilkenny.

River Barrow at Borris, Co. Carlow

Rothe House, Kilkenny, Co. Kilkenny

Edmund Ignatius Rice, founder of the Christian Brothers, was born in an old farmhouse here, which can by seen daily, by arr. with the adjoining monastery. *Tel. (056) 25141.*

Carlow

38 km (24 miles) NE of Kilkenny. TIO tel. (0503) 31554 all year.

This modest town was formerly an Anglo-Norman stronghold and is the capital of one of Ireland's smallest counties. Interesting walks through the narrow laneways and along the banks of the River Barrow. **Carlow Castle**: ruins of this 13th c. edifice are in the grounds of Corcoran's mineral water factory by the bridge. Much of the castle was destroyed in the early 19th c. when a local doctor used explosives while he was trying to turn the place into a lunatic asylum. *Open 9.30am-5pm Mon-Fri, all year.*

County Museum, *open 9.30am-5.30pm Tues-Sat, 2.30pm-5.30pm, Sun, all year. Tel. (0503) 31324.* Located in the town hall, the museum has many local history exhibits, including a blacksmith's forge, a dairy and country kitchen. Also an old printing press once used by the local *Nationalist and Leinster Times* newspaper. **Cathedral of the Assumption (C)**, *off Tullow Street.* Consecrated in 1833, this edifice has windows by Harry Clarke and a distinctive spire.

Oak Park Agricultural Research Station, *3 km (2 miles) N of Carlow, open 9am-5pm Mon-Fri, all year, tel. (0503) 31425.* Run by Teagasc, it has extensive woodland lakes and a wildfowl sanctuary. **Browne's Hill Demesne**, *3 km (2 miles) E of Carlow* has a magnificent dolmen; its capstone is the largest in Ireland.

Castlecomer

20 km (12 miles) N of Kilkenny.

Built to a classical design in the 17th c., it still has a gracious air, despite its one-time coalmining industry. Reddy's pub has relics of old coal mines.

Castledermot

14 km (9 miles) SE of Athy.

Two well-preserved medieval high crosses and a 10th c. round tower equally good condition. Unfortunate only the chancel walls remain of th 14th c. Franciscan friary.

Dunmore Cave

11 km (7 miles) N of Kilkenny. Ope 10am-5pm Tues-Sat, 2pm-5pm Su mid-Mar – mid-June, 10am-7pm dai mid-June – mid-Sept, 10am-6pm dai mid-Sept – Oct, 10am-5pm Sat, St and bank holidays, Nov-mid-Mar. T (056) 67726.

Arguably the finest limestone caves Ireland, made up of a series of cavern There was a Viking massacre here 928. Exhibitions and displays in th visitor centre.

Graiguenamanagh

32 km (20 miles) SE of Kilkenny.

Attractive village set on banks of th River Barrow. Duiske Inn, near th bridge, has many photographs of th old village. **Duiske Abbey**, the large Cistercian foundation in Ireland, bu in the 13th c., has been restored to original glory.

nistioge

km (5 miles) SW of Thomastown.
Thoroughly unspoiled and attractive village by banks of the River Nore. Treelined square and walks by the river. Two interesting churches: one is Catholic, the other Church of Ireland. In the graveyard of the latter church, Mary Tighe, the celebrated late 18th/early 19th c. poetess is buried. Ruins of 13th c. castle. Armillary sphere in square is ancient Greek device to depict the progress of the earth and moon.

Woodstock Park, *1.5 km (1 mile) of the village* was once the estate of the local landowner. The ruins of the mansion, which burnt down over 70 years ago, stare out over what had been the formal gardens and arboretum. Visitors can walk through the grounds.

erpoint Abbey

km (2 miles) SW of Thomastown. Open 10am-5pm Tues-Sun, mid-Apr – May, end Sept – mid-Oct, 9.30am-5.30pm daily, June-end Sept. Tel. (056) 4623.
Cistercian foundation dating from late 12th c. is one of Ireland's finest monastic ruins. Unique cloister carvings. Small visitor centre.

ells Priory

3 km (8 miles) S of Kilkenny.
Founded in 12th c., the extensive ruins run down to the King's River.

ilkenny

17 km (73 miles) SW of Dublin. Pop 500. TIO Rose Inn Street, tel. (056) 1500 all year.
This medieval city, set on the banks of the River Nore, is now designated as one of Ireland's main heritage towns, with a wealth of sites and facilities for visitors. During the 17th c., Kilkenny came close to upstaging Dublin as the administrative centre of Ireland, but now it is renowned as a cultural and historical centre, well worth the time spent in exploration. Kilkenny has a very varied and comprehensive arts festival in August.

The **Kilkenny CityScope Exhibition**, *Rose Inn Street, open 9am-6pm Mon-Sat, 10am-5pm Sun, May-Sept, 9am-5pm Tues-Sat, Oct-Apr. Tel. (056) 1500.* The best place to start a tour of the city. This audio-visual presentation in the former Shee Alms House is

centred around a model of Kilkenny as it was in 1640.

Kilkenny Castle, *open 10.30am-5pm daily, Apr-May, 10am-7pm daily, June-Sept, 10.30am-5pm Tues-Sat, 11am-5pm Sun, Oct-Mar. Tel. (056) 21450.* Built in the 12th c. and was extensively remodelled in the 19th c. The rooms have been restored and are open to view, including the Long Gallery. A suite of servants' rooms has been turned into the **Butler Art Gallery**, a fine venue for contemporary art exhibitions. The castle is soon to be the location for the National Furniture Collection. The grounds, with woodland walks, lake and formal terraced garden, have also been restored.

St Canice's Cathedral (CI). *Open 9am-6pm Mon-Sat, 2pm-6pm Sun, Easter -Oct, 10am-4pm Mon-Sat, 2pm-4pm Sun, Oct-Apr.* Built in the 13th c., St Canice's is one of the most striking medieval churches in Ireland. The view from the top of the round tower, next to cathedral, is equally impressive, provided you have a head for heights.

Rothe House, *Parliament Street, open 10.30am-5pm Mon-Sat, 3pm-5pm Sun, Apr-Oct, 3pm-5pm Sun, Nov-Mar. Tel. (056) 22893.* Three houses make up this Tudor masterpiece, meticulously restored to form an elaborate museum of Kilkenny history. Items on show are many and varied, from old picture postcards to an 1850 Kilkenny-made double bass. Also includes an interpretative and genealogy centre. Gardens being restored.

Kyteler's Inn, *St Kieran's Street*, has been an inn since 1324. Dame Alice Kyteler, a noted Kilkenny witch, was born here in 1280. **Black Abbey (C)**, *Abbey Street*. Built in 1225, the nave and transept have been restored as a Dominican church. **Smithwick's Brewery**, *open Mon-Fri, all year. Tel. (056) 21021.* Video of brewery and tour of the 14th c. abbey in its grounds. **Kilkenny Design Workshops**, *opposite the castle, open daily, all year.*

Tynan's Bridge House bar, near the castle, has an authentic Edwardian interior, with marble counter and gas lights, while the **Club House Hotel**, *Patrick Street*, has intriguing collection of 19th c. political cartoons.

Leighlinbridge

11 km (7 miles) S of Carlow.

Attractive village set on banks of River Barrow, with ruins of 16th c. tower. Walks along the river bank.

Moone

19 km (12 miles) NE of Carlow.
Moone High Cross has 51 elaborate carved panels. The walls of the nearby Moone High Cross Inn are lined with fascinating historical newspaper cuttings and photographs.

Thomastown

18 km (11 miles) S of Kilkenny.
Delightful but traffic-congested market town on banks of the River Nore. Walks in town and in surrounding demesnes. **Water Garden**, *open 10am-6pm daily, May-Sept, tel. (056) 24478,* is small and very peaceful, with lots of aquatic plants.

Tullow

12 km (7 miles) SE of Carlow.
Tullow Museum, beside bridge over River Slaney, *open 2pm-5pm Wed, summer, 2pm-5pm Sun, all year.* Display of historical items, including vestments of Fr John Murphy, who led the insurrection at Vinegar Hill in 1798. Annual agricultural show in Tullow on August 15.

Wicklow Mountains

Arklow

14 km (9 miles) S of Wicklow Town.
Maritime Museum, *St Mary's Road, open 10am-5pm Mon-Fri, summer only, and by arr. Tel. (0402) 32868.* Display of many items relating to Arklow's long maritime history. **Arklow Pottery**, *tel. (0402) 32401,* has guided tours and shop. Riverside, harbour walks.

Aughrim
14 km (9 miles) NW of Arklow.
Pleasant riverside village, surrounded by forests, excellent for walking.

Avoca
26 km (16 miles) S of Wicklow Town.
See Tom Moore's tree, near the **Meeting of the Waters**, where he spent many hours lost in contemplation. The mill at **Avoca Handweavers**, *tel. (0402) 35105*, dates back to 1723. Also shop and restaurant.

Avondale Estate
2.5 km (1.5 miles) S of Rathdrum. Open 10am-6pm daily, May-Sept, 11am-5pm, Oct-Apr. Tel. (0404) 46111.
Charles Stewart Parnell, the great late 19th c. political leader who fell from grace, lived in this charming house which was built in 1799 and has now been restored. An audio-visual presentation details his life and the main rooms display fascinating mementoes. The estate has an arboretum, river walks, car parks and a tea-shop.

Baltinglass
30 km (19 miles) SW of Blessington.
Impressive ruins of a 12th c. abbey on the banks of River Slaney. **Baltinglass Hill**, *2 km (1 mile) east of Baltinglass* is worth the climb to see the Bronze Age cairn and enjoy the excellent views. **Hume Castle** at nearby *Kiltegan, open 10am-2pm daily, Apr, Sept. Tel. (0508) 73215.* This exotic, castellated, 19th c. mansion has an extensive walled estate and two lakes.

Blessington
27 km (18 miles) SW of Dublin.
Broad, tree-lined Main Street is very French in appearance. **Ardenode Deer Farm**, *Ballymore Eustace, open Wed and Sat. Tel. (045) 64428.* **Cruises** on Blessington Lake, *daily (in season), tel. (045) 65850.*

Bray
12 km (8 miles) S of Dublin.
Seaside town with long promenade and shingle beach. **Bray Heritage Centre**, *Lower Main Street, next to Royal Hotel, open 10am-4pm daily, summer. Tel. (01) 286 7128.* Has many local artefacts and mementoes and the building also houses the Bray TIO.

Brittas Bay
13 km (8 miles) S of Wicklow Town.
Popular sandy beach stretching for 5 km (3 miles) backed by dunes.

Glendalough
24 km (15 miles) W of Wicklow Town. Open 9.30am-5pm daily, mid-Oct – mid-Mar, 9.30am-6pm daily, mid-Mar – May, 9am-6.30pm daily, June-Aug, 9.30am-6pm daily, Sept – mid Oct. Tel. (0404) 45325/45352.
One of Ireland's most attractively set and extensive monastic sites. The principal ruins, just east of the Lower Lake, are the cathedral, an 11th c. nave, chancel and **St Kevin's Church**, usually called St Kevin's Kitchen, which is a fine example of early Irish barrel-vaulted oratory. Beside the church is an almost-perfect round tower. Less accessible, on the south shore of the Upper Lake, are **Teampall na Skellig** (Church of the Rock) and **St Kevin's Bed**, cut into the rock face.

The **Visitor Centre** has exhibitions and an audio-visual show. **Craft Centre**, *open daily, tel. (0404) 45156*, featuring jewellery making and weaving, gallery and tearoom. **Glendalough Woods**, *1.5 km (1 mile) west of Laragh*, have nature trails and forest walks. There are guided walks from the information point at the Upper Lake through **Wicklow National Park**, which is currently being developed.

Glen of Imaal
Dwyer McAllister Cottage, Derrynamuck. Open 2pm-6pm daily, mid-June – mid-Sept.
Walks in four forests: Leitrim, Knickeen, Knockamunnion and Stranahely. **Dwyer McAllister Cottage**, *Derrynamuck*, is where the famed rebel, Michael Dwyer, held out against British troops before escaping over the snow-covered mountains.

Greystones
8 km (5 miles) S of Bray.
Attractive seaside village with harbour and walk along seafront.

Kilruddery Gardens
2 km (1 mile) S of Bray. Open 1pm-5pm daily, May-June, Sept, tel. (01) 268 3405.
Ireland's only 17th c. gardens, set at the foot of the Little Sugar Loaf mountain.

Mount Usher Gardens
Ashford, 8 km (5 miles) NW of Wicklow Town. Open 10.30am-6pm Mon-Sat, 11am-6pm Sun, Mar 17-end Nov. Tel. (0404) 40116/40205.
These attractive gardens beside the Dargle river have more than 5,000 species of plants from azaleas to rhododendrons. Tea room, craft shops.

National Garden Centre
Kilquade, 8 km (5 miles) SE of Greystones. Open 10am-6pm Mon-Sat, 1pm-6pm Sun. Tel. (01) 281 9890.
15 garden layouts, mountain streams and ponds.

Powerscourt Estate
Enniskerry, 19 km (12 miles) S of Dublin. Gardens open 9.30am-5.30pm daily, Mar-Oct. Waterfall, open 9.30am-7pm daily, summer, 10.30am-dusk, winter. Tel. (01) 286 7676.
Vast estate in the shadow of the Wicklow mountains has Italian and Japanese gardens, complete with sweeping terraces, antique sculpture and fountains. Ruined great house is due to be restored. Craft shops, garden centre, café.

Agricultural Heritage Display Centre, *Coolakay House, Enniskerry. Tel. (01) 286 2423.* Working farm with displays of old implements and machinery, from early 18th c. Tearoom.

Rathdrum
16 km (10 miles) SW of Wicklow Town.
Small, attractive town surrounded by forests. **Parnell Memorial Park** commemorates the great leader. **Clara Lara Fun Park**, *Vale of Clara, near Rathdrum. Open daily, tel. (0404) 46161.* Water-based sports, picnic, restaurant.

Roundwood
19 km (12 miles) SW of Bray.
Highest village in Ireland, 238 m (781 ft) above sea level. Walk along Main Street for distant glimpses of reservoir. Market in parish hall on Sunday afternoons. **Ballinastoe Studio Pottery**, *Enniskerry Road, 5 km (3 miles) from Roundwood. Open 10am-6pm daily, all year. Tel. (01) 281 8151.* Close by are **Loughs Tay and Dan**, *3 km (2 miles) W of Roundwood.* The countryside which surrounds them

Glendalough, Co. Wicklow

surely the most desolate and remote in eastern Ireland and is very Scandinavian looking.

Russborough House
3 km (2 miles) SE of Blessington. Open 10.30am-5.30pm Sun and bank holidays, Apr-May, Sept-Oct, 10.30am-5.30pm daily June-Aug. Tel. (045) 65239.
Great Palladian house, built 1740-1750, has Beit art collection with works by Goya, Rubens, Velasquez, Vermeer. Irish silverware, magnificent Francini plasterwork. Furniture, carpets, tapestries. Shop, restaurant, children's playground.

Shillelagh
8 km (5 miles) S of Tinahely.
Good walks in the hills surrounding this attractively set village. A portion of the nearby ancient oak forest at Coolattin Woods has been saved for posterity.

Wicklow Gap
The R756 runs for some 32 km (20 miles) across some of the most spectacular mountain landscapes in Ireland, including the Wicklow Gap, between Hollywood in west Wicklow and Glendalough.

Wicklow Town
48 km (30 miles) S of Dublin. Pop. 6,000. TIO Fitzwilliam Square, tel. (0404) 69117, all year.
The administrative centre of Ireland's garden county, Wicklow Town has a strong maritime feel, enhanced by its busy harbour and two piers. Its best-known son is Captain Robert Halpin, born in the Bridge Inn in 1836, who became captain of the Great Eastern cable laying ship. The **Fitzwilliam Square Memorial** commemorates Capt Halpin. Many historic items relating to Halpin can be seen at **Tinakilly Country House and Restaurant**, *2 km (1 mile) north of the town*, which he built as his retirement home.

The town's busy and straggling Main Street has many small craft and gift shops, and is divided into two levels. **St Lavinius Church (CI)** has a Norman doorway, an informative memorial to the aforesaid Halpin and a Russian-style copper dome. On the headland beyond the harbour are the remains of the castle, begun in the late

12th c. In the town, directly opposite the **Grand Hotel**, the ruins of the 13th c. Franciscan friary can be seen by arr. with the parish priest in adjoining presbytery.

Wicklow's old jail is currently being converted into a museum and heritage centre and this should be completed in 1995. Enjoyable walks beside the river Leitrim, along the west quays, the breakwater and pier. **Hunter's Hotel** *in Rathnew, 3 km (2 miles) N of Wicklow*, has fine riverside gardens and some interesting historical photographs inside. South of Wicklow Head is **Silver Strand**, an attractive and popular sandy beach.

Woodenbridge
8 km (5 miles) NW of Arklow.
One of the most attractive villages in Ireland, set where three valleys meet.

Wexford Shores

Ballyhack
1.5 km (1 mile) E of Passage East, across Waterford Harbour.
Attractive seaside village. **Ballyhack Castle**, *open 12 noon-6pm Wed-Sun, Apr-June, Sept, 10am-6pm daily, July-Aug. Tel. Pierce McAuliffe (051) 89468/ 88348*. This large tower house is believed to have been built about 1450 by the Knights Hospitallers of St John at the time of the Crusades.

Bunclody
21 km (14 miles) NW of Enniscorthy.
Spaciously laid-out town with broad main square divided in two by fast-flowing stream. Attractively set in the shadow of the Blackstairs mountains.

Courtown
6 km (3. 5 miles) SE of Gorey.
Popular seaside resort, with small bu interesting harbour and entertainments

Dunbrody Abbey
20 km (12 miles) S of New Ross. Nea Campile.
Great roofless church dating from the 12th c., built by Cistercian monks from St Mary's Abbey, Dublin. Key at cottage by main road entrance.

Enniscorthy
24 km (15 miles) N of Wexford.
Delightful town set beside the Rive Slaney; the main part of the town rise up steeply from the river. Lots o historical atmosphere, it is worth exploring the quaysides and man narrow laneways. Castle rebuilt in lat 16th c. houses the **Town Museum** *open 10am-6pm Mon-Sat, 2pm-5.30pm Sun, June-Oct, 2pm-5.30pm daily, Nov May. Tel. (054) 35926*. Folk section relics of 1798 and mementoes of Ennis corthy's industrial history. **Vinegar Hil** on east outskirts of the town is wher the decisive 1798 battle was fought an offers fine views over the town. S **Aidan's Cathedral (C)** was designe by Pugin in the 1840s.

There are three fascinating potterie near Enniscorthy. The oldest, goin back over 300 years, is **Carley's Bridg Pottery**, *open 8.30am-5.30pm Mon-Fr all year, tel. (054) 33512*. The nearb **Paddy Murphy's Hillview Pottery** *open daily, all year, tel. (054) 3544* makes pots the traditional way. **Kiltre Bridge Pottery**, *open daily, all yea tel. (054) 35107*, does very moder stylish pottery, mostly glazed. Als weaving workshop.

Ferns
34 km (21 miles) N of Wexford.
Once the capital of Leinster, this sma village has some impressive ruins including a 13th c. castle, a 12th c Augustinian abbey and a cathedral.

Hook Peninsula
E side of Waterford harbour.
This narrow finger of land conclude with the **Hook Head lighthouse**, on of the oldest lights for shipping in th world. Now that it has been automated there are plans to turn it into a mar time heritage centre.

The main town is **Fethard-on-Sea**

with its "shell" garage, the façade of which is covered in sea shells. **Tintern Abbey**, the impressive ruins of a 13th c. Cistercian foundation, is 6 km (3.5 miles) north of Fethard-on-Sea. On the east side of the peninsula is Slade, with its tiny harbour, 18th c. fish house and 14th c. castle. **Baginbun Bay** is the site of the first Norman landing in Ireland in 1169. On the west side of the peninsula is Dollar Bay, one of several sandy bays which are reputed to hide Spanish treasure.

The large crack in the ceiling of the 18th c. **Loftus Hall** is supposedly the spot where the Devil exited in a hurry and as a result cannot be repaired. The old military fort at Duncannon is also being restored. The entire Hook Peninsula drive is well signposted.

Irish National Heritage Park
5 km (3 miles) N of Wexford. Open daily. Tel. (053) 41733.
Full sized replicas of the homesteads, burial locations and places of worship used in prehistoric Ireland. This living history lesson goes up to Viking and Norman times. Lectures, guided tours.

John F. Kennedy Park
8 km (5 miles) S of New Ross. Open 10am-8pm daily, May-Aug, 10am-7.30pm daily, Apr, Sept, 10am-5pm daily Oct-Mar. Tel. (051) 388171.
This 165 ha (410 acre) park commemorates the late J.F. Kennedy, US President from 1961-1963, whose ancestors came from this immediate area. Arboretum with large selection of trees and shrubs from around the world, forest garden. Tremendous views from summit of nearby Slieve Coillte hill. Visitor centre, pony and trap rides, miniature railway, café. At nearby Dunganstown, the one room Kennedy homestead is shrine to JFK's 1963 visit to Ireland.

Johnstown Castle
6 km (4 miles) S of Wexford.
The castle itself, which contains an agricultural research centre, is not open to visitors, but the ornamental grounds, with over 200 species of trees and shrubs, together with a large lake, can be seen. On working days, visitors can also see the walled gardens and hothouses.

The **Irish Agricultural Museum**, *open 9am-5pm Mon-Fri, 2pm-5pm*

Sun, June-Aug, 9am-5pm Mon-Fri, Apr, May, Sept, 9am-5pm Mon-Fri, Sept-Mar. Tel. (053) 42888. This is an excellent presentation of the old rural way of life, with sections on transport, dairying and farming, besides farmhouse interiors and country furniture. Replica workshops on rural crafts, including the blacksmith's forge, basket and harness makers.

Kilmore Quay
16 km (10 miles) S of Wexford. Open 12 noon-6pm daily, May-Oct. Tel. (053) 29655/29832.
A long, straggling Main Street with a dozen thatched cottages, runs down to the harbour. The old Guillemot II lightship in the harbour has been turned into a full-scale **maritime museum**, with sections on lightships, the Irish Navy, the old Irish Shipping fleet and modern fishing. Also ships' models. In calm summer weather, boats will take visitors to the two offshore **Saltee Islands**, renowned bird sanctuaries.

Lady's Island
10 km (6 miles) SW of Rosslare. Just W of Carnsore Point.
A place of pilgrimage on 15 August. A causeway joins the island to the mainland. Ruins include a Norman tower that leans at greater angle than Leaning Tower of Pisa.

New Ross
37 km (23 miles) E of Wexford. TIO tel. (051) 21857, June-Aug.
The streets of this town set on the River Barrow are positively medieval. The town rises steeply from the quaysides, with its Dutch-style buildings, to the hilltop area of New Ross, which is full of Middle-Ages fortifications. There are substantial ruins of the 13 c. parish church at St Mary's, Church Lane. **Tholsel** (Town Hall) has civic insignia and documents, including charter of King James II. **Berkeley Doll and Costume Museum**, *open daily 11.30am-5.30pm*, includes collections of dolls and rocking horses. New Ross is scheduled to have a heritage centre linked to the JFK theme and this should be ready for 1995. River cruises along River Barrow and River Nore, with dinner served on board, summer only. Tel. (051) 21723.

Rosslare Harbour
25 km (16 miles) S of Wexford. TIO, tel. (053) 33622, all year.
The port may be the busy terminal for ferries from Wales and northern France, but the town will repay a closer inspection. There are many fine sandy beaches and cliff walks in this area. The bar of the Hotel Rosslare has a well-presented maritime museum, with many relics, documents and photographs of local shipping and the local lifeboat, even an old-style diving suit.

Tacumshane Windmill
3 km (2 miles) W of Lady's Island lake.
This 19th c. windmill, complete with sails, was restored about 40 years ago. Both sails and interior are in perfect condition. Key at adjoining house.

Wexford
144 km (90 miles) S of Dublin. Pop 10,000. TIO The Crescent tel. (053) 23111 all year.
An ancient town whose name is derived from its Viking title, set on the broad expanses of the River Slaney estuary. The narrow Main Street with many slate-fronted buildings winds its way through the town. Many laneways run off the Main Street, some to the wooden quaysides, others to the heights of the town. In summer, Wexford is understandably popular, packed with cars and people, while in the autumn, the **Wexford Opera Festival**, *tel. (053) 22144/22240*, attracts the cosmopolitan black-tie crowd to the tiny but gloriously refurbished **Theatre Royal**. Many fringe events and exhibitions are also staged during the festival.

Westgate Heritage Centre, *open 9.30am-5.30pm, Mon-Sat, all year, 2pm-5pm, Sun, July-Aug. Tel. (053) 42611*, uses audio-visual techniques to detail the long and tortuous history of this seafaring, culture-loving town. See the adjoining town walls dating back to Norman times, which are now restored. Substantial ruins of 12th c. **Selskar Abbey**, *Westgate*. Henry II spent Lent here in 1172 as penance for the murder of Thomas à Becket.

Wexford has some fine churches, including the so-called "Twin Sisters", the **Church of the Immaculate Conception (C)**, *Rowe Street* and the **Church of the Assumption (C)**, *Bride Street*, both 19th c. and almost identical in external appearance. **St Francis (C)**,

Late evening, Wexford town

School Street is a Franciscan friary church founded in 1230, plundered in Cromwell's time and remodelled in 1784. **St Iberius' Church (CI)**, *North Main Street*, was built in the 17th c. and has been substantially restored, but there has been a church on this site for 1,500 years.

White's Hotel, where the opera festival was founded, has many interesting historical photographs, while the town library, next door, also has much material on Wexford. **Wexford Arts Centre**, *Cornmarket, open daily, all year, tel. (053) 23764*, hosts concerts, exhibitions and other events.

Wexford Wildfowl Reserve

North Slob, Wexford. Open 9am-6pm daily, mid-Apr – Sept, 10am-5pm daily, Oct – mid Apr. Tel. (053) 23129.
Over a third of the world's population of white-fronted Greenland geese winter here. The visitor centre has an audio-visual show, exhibitions and guided tours.

Yola Farmstead

Open daily, June-Sept. Tel. (053) 31177.
This tourist-related development commemorates the Yola dialect developed in Wexford by the Normans from the 12th c. onwards. By the early 19th c. it had largely died out. The farmstead has several thatched buildings and out buildings, including a privy made for two! Crystal glass making, a café, and nightly entertainment in summer.

The South

Travelling south, into Tipperary and on to Cork, one of Ireland's great
sights suddenly comes into view: Cashel's massive ruins perched, Acropolis-
like, on a rock outcrop that dominates the surrounding plain. Cashel has
smaller delights too, like Brú Ború, its folk village and the Bothán Scoir, a
venerable one-roomed thatched cottage. The south is like that, set pieces
that startle and surprise besides innumerable smaller places. Cork, both
city and county, has an immense variety of sights. East Cork contains
Midleton's whiskey heritage centre and the Queenstown Experience in
Cobh, while Youghal, with its unsurpassed town walls, has rediscovered its
rich past. The bays, inlets and peninsulas of West Cork have their own
natural magic, culminating in the unspoiled, desolate splendour of the
Beara peninsula. The most spectacular vistas of all in the south are to be
found from one end to the other of the Ring of Kerry, a spectacular coastal
route, while all through the Dingle peninsula more mountains
and deserted beaches entice the traveller.

Tipperary Castles

Athassel Abbey
8 km (5 miles) W of Golden.
Extensive ruins of 12th c. Augustinian foundation in delightfully rural location.

Cahir
17 km (11 miles) S of Cashel. TIO, tel. (052) 41453, May-Sept.
Small, quiet town beside the River Suir, with Georgian buildings and unusual churches. **Cahir Castle**, *open 10am–6pm daily, Apr–mid-June, mid-Sept–mid-Oct, 9am-7.30pm daily, mid-June–mid-Sept, 10am-4.30pm daily, mid-Oct–Mar. Tel. (052) 41011.* This magnificent 12th c. structure has been elaborately restored and features include a courtyard and hall, a massive keep and high enclosing walls. Good views of the river and town from the parapets. Audio-visual show on all main sites in the area.
The **Swiss Cottage**, *open 10am-4.30pm Tues-Sun, Mar, Oct, Nov, 10am-5pm Tues-Sun, Apr, 10am-6pm daily, May-Sept. Tel. (052) 41144.* A cottage ornée built in early 19th c. to a design by John Nash, the noted Regency architect. It has been lovingly restored in recent years, both interior and exterior. **Cahir Park**, *immediately south of the town* offers walks and scenic views by the River Suir.

Carrick-on-Suir
27 km (17 miles) NW of Waterford.
Scenically set on the banks of the River Suir, with Comeragh Mountains to the immediate south. **Ormond Castle**, *open 9.30am-6.30pm daily, mid-June–Sept. Tel. (051) 640787.* Splendidly restored, this 15th c. castle is fronted by a 16th c. Elizabethan manor house with some of the finest Tudor plasterwork in Ireland, and is surrounded by parkland. **Heritage Centre**, *open daily, tel. (051) 640200,* has historical and genealogical details on the area, together with exhibitions. **Tipperary Crystal**, *5 km (3 miles) E of Carrick-on-Suir. Open 8am-7pm Mon-Sat, 11am-6pm Sun and bank holidays. Tel. (051) 641188.* Former Waterford Crystal craftsmen run this crystal glassmaking company, which has gained a fine reputation for itself. Factory tours and showrooms.

Cashel
160 km (100 miles) SW of Dublin. Pop 2, 500.
The Rock of Cashel. *Open 9.30am-4.30pm daily, mid-Sept–mid-Mar, 9.30am-5.30pm daily, mid-Mar–early June, 9am-7.30pm daily, early June–mid Sept. Tel. (062) 61437.* The Rock dominates the town and the surrounding plain and is one of Ireland's great historic sites, the country's equivalent to the Acropolis. Main features are the 12th c. round tower, **Cormac's Chapel**, styled as a miniature cathedral, **St Patrick's Cross** and the **Cathedral of St Patrick**. In the Hall of the **Vicar's Choral**, which you go through on entering the site, there are many fascinating relics and replicas, which will give you a feel for the site and prepare you for scrambling round these extraordinary ruins. Audio-visual presentation, full guide service.
Brú Ború, *open 9am-12 midnight daily, mid-June–mid-Sept (entertainment at 9pm), 9am-5pm daily, mid-Sept – mid-June (no shows). Tel. (062) 61122.* In the shadow of the Rock, has a genealogy centre, folk theatre and restaurant. **Cashel Folk Village**, *open daily, Mar–Oct, tel. (062) 61947.* Located in Chapel Lane, the village has many historical artefacts, a 19th c. house and shop fronts. **Bothan Scoir**, *Clonmel Road, tel. (062) 61360,* is a totally authentic single room 17th c. thatched cottage and is well worth a visit. **Cashel Palace Hotel**, built in Queen Anne style in 1730, was formerly a residence of Church of Ireland archbishops and has magnificent interiors with original panelling and carvings. The sumptious food and wine complement those interiors well. **Bolton Library**, *open 9.30am-5.30pm Mon-Sat, 2.30pm-5.30pm Sun, all year. Tel. (062) 61944.* Set in the precincts of the Church of Ireland Cathedral, the library has one of the finest collections of 16th and 17th c. books in Ireland, together with ancient maps. **Hore Abbey**, just west of the Rock of Cashel, is the ruin of a Cistercian abbey, while Dominican friary ruins can be seen in Chapel Lane, opposite the folk village. **Padraig O Mathuna**, *Main Street,* creates exquisite jewellery with Celtic themes, together with paintings and sculptures.

Clonmel
48 km (30 miles) NW of Waterford. TIO, tel. (052) 22960 all year.
Tipperary's main town, set most attractively beside the River Suir, is an excellent base for exploring the Comeragh and Knockmealdown mountains. The **Museum and Art Gallery**, *Parnell Street, open 10am-5pm Tues-Sat, all year, tel. (052) 21399,* has large collection of local historical material and paintings. **St Mary's Church (CI)** is mainly a 19th c. structure but includes part of an earlier 14th c. church and is surrounded by extensive sections of the old town walls. Other interesting churches in the town include the **Franciscan (C)** in *Abbey Street,* a 19th c. church which has been restored.
Hearn's Hotel, *Parnell Street,* recently refurbished, saw the start of Bianconi's horse-drawn car service in 1815. **The Main Guard**, about 350 years old, is being restored. Facing it, at the other end of O'Connell Street, is **West Gate**, a 19th c. reconstruction of the 14th c. original. Enjoyable walks along the quaysides and park which skirt the River Suir.

Dromineer
10 km (6 miles) W of Nenagh.
Fine resort on the eastern shores of Lough Derg, a sailing mecca in summer.

Fethard
14 km (9 miles) NW of Clonmel.
Large sections of town wall in this atmospheric medieval settlement have been restored. The **Farm, Folk and Transport Museum**, *open 10am-6pm daily, June-Aug, Sun, Sept–May, tel. (052) 31516.* Based beside the old railway station, the museum has a wealth

of items, over 2,500, from old farm implements and craft tools to prams and a Victorian hearse.

Holy Cross

5 km (4 miles) S of Thurles. Open 10am-6pm daily, all year. Tel. (0504) 43241.
The restored abbey was founded in 1168 by the Benedictines but was soon afterwards transferred to the Cistercians. Set on the banks of the River Suir it is an impressive institution.

Nenagh

39 km (24 miles) NE of Thurles. TIO tel. (067) 31610 May-Sept.
Nenagh Heritage Centre, open 10am-5pm Mon-Fri, 2.30pm-5pm Sun, May-Sept, tel. (067) 32633. The former governor's house of the old county jail has been turned into a fascinating reconstruction of aspects of the old way of life, including a shop and a schoolroom. Also hosts temporary exhibitions. **Nenagh Castle**, nearby, has circular keep that was part of a larger early 13th c. castle.

Roscrea

34 km (21 miles) N of Thurles.
Interesting market town with strong heritage that has been well preserved. **Damer House**, early 18th c., was saved from demolition and fully restored, its richly carved main staircase is a notable feature. The formal garden at the rear of the house has also been restored. However the most recent restoration has been of **Roscrea Castle**, *open 9.30am-6.30pm daily June-Sept. Tel. (0505) 21850.* Dating from the late 13th c., it comprises a gate tower, curtain walls and two corner towers.

The round tower, on the main road into Roscrea from Dublin can now be seen to full advantage, since its surroundings have been cleared and landscaped. **Mount St Joseph's**, *3 km (2 miles) W of Roscrea, tel. (0505) 21711*, is Ireland's only silk farm. A Cistercian abbey, it is the sister foundation of Mount Melleray in Co Waterford.

Terryglass

24 km (15 miles) N of Nenagh.
This lakeside village at north-east corner of Lough Derg is full of character and includes a 13th c. castle.

Thurles

21 km (13 miles) N of Cashel.
Market town on banks of the River Suir. Remnants of two Norman castles by the bridge, while in the spacious Liberty Square, the **Hayes Hotel** was the building in which the Gaelic Athletic Association was founded in 1884. **GAA Museum** is now open; strong on the history of the Association, with models and memorabilia. The **Cathedral (C)** built in late 19th c. has a richly-decorated interior, while its campanile is a landmark for miles around.

Tipperary Town

40 km (25 miles) SW of Thurles. TIO tel. (062) 51457 all year.
Tipperary was immortalised in the World War I marching song "It's a Long Way to Tipperary", which has been sung around the world ever since. That song and many other aspects of Tipperary's heritage are due to be

Cahir Castle, Cahir, Co. Tipperary

commemorated in the town's new heritage centre, which will reflect the cultural and social life of Tipperary Town and its hinterland. The old jail is also due to be restored.

There are interesting riverside walks and some streets in the centre of the town have fine old shopfronts. The **Celtic Plantarum** *Dundrum, 12 km (8 miles) NE of Tipperary Town, open daily, all year, tel. (062) 71303,* and has over 2,500 species of trees, plants, shrubs. The **Glen of Aherlow,** *immediately S of Tipperary Town,* is a noted beauty spot with outstanding mountain views.

Toomyvara
16 km (10 miles) E of Nenagh.
The folk museum features many items from rural way of life now vanished. Daily, key at next door house.

Waterford City and Coast

Annestown
20 km (12 miles) W of Tramore.
Small resort with good sandy beach, on the coast road from Tramore to Dungarvan. Beware of disused mine workings in the area.

Bunmahon
18 km (11 miles) W of Tramore.
Tiny fishing village with sandy beach surrounded by cliffs.

Cappoquin
30 km (19 miles) N of Youghal.
Cappoquin House and Gardens *open 9am-1pm Mon-Sat, Apr-July, tel. (058) 54275.* Noted coarse fishing location at head of tidal section of River Black-

water. Excellent views of the nearby Knockmealdown mountains and an impressive drive over the mountains to Clogheen. On the slopes north of Cappoquin is **Mount Mellerary Abbey** where the monks follow various crafts including baking. Details of visitations are recorded in the nearby grotto. Visitors can attend services in the chapel. The abbey offers impressive views over the Blackwater valley.

Cheekpoint
13 km (8 miles) E of Waterford.
Small riverside village has peaceful atmosphere. Nearby Cheekpoint Hill gives fine views of Waterford city and harbour.

Clonea
5 km (3 miles) E of Dungarvan.
Fine sandy beach.

Curraghmore House
Portlaw 16 km (10 miles) W of Waterford. Open 2pm-5pm Thurs and bank holidays, Apr-Sept. Tel. (051) 387101/387102.
Gardens in beautiful setting, but only the shell of house remains.

Dungarvan
30 km (19 miles) NE of Youghal.
'Capital' of West Waterford, this attractive town is set on the coast where the River Colligan broadens into Dungarvan harbour. Fine walks along the harbour and promenade. **Dungarvan Castle** is late 12th c., while Abbeyside, on the east bank of the river, has a tower from a 13th c. Augustinian priory which is used as belfry by next door church. The west wall is all that is left of 12th c. **Abbeyside Castle. Shell Cottage** has exterior walls covered in thousands of sea shells.

Dungarvan Museum, *Lower Main Street, open 9am-5pm Mon-Fri, all year, tel. (058) 41231,* is housed in a 17th c. Market House and contains many relics and mementoes of Dungarvan's maritime history. The **Seanachie Inn,** *off the Cork road,* west of Dungarvan, has historical relics, including old furniture and kitchen implements. A railway once connected Dungarvan to Waterford, and there are plans to use the track to once again run steam trains.

Touraneena Heritage Centre, *Ballinamult, 16 km (10 miles) NW of*

Dungarvan. Open daily, all year. The now vanished rural way of life is depicted here, including buttermaking, dairy, blacksmith's forge.

Dunmore East
14 km (9 miles) SE of Waterford.
Attractive fishing village with busy harbour. Neat, Breton-style thatched cottages along the Main Street. Walks around harbour area, including breakwater, down to the coves. Small sandy beach.

Lismore
6 km (4 miles) W of Cappoquin.
The Lismore Experience, *open daily, Apr–Sept, Sun, Tel. (058) 54975.* This impressive new heritage centre in the old courthouse uses multi-media techniques to tell the story of the town since the arrival of St Carthage in 636. Historical display room.

St Carthach's Cathedral (CI) is a striking medieval church, with Gothic vaulting and impressive memorials, a complete contrast to the very Italianate Catholic cathedral nearby. Also see streets with English-style Tudor houses and **Lismore Castle Gardens,** *open 2pm-5pm daily except Sat, May-Sept. Tel. (058) 54424.* Magnificent verdant setting overlooking the River Blackwater.

Passage East
11 km (7 miles) E of Waterford.
Old world riverside village with fine views of Waterford harbour from the quays and from the hill close to the village. Regular daily **car ferry to Ballyhack** on far side of estuary, *tel. (051) 382488.* **Geneva Barracks,** *5 km (3 miles) S of Passage East,* is a settlement founded in 1785 by gold and silversmiths from Geneva but was never completed. It was later used to hold prisoners after the 1798 rising, and the extensive walls can still be seen. **Woodstown Strand,** *5 km (3 miles) S of Passage East,* is a pleasant, secluded beach.

Stradbally
10 km (6 miles) NE of Dungarvan.
Small, attractive village that is a mass of flowers in summer. Interesting coves and fine cliff walks in the vicinity.

Tramore
13 km (8 miles) S of Waterford. TIO

Waterford city

old railway station, tel. (051) 381572 June-Aug.
Busy seaside town with many new amenities for visitors. **Celtworld**, *open daily, Apr-Sept, Sat and Sun, Oct-Mar, tel. (051) 386166,* uses modern, computer-driven, audio-visual techniques to depict ancient Celtic mythology. Interactive area, theme shop and Laserworld; electronic games with Celtic theme. **Splashworld**, *open daily, all year, tel. (051) 386565,* is a futuristic water-based leisure centre.

Other Tramore attractions include an amusement park covering more than 20 ha (50 acres), a racetrack which provides horse racing all through the year, including the main event in August. Walks along the promenade and to the nearby coves. **The Majestic Hotel**, opposite the TIO, has interesting old photographs of the town. There are also walks along both sides of Tramore Bay to see the old style navigation marks, including the most famous, the early 19th c. Metal Man, on the west side of bay. Waterford regional airport, between Tramore and Dunmore East,

has an **Aviation Museum**, *open daily,* in old DC3 aircraft. **Knockeen Dolmen**, *5 km (3 miles) N of Tramore,* is an excellently preserved dolmen.

Waterford

166 km (103 miles) SW of Dublin. Pop 40,000. TIO 41 The Quay, tel. (051) 75788, all year.
This busy port mainly on south bank of the broad River Suir has many interesting historical buildings and some fascinating laneways. In recent years, the city centre's facilities have been radically upgraded.

The **Waterford Heritage Centre**, *open 10am-8pm Mon-Fri, 10am-5pm Sat, June-Sept, 10am-6pm Mon-Fri, 10am-1pm Sat, Apr, May, Oct. Tel. (051) 71227.* Just off the quays, near Reginald's Tower, the centre has many relics of Viking and Norman Waterford which were discovered during recent excavations.

Reginald's Tower, *on the quays, open 10am-8pm Mon-Fri, 10am-5pm Sat, June-Sept, 10am-6pm Mon-Fri, 10am-1pm Sat, Apr, May, Oct. Tel.*

(051) 73501. Built in 1003 by the Vikings, it now houses the civic museum with collections of archive material and regalia.

The **French Church**, *Greyfriars Street,* built in 1240 as a Franciscan foundation, later housed Huguenot refugees. **Holy Trinity Cathedral (C)**, *Barronstrand Street,* has fine late 18th c. interior. **Christ Church Cathedral (CI)**, *off the Mall,* is equally impressive inside and dates from 1773. The square tower is the only major remnant of the 13th c. **Blackfriars Dominican Friary** *in Arundel Square,* while the **Chamber of Commerce** building in *George's Street* has a fine late 18th c. interior. Also see the council chamber in the **City Hall** and sections of old city walls. The Waterford Room in the **City Library**, *Lady Lane* can provide the visitor with a good range of material on the city's ancient and modern history.

The **Theatre Royal**, *The Mall,* has a lovely Victorian interior, one of only three in Ireland (the others are the Grand Opera House, Belfast and the

Gaiety Theatre, Dublin). **Garter Lane Arts Centre**, *22A O'Connell Street, open daily, tel. (051) 77153*, has regular exhibitions, cultural events, cinema and theatre performances. The **Waterford Light Opera Festival** is staged every September.

The **People's Park**, *off Dunmore East Road*, has fine open spaces, and **Mount Congreve Demesne**, *8 km (5 miles) W of Waterford, tel. (051) 384115*, offer attractive gardens in a woodland setting. **Tory Hill**, *13 km (8 miles) N of Waterford*, affords superb views of the surrounding plain, Waterford city and harbour.

East Cork

Ardmore
13 km (8 miles) E of Youghal.
Pleasant seaside resort with some thatched cottages and long, sandy beach. Cliff walks above the village. St Declan's 7th c. monastic settlement includes a round tower. Amusement park.

Ballycotton
32 km (20 miles) W of Youghal.
Fishing village overlooking bay and lighthouse. Sandy beaches, cliff walks, good views.

Carrigtwohill
12 km (8 miles) E of Cork city.
Barryscourt Castle *between Fota Island and Cobh, open 10.30am-6.30pm daily, Apr-Oct, tel. (021) 883864*, is a 13th c. castle with courtyard and towers which has been restored recently. Craft and coffee shop.

Cloyne
29 km (18 miles) E of Cork.

Cloyne Cathedral (CI) is a restored, spacious 14th c. building, with a monument to the one-time bishop of Cloyne, the philosopher, George Berkeley (1685–1753). **Cloyne Round Tower**, *opposite the cathedral*, was built in 900 but is still in sound condition and can be climbed. Key from house in corner of the cathedral grounds.

Cobh
24 km (15 miles) E of Cork.
This fine 19th c. seaside town, with a Brighton-style "Crescent" (terrace of Georgian houses), is enjoying a revival. The main reason for Cobh's resurgence is the **Queenstown Story**, *open daily, 10am–6pm, all year, tel. (021) 813591*. Located in part of the railway station., it tells how innumerable people emigrated through Cobh and Queenstown to North America during the past two centuries. It also records details of the great trans-Atlantic liners that once called to Cork Harbour, and the sinking of the Lusitania off Kinsale in 1915. The **Lusitania Memorial**, *on the quayside*. Many victims of the tragedy are buried at Cobh's Old Church Cemetery.

Cobh Museum, *open 3pm-6pm Wed, May-Sept, 3pm-6pm Sun, all year, tel. (021) 811562*, in the former Presbyterian Church has many items relating to Cobh's history. **St Colman's Cathedral (C)** on a hill above the town is a magnificent 19th c. Gothic edifice with carillon to match. Recitals are often given in summer. Regular **harbour trips** are run from *Kennedy Pier, Cobh. Tel. Marine Transport (021) 811485*. A new car ferry connects Cobh to Ringaskiddy, across Cork Harbour, which means you can avoid driving through Cork city.

Fota Island
16 km (10 miles) E of Cork.
Wildlife Park, *tel. (021) 812678*, has many species, including antelopes, giraffes, emus and ostriches, and is unaffected by the current development plans for the site. The arboretum is one of the finest in Ireland. **Fota House** is occasionally open to visitors.

Glanmire
6 km (4 miles) E of Cork
Dunkathel House, *open 2pm-6pm Wed-Sun, May-Oct, tel. (021) 821014*,

is an attractive 18th c. building full of antiques and paintings. **Riverstown House**, *open 2pm-6pm Thurs-Sat, May-Sept, tel. (021) 821205*. Built in 1602 and rebuilt in 1745, the house features fine plasterwork and an art gallery.

Midleton
22 km (14 miles) E of Cork.
Jameson Heritage Centre, *open 10am-6pm daily, Mar-Nov. Last tour at 4pm, tel. (021) 661551/682821*. The old whiskey distillery, in use between 1825 and 1975, has been turned into this comprehensive centre which details the history and methods of whiskey distillation.

Shanagarry
3 km (2 miles) NW of Ballycotton.
This castle which belonged to William Penn, 17th c. Quaker who founded the US State of Pennsylvania, has been restored by Stephen Pearce, owner of the nearby pottery.

Youghal
48 km (30 miles) E of Cork. Pop. 5,500. TIO tel. (024) 92390, June-Sept.
This historic walled town and seaport is starting to realise its tourist potential, with the opening of its new heritage centre. Youghal is most attractively set, between steep hillsides and the broad expanse of the Blackwater estuary. Founded by the Anglo-Normans in the 13th c., many of the town's medieval buildings can still be seen along the 1.5 km (1 mile) long Main Street. In many ways, the town still has the air of a 1950s seaside resort.

The **Heritage Centre** *in the Old Market House, open 9.30am-5.30pm Mon-Fri, all year, tel. (024) 92390*, tells the story of Youghal and its seaborne trade. The four-storey clock tower nearby, was built in 1777 to straddle the Main Street, and during a period of insurrection in the late 1790s, rebels were often hung from the windows as an example to the populace. The **Devonshire Arms Hotel** *in Pearse Square, at the south end of Main Street*, has many photographs of the old Youghal sailing schooners. The **Moby Dick pub**, *just off the quays*, has film stills and other photographs of the making of the film 'Moby Dick' in Youghal in 1954.

St Mary's Collegiate Church (CI)

Midleton whiskey distillery, Midleton, Co. Cork

was built in the 11th c. and is one of Ireland's finest medieval churches, standing in the shadow of the town walls. **Myrtle Grove House** *tel. (024) 92274*, is where Sir Walter Raleigh, the man who brought the potato and tobacco to this part of the world, lived when he was Mayor of Youghal in the 16th c. Regular guided tours.

Perk's Amusement Park is on the south side of the town, near former railway station for old Cork-Youghal passenger line. There are also some 8 km (5 miles) of sandy beaches in the vicinity of Youghal.

North Cork & the Blackwater Valley

Annes Grove Gardens
1. 5 km (1 mile) SE of Castletownroche. Open 10am-5pm Mon-Fri, 1pm-6pm Sat and Sun, Easter-Sept. Tel. (022) 26145.
The gardens sweep down to the River Awbeg, a tributary of the Blackwater. Several of them, including the cliff garden and the walled garden, contain many rare trees and shrubs which are displayed in a naturalistic style, a 'must' for every true gardener.

Ballyporeen
13 km (8 miles) E of Mitchelstown.
The great-grandfather of Ronald Reagan, US President 1981–1989, lived here over 150 years ago, and Ronald and Nancy Reagan visited the area in 1984. The heritage centre at the cross-roads has material commemorating that visit.

Buttevant
11 km (7 miles) N of Mallow.
Buttevant Friary, beside the River Awbeg, was an Augustinian foundation built in the 13th c. Its chancel walls are still largely intact, as is the dovecot.

Doneraile
10 km (6 miles) NE of Mallow.
Canon Sheehan, the author, was parish priest here 1895–1913 and is com-memorated by a memorial. **Doneraile Wildlife Park**, *open daily*, has herds of deer in mature parkland setting.

Fermoy

30 km (19 miles) E of Mallow.
Delightfully situated on the banks of the River Blackwater, the town has some fine riverside walks. The promenade is lined with stately trees, while on the opposite side of the river are the wooded grounds of **Castlehyde House**.

Kanturk

16 km (10 miles) NW of Mallow.
This attractive market town is set on the Rivers Allua and Dallua which are spanned by three bridges. The main bridge has interesting 18th c. poetic inscriptions carved on its parapet. Work on **Kanturk Castle** stopped about 1609, because the English Privy Council decided it was too grand for an Irish subject (the local chieftain MacDonagh MacCarthy). Consequently the building was never finished though the ruins can still be seen. **Assolas House**, a 17th c. manor house which is now a hotel, has many fine furnishings and a well-tended garden.

Kilcoman

5 km (3 miles) NW of Doneraile.
The 16th c. English poet, Edmund Spenser, lived in **Kilcoman Castle** for eight years and was said to have written much of the "Faerie Queen" here. Access to the ruins is difficult and in any case they are best seen from afar. **Kilcoman Bog**, *tel. (022) 24200*, is a bird observatory, with many rare species, including Greenland white-fronted geese.

Kildorrery

13 km (8 miles) W of Mitchelstown.
Site of **Bowen's Court**, where the distinguished novelist Elizabeth Bowen once lived. The location is marked, though the house was sold in 1959 and was later demolished.

Killavullen

10 km (6 miles) E of Mallow.
This 250 year-old house, once the ancestral home of the Hennessy brandy distilling family, stands on a cliff overlooking the River Blackwater. There are caves nearby, though they have not been developed as a tourist attraction and should only be explored by experts.

Near Mallow, Co. Cork

Longueville House

5 km (3 miles) W of Mallow.
This fine early 18th c. house has been converted into a hotel. It has its own vineyard, one of two in the area. The restaurant has portraits of all the Presidents of Ireland.

Macroom

37 km (24 miles) W of Cork
Lively mid-Cork town which was once the property of Admiral Sir William Penn, whose son founded Pennsylvania. Penn Castle, now mostly demolished, stands in the town square.

Mallow

35 km (22 miles) NW of Cork. Pop. 6,000. Tourist Information Point, Bridge Street.
Now a prosperous market town and agricultural processing centre, Mallow had a much livelier reputation in the 18th and early 19th c., when many visitors would come to take the waters and indulge in riotous living. Their antics were reflected in the song "The Rakes of Mallow". The present day town is altogether more sedate. **Mallow Castle** is not open, but visitors can wander the grounds, which extend to the River Blackwater, and see the herds of deer on the estate. Thomas Davis, the 19th c. patriot writer, was baptised in 1814 in **St Anne's Church** which dates from the 13th c. The ruins of a 17th c. church can be seen at the entrance to the demesne. **Nano Nagle Heritage Centre**, *12 km (7 miles) E of Mallow*. The centre commemorates the 18th c. educational pioneer, who founded the Presentation Sisters in Cork and was a formative influence on Irish education.

Mitchelstown

34 km (21 miles) NW of Mallow.
This undistinguished-looking town with its broad Main Street is a busy agricultural processing centre. The monument in the main square commemorates men shot at a Land League meeting in 1887. See also **St Fanahan's Holy Well**; the saint died over 1,500 years ago, and the water is said to have curative properties. **Burncourt House**, *13 km (8 miles) NE of Mitchelstown*. See the shell of the 17th c. house which the owner burned before he would allow Cromwell to occupy it.
    Mitchelstown Caves, *16 km (10*

miles) NE of Mitchelstown. Open 10am-6pm daily, all year. Tel. (052) 67246. Access to the new cave is easy and a guide will take you on a 3 km (2 miles) tour of the passages and chambers. The old cave can only be reached by rope or ladder.

Cork City and Leeside

Ballincollig

8 km (5 miles) W of city centre.
The late 18th c. gunpowder mills have been restored as a **Heritage Centre**, *open 10am-6pm daily, Apr-Sept. Tel. (021) 874430.*

Blackrock

3 km (2 miles) SE of city centre.
Cork Heritage Park has a centre detailing many aspects of local history, including the fire service, transport and the Pike family – Quakers in the area who gave sustenance during the 19th c. famine. The **Maritime Museum**, *open 10am-5.30pm daily, Apr-Sept, tel. (021) 358854*, has history of Cork Harbour.

Blarney

8 km (5 miles) NW of Cork city.
Blarney Castle and Stone, *open from 9am daily, all year. Closing time varies. Tel. (021) 385282.* Climb over 100 steps to the battlements of the central keep, which is all that's left of this 15th c. castle. Hang upside down, with an attendant holding your feet, and kiss the stone, whereupon you'll be blessed with the gift of the gab. If you want to stay a strong, silent type, simply admire the lush pastoral views. The castle grounds have pleasant walks

and include a grove of ancient yew trees.

Blarney Castle House, *open 12 noon-6pm Mon-Sat, June-Sept.* Built in the Scottish baronial style, complete with turrets and gables. The interior has been fully refurbished and has many family portraits. Many craft shops are clustered around the green, near the castle entrance. The biggest store is the **Blarney Woollen Mills**, in a converted 19th c. factory. **Blarney Woodland Farm**, *Waterloo Road, open 10am-6pm daily, tel. (021) 385733.* Has many farmyard pets, plus a tearoom.

Cork

259 km (161 miles) SW of Dublin. Pop. 127,000. TIO Grand Parade. Tel. (021) 273251, all year.
The second city of the Republic maintains a strong hold on its originality and separateness. In the 19th c., it emerged as a centre of the Fenian movement, earning Cork the title of "Rebel City". A large portion of the city centre was burned down during the War of Independence, only to be rebuilt in a flat, dull style. Today, Cork is a city keenly aware of its cultural, social and literary heritage, and this is reflected in various new developments. The **Cork Choral and Folk Dance Festival** in May, its **Film Festival** in October and the **Jazz Festival**, also in October, are three of the year's cultural highlights.

St Finbarre's Cathedral (CI), near the South Mall, was built in early French Gothic style over a century ago and has fine carvings and mosaics. See the cannon ball fired during the 1690 siege of Cork, which was found embedded in the tower of the previous church on this site. **Christ Church** is now an archives centre at South Main Street; built in 1702 some of its foundations date from the Norman church built on this site about 1270 and badly damaged in the 1690 siege. This archives centre is shortly to be moved to the former Albert Quay railway station, near the City Hall. **Church of Christ the King (C)**, *Turner's Cross, north-west Cork*, is one of Ireland's most stunning modern churches, with equally impressive views over the city. **Red Abbey**, *between George's Quay and Douglas Street*, the square tower is all that is left of this medieval abbey, the oldest

structure in Cork. **St Anne's (CI)**: would-be Quasimodos can ring the tunes on the Shandon bells. The church has a small but interesting historical exhibition, including old books. **Honan Chapel, University College**, was built in 1915/16 and has superb stained-glass windows by Harry Clarke and Sarah Purser.

Public Museum, *open 11am-5pm Mon-Fri, 3pm-5pm Sun, all year. Closed on bank holidays, Sundays and all other public holidays. Tel. (021) 276871.* Located in Fitzgeralds Park, the museum has a natural history section, an ogham stone collection, old photographs, notably of 1916–1922 period, old documents, silverware and a reference library. The former **Women's Gaol**, *Sunday's Well*, which was the improbable setting for Cork's first radio station, in the mid-1920s, now has another use as a **Heritage Centre**, *open 9.30am-8pm daily, Apr-Oct, 10am-4pm Sat, Sun, Nov-Mar.* The audio-visual show details Cork life in the 19th c. A second phase of the project is due to include, appropriately, RTE's historical broadcasting collection. **Collins Barracks** has Michael Collins memorabilia, *tel. (021) 397577.* Cork's mainline railway station has an 1848 steam locomotive that clocked up nearly half a million miles for the Great Southern Railway.

Triskel Arts Centre, *Tobin Street, off South Main Street, tel. (021) 272022* has regular performances, exhibitions, restaurant, wine bar. **Crawford Municipal School of Art**, *open 10am-5pm Mon-Sat, 10am-1pm Sat, all year.* Displays of many local scenes depicted in water and oil, together with sculptures and a collection of classical casts from Vatican. Restaurant. There are also frequent exhibitions at the **Cork Arts Society Gallery**, *16 Lavitt's Quay, open 11am-6pm Tues-Sat, tel. (021) 277749.* The **Opera House**, *Emmet Place, tel. (021) 270022* has regular performances of drama, opera, variety. **Everyman Palace Theatre**, *MacCurtain Street*, is revival of 19th c. theatre originally built as a music hall. **University College, Cork**, is planning a new theatre at the Mardyke and the **Cork School of Music**, *Union Quay*, has regular evening recitals.

Elizabeth Fort, *near the Beamish & Crawford brewery*, was built in the early 17th c. and has had many changes

of use since then. There are excellent views over the city from its parapets. Daly's Suspension Bridge, Sunday's Well, also offers fine vistas of the River Lee, and the Tanto Footbridge at Blackrock, also gives good river views. Carey's Lane, off Patrick Street, was once the heart of Cork's Huguenot settlement, and now houses interesting craft shops.

An Sraidbhaile, *Grand Parade Hotel*, recreates folk life 100 years ago, with entertainment. **Shandon Craft Centre**, *opposite St Anne's Church*, has interesting workshops. The **English Market** dates from Victorian times and is a fine, covered food emporium. Food specialities sold here include two that are unique to Cork, *crubeens* (pigs trotters) and *drisheen* (a type of black pudding). For those unaccustomed to such delicacies, a strong stomach is recommended! There is also an open-air market at Coal Quay.

Cork has a good selection of pubs, including Le Chateau, Patrick Street, frequented by Cork Examiner journalists, also opera singers; An Bodhran, Oliver Plunkett Street, for traditional Irish music; Dan Lowrey's, MacCurtain Street, with period atmosphere and the Long Valley, Winthrop Street, a traditional pub.

The **Lee Walk Fields** offer good riverside walks opposite the County Hall on the western approaches to the city and there are excellent strolls along the riverside quays upstream from the city centre. **Fitzgerald Park** has sculptures as a diversion from walking. The **Marina Park** *3 km (2 miles) downstream from the city centre*, and the Lough south of the city centre is a wildlife habitat full of bird species.

Crosshaven

27 km (17 miles) SE of Cork.
The narrow main street of this delightful seaside town has interesting pubs and shops. Walk up the hill to **St Brigid's Church (C)** for fine views of the surrounding area. The **Royal Cork Yacht Club** was founded in 1720 making it the oldest in the world. Climb the headland road from Crosshaven to **Fort Camden**, a great military fortification built in the late 18th c. and scheduled to be converted into a military history museum.

St Finbarre's cathedral, Cork city

Kilcrea Abbey
km (5 miles) W of Ballincollig.
Grave of Noble Art O'Leary, murdered in 1773 because he wouldn't sell his horse for £5. At that time, Catholics were prevented from owning a horse worth more. Opposite the abbey are the ruins of **Kilcrea Castle**.

racton
km (3 miles) S of Carrigaline.
See the aptly-named 'Overdraft' pub and enjoy extensive forest walks.

West Cork

drigole, Beara Peninsula
0 km (12 miles) SW of Glengarriff.
The road over the **Healy Pass** was started during the great mid-19th c. famine and only completed in 1931. It is a difficult drive, but if the weather is clear you will be rewarded with tremendous views.

hakista
8 km (12 miles) SW of Bantry.
Just before the tiny windswept village is the impressive memorial to the 329 victims of the Air India jumbo jet that crashed into the Atlantic in 1985. The narrow, winding road continues for a further 16 km (10 miles) to the tip of the **Sheep's Head peninsula**.

llihies
km (6 miles) W of Castletownbere.
The remains of the 19th c. copper mine should be explored with care. Near the village is a fine strand.

allinascarthy
km (5 miles) N of Clonakilty.

West Cork landscape

Ballydehob
16 km (10 miles) S of Bantry.
Quaint harbour. The winding and decorative village streets have craft workshops, but the main highlight is the former railway viaduct now converted into a walkway, giving panoramic views of **Roaring Water Bay**.

Baltimore
13 km (8 miles) SW of Skibbereen.
Centuries old fishing village, full of atmosphere. From the White Beacon atop the cliffs above Baltimore, you get fine views of the harbour and Sherkin Island. From the **Baltimore Diving and Water Sports Centre**, tel. (028) 20300, visitors can go down to explore the many wrecks in the area.

Bandon
21 km (13 miles) NW of Kinsale.
Busy market town. **Heritage Centre** in *former Christ Church (CI)*, built in 1610, reputed to have been the first church built in Ireland for Protestant worship. **Bandon Weir**, *open by arr.*, tel. (023) 41533, has a salmon leap viewing area and a wildlife sanctuary. See pottery being made at **R & J Forrester's Craft Shop and Gallery**, *83 North Main Street, tel. (023) 41360.*

Bantry
92 km (57 miles) W of Cork. TIO The Square, tel. (027) 50229, June-Sept.
Delightfully placed town at head of Bantry Bay. **Bantry House** was built in the mid-18th c. and is exquisitely furnished with tapestries and furniture. The hall, dining and drawing rooms are especially interesting. Some upstairs bedrooms are open to visitors. The gardens, with their Italianate terraces more than repay exploration, particularly with the stunning views across the bay. Craft shop, tea room. The new **French Armada Centre**, *open 10am-6pm daily, tel. (027) 51796*, details the abortive French landing in Bantry Bay in 1796. The **Kilnaurane Inscribed Stone**, near the West Lodge Hotel, has an early 7th c. carving and is unique to West Cork.

Béal-na-mBláth
3 km (2 miles) SW of Crookstown.
Memorial to General Michael Collins, killed here in 1922. The house where Collins was born, at **Woodfield**, *8 km (5 miles) SW of Clonakilty*, has been turned into a Collins memorial centre.

Bere Island
3 km (2 miles) E of Castletownbere.
Ferries from Castletownbere take about 30 minutes in calm weather. Tourist accommodation on this island with a permanent population of about 230 is limited. Explore the ruins of the former Royal Navy base, abandoned in 1938. Sailing tuition at the **Glenans Sailing Centre**, tel. (027) 75012. Sea-angling.

Castletownbere
51 km (32 miles) SW of Bantry.
This small fishing town is a good centre for exploring the rugged beauties of the Beara Peninsula. The large town square is surrounded by some interesting shops and pubs. Just south of the town is the great ruined shell of **Dunboy Castle**, built in the 19th c. by the Puxley family who owned the copper mines at Allihies. The castle was burned down in 1921, during the War of Independence.

Castletownshend
8 km (5 miles) SE of Skibbereen.
Very attractive single street village. The road descends steeply to the tiny harbour and used to have two great trees that divided the street halfway. Edith Somerville and Violet Martin, co-authors of *The Irish RM and his Experiences*, and other humorous stories of the old Anglo-Irish way of life in West Cork, lived in the village and are buried in the graveyard of **St Barrahane's Church (CI)**, at the end of the main street.

Charles Fort
5 km (3 miles) S of Kinsale on E shores of estuary. Open 9am-4.30pm Tues-Sat, 11am-5.30pm Sun, Apr-June, 9am-6pm daily, July-Sept, 9am-5pm Mon-Sat, 10am-5pm Sun, Oct. Tel. (021) 772263.
This star-shaped fort, built in late 17th c., is in a good state of preservation. Fine views out to sea. Enjoyable walk back to Kinsale, taking in Bulman's pub and the Church of Ireland graveyard in nearby Summercove and concluding

Site of the homestead (private property), where William Ford, father of Henry Ford, the US motor pioneer, was born. Plans for developing the area.

in the Spaniard Inn, Kinsale.

Clear Island

10 km (6 miles) SW of Baltimore. Ferry from Baltimore all year and from Schull in summer. Tel. (028) 20125.
The new pier on the island also improves access. A tiny museum with relics of the island's history and a bird observatory are virtually the only man-made attractions on the island, which is one of the last places in West Cork where Irish survives as a living language.

Clonakilty

35 km (22 miles) SW of Kinsale. TIO Rossa Street, tel. (023) 33226, June-Aug.
An attractive angling centre at the head of Clonakilty Bay. Many of the shop-fronts in its winding streets have their names in traditional Irish lettering. The Wheel of Fortune, a cast iron contraption, dates from about 1840 when the town got its first proper water supply. **Emmet Square** has well-preserved Georgian-style houses near Kennedy Gardens. **West Cork Regional Museum**, *Western Road, open 10.30am-5pm Mon-Sat, 2.30pm-5.30pm Sun, May-Sept,* has archaeological relics, mementoes of the town's industrial past, including brewing, the post office, social life and much on Michael Collins. The new highlight in the town is the **Model Village**, *open daily, all year, tel. (023) 33224.* Opened in 1994 and scheduled to be completed by 1996, the village has models of the main buildings in West Cork's towns and also a miniature of the much-missed West Cork Railway. The station building, which houses a restaurant, is a full-sized replica of Clonakilty's original station on the line. **Lisselan Castle**, *3 km (2 miles) from Clonakilty on the Bandon road* has homestead farm and gardens. *Open 10am-5pm Thurs, Apr-Sept, tel. (023) 33249.*

Coppinger's Court

3 km (2 miles) SW of Ross Carbery.
Ruins of the 1610 mansion which burned down 30 years after it was built. It was said to have had a chimney for every month, a door for every week and a window for every day of the year.

Courtmacsherry

5 km (3 miles) E of Timoleague.

Attractive seaside village looking out on the estuary and backed by woods. Sea-angling centre.

Creagh Gardens

6 km (4 miles) SW of Skibbereen. Open 10am-6pm daily, Easter-Sept. Tel. (028) 21267.
These privately-owned gardens covering about 12 ha (5 acres) run to the banks of the River Ilen. They have a variety of trees and shrubs.

Crookhaven

20 km (12 miles) SW of Schull.
This tiny harbour is near the end of the Mizen Head Peninsula. Just west of the harbour is the site of the Pilchard Palace, once used for storing fish. Nearby Barley Cove, with its magnificent sandy beach, is a popular resort.

Derreen Woodland Garden

Near Lauragh, on N shores of Beara peninsula. Open 2pm-6pm Sun, Tues, Thurs, Apr-Sept. Tel. (064) 83103.
First planted over a century ago, a splendid location for many specimen trees and shrubs.

Dursey Island

25 km (15 miles) W of Castletownbere.
This small, sparsely populated island has few facilities for visitors, but the trip across on the cable car is an experience in itself. There are regular daily services, *tel. (027) 73018.* There is only one tiny village on the island, Kilmichael. The island has only one road, but it leads to the old and new lighthouses at the west end. Otherwise, the main delight is plenty of fresh sea air!

Garinish Island, off Glengarriff

Open 10am-4.30pm Mon-Sat, 1pm-5pm Sun, Mar, Oct, 10am-6.30pm Mon-Sat, 1pm-7pm Sun, Apr-June, Sept, 9.30am-6.30pm Mon-Sat, 11am-7pm Sun, July and Aug. Tel. (027) 63040.
Regular boats from the mainland, last landing 30 mins before closing. Marvellous Italianate gardens designed early this century, with Grecian-style temple, old Martello Tower, shrubberies, miniature Japanese and rock gardens.

Garretstown, Courtmacsherry Bay

10 km (6 miles) SW of Kinsale.
Good beaches on the shores of the bay

and woodland walks. See what is le of the Manor House that once stoo here and the orange groves.

Glandore

6 km (4 miles) W of Ross Carbery.
Extravagantly set village overlookin Glandore harbour. The higher part c the village, with its broad street, give fine views of the harbour.

Glengarriff

18 km (11 miles) W of Bantry.
Small coastal village set in a glen. Th Eccles Hotel, built in early 19th c., an refurbished, has mementoes of Georg Bernard Shaw, the author an dramatist. Glengarriff Woods offe excellent walks.

Goleen

15 km (9 miles) SW of Schull.
This tiny village on the Mizen Hea peninsula has a new **Heritage Centre** *in the former Church of Irelan Church, is open daily during th summer, tel. TIO (028) 21766.* Has ol agricultural implements and quirk local historical items.

Gougane Barra

24 km (15 miles) NE of Bantry.
This lake, surrounded on three side by mountains, is the source of the Rive Lee. Oratory on the island is reache by short causeway.

Inchadoney Island

3 km (2 miles) S of Clonakilty.
Despite its name, this is actually par of the mainland. The long, golde sands are ideal for bathing and surfing

Inishannon

13 km (8 miles) NW of Kinsale.
This small village is home of Alice Tay lor, well-known Irish author. The ruir of the 15th c. **Dundaniel Castle** stan on the banks of the River Bandon.

James's Fort

4 km (2.5 miles) SW of Kinsale.
On the west side of the estuary a Kinsale, James's Fort was built in th early 17th c. and is approached by th bridge over the Bandon River. An olde structure, Charles's Fort, is on th opposite side of the estuary. Free acces at all times.

Kinsale, Co. Cork

Kinsale
29 km (18 miles) SW of Cork. Pop. 1,800. TIO Pier Road, tel. (021) 772234, Mar-Nov.
Kinsale is an extravagantly set town overlooking the Bandon River estuary. It is a consistent winner in the Tidy Towns competition and is popular with holidaymakers, the yachting and sea-angling fraternity and gourmets. The Spanish captured the town in 1601-2 and held it against English armies, and somehow that Spanish flavour seems to have lingered. The narrow, winding streets of Kinsale have been compared to those of Toledo.

St Multose Church (CI) has a fine interior, with old town stocks and flags from the Battle of Waterloo. Some victims of the Lusitania sinking off the Old Head of Kinsale in 1915 are buried in the graveyard. **St John the Baptist Church (C)**, *Friar's Street*, has an ornate, T-shaped, 19th c. interior. There are excellent views over the town from the front of the Carmelite Friary.

Desmond Castle, *open 9am-6pm daily, June – mid-Sept, 9am-5pm Mon-Sat, 10am-5pm Sun, mid-Sept – early Oct. Tel. (021) 774855*. Also known as the "French Prison", the castle is a three-storey town-house built around 1500 which has now been restored.

Kinsale Museum, *in the 17th c. courthouse, open 11am-5pm Mon-Sat, 3pm-5pm Sun, all year, tel. (021) 772044*, has many relics and memorabilia on the town's history, besides much material relating to the 'Lusitania'. Kinsale is scheduled to build both a heritage centre, and a wine museum. **The Bowling Green** is a delightful small, tree-lined park halfway up the hill on the west side of the harbour, and offers fine views of the town.

A wine museum planned for Kinsale is due to open in 1995 in part of the Desmond Castle. It will feature the Wine Geese-Irish people who were prominent in the wine trade in France and Spain, especially in the 18th c. Also planned for the town is a Heritage Centre to be located in the old mill opposite St Multose's Church. It should be completed in 1995.

Lough Hyne
6 km (4 miles) S of Skibbereen.
This enclosed lake, with a narrow outlet to the sea, is a marine nature reserve with many rare species. It is not suitable for bathing. The vantage point in the forest on the north side of the lake offers fine views.

Mizen Head
25 km (15 miles) SW of Schull
The old lighthouse on the head has been turned into a **Heritage Centre**, *open daily in summer, tel. (028) 21766*. It details local history and nature, and the building of the Fastnet lighthouse. Wrecks in the area are also detailed.

Old Head of Kinsale
15 km (9 miles) SW of Kinsale.
Although part of the area is due to be turned into a golf course, the Old Head still has plenty of good walks and seascapes, plus the ruins of a 15th c. de Courcey castle.

Ross Carbery
21 km (13 miles) E of Skibbereen.
Set around a square of enormous proportions, Ross Carbery has striking 17th c. cathedral (CI) and some ruins of a 6th c. monastery. Safe, sandy beaches in the vicinity.

Schull
6 km (4 miles) SW of Ballydehob.
Delightful village set around an almost totally enclosed harbour, replete with craft shops, restaurants and bookshops. **Planetarium**, *tel. (028) 28552*, has frequent shows.

Sherkin Island
Just off Baltimore, the crossing takes about 10 minutes. Attractions include an outdoor pursuits centre, marine station, natural history museum and the ruins of 15th c. Franciscan friary. Some safe, sandy beaches.

Skibbereen
34 km (21 miles) SW of Bantry. TIO North Street, tel. (028) 21766 open all year.
Busy market town on the River Ilen. The **West Cork Arts Centre**, *North Street, tel. (028) 22090*, has frequent events and exhibitions all year. The **Southern Star newspaper offices**, *Ilen Street*, have files of the old Skibbereen Eagle newspaper, which kept an eye on the Czar of Russia. They can be inspected by arr, tel. (028) 21200. The **Pro-Cathedral** dates from 1826.

At **Abbeystrewery**, on wester outskirts of Skibbereen, many loc victims of the famine are buried. Th story of the famine in the locality being developed for visitors. **Sk Gardens**, *3 km (2 miles) W c Skibbereen. Open 2pm-6pm Tue, Thurs, all year, tel. (028) 22368*. natural wildlife garden, complete wit waterfall and wildflower meadow, being developed. Also a venue fo contemporary sculpture.

Timoleague
16 km (10 miles) W of Kinsale.
Small village on the estuary of th Argideen River. **Timoleague Abbey** a Franciscan foundation built aroun 1240. Much of present building date from early 16th c. and substantial ruir can still be seen. **Timoleague Castl Gardens**, *open 12 noon-6pm dail Easter weekend and mid-May – mic Sept, tel. (028) 46116*. The garder have been devcloped over the past 15 years and include palm trees, beside two old-style walled gardens, one fo flowers, the other for fruit an vegetables

Unionhall
15 km (9 miles) E of Skibbereen.
On the opposite side of the harbour t Glandore. **Ceim Folk Museum**, *ope daily, tel. (028) 36280*, is a uniqu collection of historical artefact: including Stone Age, collected by on person, Therese O'Mahony.

Ring of Kerry & Killarney's Lakes

Aghadoe Hill
5 km (3 miles) N of Killarney.

..ins of a 7th c. church and castle, plus .agnificent views of lakes and .ountains surrounding Killarney.

allinskelligs
3 km (8 miles) NE of Waterville.
.iles of golden beaches on the shores
f Waterville Bay. See also the new Cill .alaig village Crafts Centre.

ahirsiveen
) km (25 miles) E of Killarney.
'Connell Memorial Church (C), *ain Street*, was built in 1888 to com-.emorate Daniel O'Connell, who was .orn just outside the village in 1775. .he ruins of his birthplace, **Carhan .ouse**, can still be seen. The new .eritage centre details his history and .at of the locality, including the **.alentia Weather Observatory**. The .d RIC barracks, burned during the .ar of Independence, has been turned .to a fantastic turreted creation .orthy of Euro Disney! *Open 10am-.m Mon-Sat, all year, also 10am-6pm .n, summer. Tel. (066) 72589.*

errynane House, Caherdaniel
1 km (13 miles) W of Sneem.
.pen 1pm-5pm Tues-Sun, Apr, Oct, .am-6pm Mon-Sat, 11am-7pm Sun .ay-Sept. Tel. (066) 75113.
.he house has many mementoes of the .aniel O'Connell, the great politician. .udio-visual show, tearooms. .urrounding coastal parklands, with .ature trails.

.ap of Dunloe Tour
.) km (6 miles) W of Killarney.
.irmly on the tourist trail, this makes a .emorable trip by jaunting car from .ither Killarney, or by pony and trap .om **Kate Kearney's Cottage**; also for .alkers who don't mind the busy .quine traffic.

.lenbeigh
. km (5 miles) SE of Killorglin.
.mall village surrounded by .ountains, with magnificent strand .earby. The bar of the Tower Hotel has .any old photographs of the locality. .he **Kerry Bog Village Museum**, *open .am-6pm daily, Mar-Nov*, has .aditional 19th c. thatched cottages .nd blacksmith's forge.

.ells
3 km (8 miles) W of Glenbeigh.
Midway between Glenbeigh and Cahirsiveen with panoramic views of Dingle Bay and the Blasket Islands. The old tunnels in the hillside were part of the railway that used to run from Cahirsiveen to Farranfore Junction.

Kenmare
34 km (21 miles) S of Killarney.
This delightful town was founded in 1670 and laid out with the three main streets forming a triangle. The new **Heritage Centre**, in the same building as the TIO, *open 10am-6pm Mon-Sat, May-Sept, tel. (064) 41233*, details Kenmare's history, including its Bronze Age stone circle, local industries and personalities. Baroness Thatcher, a former British prime minister, claims descent from a Kenmare washer-woman who emigrated to England in 1811.

Killarney
305 km (190 miles) SW of Dublin. Pop. 7,200. TIO Town Hall, tel. (064) 31633.
At first glance, a rather undistinguished-looking town, packed with jaunting cars and tourists, and owing its standing to its central location in Co Kerry's lake district. Killarney does have a good range of facilities for visitors and interesting historical buildings.
The **Cathedral of St Mary of the Assumption (C)** was designed by Pugin, the great 19th c. architect, while **St Mary's Church (CI)** in the town centre has a richly decorated Victorian interior. The modern **Prince of Peace Church (C)**, Fossa, near Killarney, was made by craftspeople from all over Ireland and its main door features dove and ark motifs by Helen Moloncy. The **Franciscan friary (C)**, *College Street*, dates from 1860 and has a fine Harry Clarke stained-glass window. Frequent arts and cultural events at the **Killarney Art Gallery**, *47 High Street, tel. (064) 34628* and the **Frank Lewis Gallery**, *6 Bridewell Lane, tel. (064) 34843*. The **Museum of Irish Transport**, *town centre, open 10am-6pm daily, all year, tel. (064) 32638*, has many veteran and vintage cars.
Reidy's traditional shop in Main Street is worth seeing. One of the last old-style grocery shops in Ireland. With its old-fashioned weighing scales, cash register ringing up pounds, shillings and pence, and hooks in the ceiling for hanging Christmas hams and turkeys, it preserves the pre-supermarket past perfectly, an ideal trip into nostalgia for visitors to the town.

Killorglin
21 km (13 miles) W of Killarney.
Though this hilly town, set above the River Laune, may look desolate it is full of warm, quixotic Kerry character. During the three days and nights of the Puck Fair in August, when a goat is hauled aloft to be crowned "King of the Fair", crowds make merry and enjoy the continuously intoxicated craic. The 17th c. **Kerry Woollen Mills**, *halfway between Killorglin and Killarney. Open 9am-6pm Mon-Sat, Apr-Oct, 9am-5pm Mon-Fri, Nov-Mar.*

Ladies' View
19 km (12 miles) SW of Killarney on N71.
Over a century ago, Queen Victoria and her ladies-in-waiting were amused by this lovely view. Today, that view is en-hanced by a tearoom and craft shops.

Leacanabuile Fort
5 km (3 miles) NW of Cahirsiveen.
Massive prehistoric fort. Excellent views of the nearby coast from the ramparts.

MacGillicuddy's Reeks
W of Killarney and Lough Leane.
Excellent mountain climbing range which includes **Carrantuohill**, Ireland's highest mountain, just over 1,040 metres (3,414 ft) high.

Mangerton
8 km (5 miles) S of Killarney, off N71.
Panoramic views of Killarney's lakes.

Meeting of the Waters
10 km (6 miles) SW of Killarney on N71 to Kenmare.
Another beauty spot, where rhododen-drons and other sub-tropical species flourish in the mild Kerry climate.

Muckross House
7 km (4 miles) S of Killarney.
Built in the Elizabethan-style in 1843, this baronial mansion has many rooms that still retain their original look. Craft workshops in the basement feature such skills as weaving, pottery, book-binding and printing, complemented by a 19th c. style pub. **Muckross**

aditional Farm, the most recent ddition, shows the old style way of rming life.

The surrounding **National Park**, ith its lake and mountain vistas, is oted for its oak woods and red deer erd. The new **Visitor Centre** is *open am-5.30pm daily, Nov – mid-Mar, am-6pm daily, mid-Mar – June, 9am-m daily, July, Aug, 9am-6pm daily, pt, Oct. Tel. (064) 31440*. The old enmare Road, from here to Kenmare, ves good walks across the mountains.

arknasilla
km (2 miles) E of Sneem.
ot a village but a fine Great Southern tel, with mementoes of George ernard Shaw, the playwright and ntroversialist, who often stayed here. e and his wife ignored everyone in eem! Many walks in grounds.

ass of Coomakista
km (5 miles) S of Waterville.
n the road between Sneem and aterville it offers fine views of Ballin-kelligs Bay and the Skelligs Islands.

ng of Kerry
he road which skirts the Iveragh eninsula from Kenmare to Killorglin, called the "Ring of Kerry". It stretches r 203 km (126 miles), and a day's rive will take in many places of terest, besides innumerable scenic ews.

oss Castle
km (2 miles) SW of Killarney. Open am-6pm daily, May, 9am-6.30pm aily, June-Aug, 9am-6pm daily, Sept, am-5pm daily, Oct. Tel. (064) 35851. robably built in the early 15th c. for he of the O'Donoghue Ross chief-ins. The castle has been extensively stored over nearly 15 years and is ow open for guided tours.

ossdohan Island
enmare Bay, 5 km (3 miles) SE of eem. Tel. (064) 45114.
his delightful island has many otanical highlights.

kellig Islands
5 km (10 miles) S of Valentia island. hese two, dramatic rocks rise sheer

e lakes of Killarney and MacGillicuddy's eks, Co. Kerry

from the sea. Little Skellig is a bird sanctuary, while Skellig Michael contains an ancient monastic settlement on its summit: Boats in season from Valentia.

Sneem
27 km (17 miles) W of Kenmare.
This charming village is situated where the Ardsheelaun River runs into Kenmare Bay. The short pier is ideal for a stroll. Two squares are connected by a narrow bridge. Two presidents are commemorated here, Chaim Herzog, the Dublin-born President of Israel, and Cearbhaill O Dalaigh, a former President of Ireland, who lived nearby and who died in 1976.

Sneem Museum, *in the west square is open daily in summer*. It has a fascinating collection of bric-a-brac and is ideal for browsing. The Church of Ireland, with its tower and exterior painted white, may look Elizabethan, but is believed to date from around 1810. Its interior has many photo-graphs from the local manor houses and the pew plates of the owners. Fr Michael Walsh, a 19th c. priest of the parish better-known as the "Fr O'Flynn" of the famous song, is buried in the graveyard of St Michael's (C).

Staigue Fort
20 km (12 miles) W of Sneem. Turn right at Castlecove.
Probably the finest dry stone fort in Ireland, dating back 2,000 years, this circular building is almost perfectly preserved.

Torc Waterfall
8 km (5 miles) S of Killarney, just off the road to Kenmare.
One of Ireland's finest waterfalls which can be seen from an adjacent footpath which ascends alongside. Magnificent lake views.

Valentia Island
SW of Cahirsiveen, road bridge from Portmagee.
The modern **Visitor Centre**, *open 10am-7pm daily, May, June, 9.30am-7pm July, Aug, 10am-7pm daily, Oct. Tel. (066) 76306*, tells the story of the Skelligs Islands in audio-visual form. The centre also has a craft shop and coffee shop. After they have seen the show, visitors are taken on a 90 minute cruise around the Skelligs. Also on the

island see the disused slate quarry, the grotto and the site of the long-abandoned Western Union cable station, where the first trans-Atlantic cable came ashore in 1866.

Bray Head on the south-western tip of the island and **Geokaun Mountain** on the north of the island, form first-class vantage points for scenic views. **Knightstown Harbour**, the main settlement on the island, has an atmospheric harbour.

Waterville
65 km (39 miles) W of Kenmare.
A popular resort town, though the main street is unimpressive. The **Butler Arms Hotel** has some fine photographs taken when Charlie Chaplin, the Hollywood film comedian, came on fishing holidays here. Fine sandy beaches and an inland drive beside Lough Currane.

Dingle Peninsula & North Kerry

Anascaul
16 km (10 miles) E of Dingle.
A road leads up for 5 km (3 miles) from this small, attractive village to the car park beside the **Anascaul Lake**, one of the most isolated places in the peninsula.

Ardfert
10 km (6 miles) NW of Tralee. Open daily, all year.
A monastery was founded here by St Brendan the Navigator in the 6th c. The earliest building on the site is the cathedral, built between the 11th and 17th c. Restoration is in progress, so work can only be seen from a viewing

In the Dingle Peninsula, Co. Kerry

platform. **Casement's Fort**, *2 km (1 mile) W of Ardfert*. Sir Roger Casement was arrested near this roadside earthern fort after landing on the nearby **Banna Strand** with German arms for the 1916 Rising. He is commemorated by a monument 2 km (1 mile) further on.

Ballybunion

34 km (21 miles) N of Tralee.
Seaside resort with wide sweep of beach, renowned for its summer **Bachelor Festival**, usually held in June, and its seaweed baths, which have restorative properties. The caves on the north side of the beach can be explored at low tide, but care is recommended. The ruins of the late 16th c. edifice, **Ballybunion Castle** can be seen on the promontory.

Ballyduff

13 km (8 miles) S of Ballybunion.
Rattoo Heritage Centre, *open daily in summer, tel. (066) 31501*, has details of the archaeology, folklore and history of the area.

Ballyferriter

W Dingle peninsula.
Heritage Centre, *Main Street, open daily in summer, tel. (066) 56100*, has many items on the 19th c. way of life in the locality. **St Vincent's (C)** on the opposite side of the street, has all its signs in Irish. **Potadoireacht na Caolóige Pottery**, *open 9.30am-7pm daily, May-Sept, tel. (066) 56229*, has fine workshops and showrooms.

Ballyheigue

16 km (10 miles) NW of Tralee.
The sandy beach is one of the finest in the country, stretching for 13 km (8 miles). Also ruins of 19th c. church.

Blasket Islands

W of Slea Head.
The only one of the seven islands which was ever inhabited permanently, is **Great Blasket** but that was abandoned in 1953. One of the smaller islands is owned by a former Taoiseach, Charles Haughey, and is closed, but the other islands can be visited by boat

from Dunquin. There are plans t restore some of the ruined building on Great Blasket, but in the meantime the new **Great Blasket Island Visito Centre** at *Dunquin, open 10am-6pr daily, Apr-Sept, tel. (066) 56444*, detai the heritage of the island, including i strong literary tradition. **The Fuair (sound) room** enables visitors t experience the sounds of the island from keening to crashing waves.

Blennerville

3 km (2 miles) S of Tralee.
A steam railway runs from Tralee on section of the old **Tralee-Dingle Rai way**, using a restored locomotive fron that line. *Open daily, Apr-Sept, tel. (06C 28888*. **The windmill**, *open 10am-6pr daily, Apr-Oct, tel. (066) 21064*, stand five stories high, a shining white be con, fully restored to its original la 18th c. state. Also audio-visual show emigration exhibition, craft work-shops pottery, restaurant. **Blennerville A Gallery and Studio**, *Main Stree Blennerville, is open 9.30am-6pm daily*

randon Bay
of Dingle peninsula.
loghane, on an inlet of Brandon Bay,
as an excellent strand and is a good
ase for climbing nearby Brandon
ountain and exploring the coastline
etween Brandon Point and Brandon
ead.

randon Mountain
Dingle peninsula.
rough track leads up to the 900 m
,000 ft) summit, which gives magnifi-
nt views of the peninsula and north
erry in clear weather. **St Brendan's**
ratory is just below the summit.

astleisland
km (11 miles) E of Tralee.
rag Caves, *open 10am-6pm daily, 17*
ar-June, 10am-7pm daily, July-Aug,
0am-6pm daily, Sept-Oct, 10am-5pm
aily, Nov-Dec. Tel. (066) 41244. The
ves form part of one of Ireland's most
npressive cave systems and have
agnificent stalactites. Craft shop,
staurant.

Connor Pass
10 km (6 miles) NE of Dingle.
Rising to a height of 450 m (1,500 ft);
in some places only a low stone wall
protects drivers and walkers from a
great fall to the valley below. There are
magnificent views in clear weather,
though in cloudy weather, it's rather
like being in an aircraft!

Dingle
50 km (35 miles) W of Tralee. TIO,
Main Street, tel. (066) 51188, Apr-Oct.
The main town on the Dingle Peninsula has a busy fishing harbour and
marina, two festivals in August, some
fine craft shops and excellent gourmet
restaurants. In recent years, "Fungie"
the dolphin has enlivened the harbour. **St Mary's (C)** was built in the
1860s and renovated in the 1960s and
1970s. The next door library has much
local historical material; some relating
to the prominent local patriot,
Thomas Ashe. Craft village on the
Dunquin Road has some fine craft
workshops.

Dingle-Dunquin Road
Some spectacular sea-views skirting
Ventry Harbour and then Slea Head.
Archaeological remains on the
mountainside, readily seen from the
road, include over 400 prehistoric
stone huts shaped like beehives.

Fenit
13 km (8 miles) W of Tralee.
Fine 1 km (0.5 mile) walk along the L-
shaped pier, giving excellent views of
Tralee Bay and the **Dingle Peninsula**
mountains. **Fenit Sea World**, *open*
10am-8pm daily, all year, tel. (066)
36544, is a water-based theme exhibition displaying many aspects of marine
life, it even includes an old shipwreck.
Visitors can also see dangerous species
such as conger eel from a safe distance.

Gallarus Oratory
3 km (2 miles) NE of Ballyferriter.
The best-preserved early Christian
church in Ireland, believed to date
from 8th c. Resembling an upturned
boat, it is accessible at all times.

an Foley's pub, Dingle, Co. Kerry

Glin Castle

48 km (30 miles) NE of Tralee on S shore of Shannon estuary. Open by arr, tel. (068) 36230.

Late 18th c. seat of the Knight of Glin, with fine neo-classical plasterwork and Adam-style ceilings. Good collection of 18th c. furniture, shop at gate.

Inch

6 km (4 miles) E of Anascaul. S Dingle Peninsula.

6 km (4 miles) long golden sandy strand at the entrance to **Castlemaine Bay** is one of best bathing places in the region.

Listowel

27 km (17 miles) NE of Tralee. TIO, St John's Church, tel. (068) 22590, June-Sept.

The amazing plaster decorations on the façades of the buildings fronting Listowel's great square are the work of a local artist in plaster, Patrick McAuliffe, who died in 1921. St John's former Church of Ireland church in the centre of the square has been turned into a literary, arts and heritage centre. It commemorates the North Kerry literary tradition, one of whose main writers, John B. Keane, runs a nearby pub.

Writers Week in early summer, is great fun for anyone with literary inclinations and a thirst to match! On the Ballybunion Road, just outside Listowel, is the mid-19th c. famine graveyard. Nearby at **Finuge**, *5 km (3 miles) SW of Listowel, Teach Siamsa* holds Irish folklore displays and provides entertainment in summer.

Lixnaw

9 km (6 miles) SW of Listowel.

The **Agricultural Museum**, *open 10am-6pm Mon-Sat, 2pm-6pm Sun, June-Sept, tel. (066) 32202*, has a collection of old farm implements.

Magharee Islands

8 km (5 miles) N of Castlegregory.

Off the northern tip of the flat, sandy peninsula that divides Tralee Bay from Brandon Bay, this group of small islands is isolated and uninhabited. Boatmen from the small harbour at the north point of the peninsula will take you across.

Smerwick Harbour

12 km (8 miles) NW of Dingle.

Good walks along both shores of this vast landlocked harbour, which turns into mudflats at low tide. There is a spectacular drive from the eastern shoreline of the bay to Ballyferriter and back to Dingle, by the Slea Head Road.

Tarbert

16 km (10 miles) NE of Listowel.

The **Tarbert Bridewell**, *open 10am-6pm daily, May-Oct, tel. (068) 36500*, is a recently restored 1830 courthouse, including cells and exercise yard. Coffee and gift shop. **Tarbert House**, *open 10am-4pm daily, May-Aug. Tel. (068) 36198*. Built in the late 17th c., the house has fine Georgian interiors and furniture, also many family portraits. Tarbert-Killimer Car Ferry Services, tel. (065) 53124. Regular crossings of the Shannon every day of the year.

Tralee

300 km (187 miles) SW of Dublin. Pop. 17,000. TIO tel. (066) 21288, all year.

A lively and attractively set out business centre geared towards catering for visitors the town is the gateway to the Dingle Peninsula. In recent years some outstanding new tourist attractions have been added.

Kerry the Kingdom and **Treasures of the Kingdom**, *Ashe Memorial Hall, Denny Street, open 10am-6pm daily, Mar-Oct, 2pm-5pm daily, Nov-Feb. Tel. (066) 27777*. Kerry the Kingdom is a spectacular visual show; a three-part interpretation of the county and its history. Geraldine Tralee uses a "time car" to recreate life in Tralee as it was in 1450, complete with sounds and smells. Treasures of the Kingdom displays the county history, from the Stone Age to the present, and has priceless archaeological treasures.

Aqua Dome, *open 10am-10pm Mon-Fri, 10am-7pm, Sat, Sun all year, tel. (066) 28899*, is a water-based leisure centre. **Siamsa Tire**, is Ireland's lively national folk theatre, with regular shows during May and September, tel. (066) 23055. **St John's (C)** *Castle Street* was built in 1870 and has a 1959 statue of the locally-born Saint Brendan the Navigator. **Holy Cross (C)** *Princes Street* was designed by Pugin in 19th c.

Ventry

10 km (6 miles) W of Dingle

Formerly a major port, Ventry boasts a good natural harbour and sandy beac with the imposing Mount Eagle in t background.

Limerick City and County

Adare

16 km (10 miles) SW of Limerick.

With its Main Street lined with thatche cottages, Adare claims to be the bes looking small town in Ireland. Th **Adare Heritage Centre**, *open dail all year, tel. (061) 396255*, has a mul media presentation on its histor including the influence of th Dunraven family in the 19th and ear 20th c. A model depicts Adare in 150 Also see the ruins of the 15th c. Fra ciscan friary and the 14th c. Desmor castle. Non-residents can explore th ground floor and demesne of **Ada Manor**, a fine 19th c. baronial buildin now restored as a luxury hotel.

The **Church of the Most Ho Trinity (C)** and **Adare Parish Churc (CI)** are worth exploring, as Stacpoole's antiquarian bookshop the Main Street. **Celtic Park**, *8 km (miles) N of Adare. Open 9am-7p daily, Mar-Oct, tel. (061) 39424* Classical garden, Mass Rock, early 6t 7th c. Christian wooden churc ancient fort, ogham stone, café.

Askeaton

26 km (16 miles) W of Limerick.

Ruins of a 15th c. Desmond Castle a well-preserved on an islet in River Dee but best seen from the banks. Extensiv ruins of 15th c. Franciscan friary.

nratty Castle, Co. Clare

llyneety
*km (5 miles) N of Kilmallock.
tween Lough Gur and Kilmallock.*
rnamental **pheasant farm**, *open
am-9pm daily, tel. (061) 351607.*
is 30 varieties on show.

nratty
km (8 miles) W of Limerick.
nratty Castle, *open 9.30am-5pm
ily, all year.* Built in 1460, the castle
is been fully-restored and now
uses one of the finest collections of
th–17th c. furniture and furnishings
Ireland. **Bunratty Folk Park**, *open
30am-7pm daily, July-Aug, 9.30am-
30pm Sept-June. Tel. (065) 361511.*
is world renowned park has
amples of houses from every part of
e region, plus a reconstructed 19th
village street. Craft demonstrations,

including basket weaving, bread and
candle making and farriery. Bunratty
Courtyard has a display of old farm implements. The **Bunratty Winery**, *open
9.30am-5.30pm daily, all year, tel.
(061) 362222*, makes mead and poteen
(legally) and has a small museum.
Durty Nelly's pub, *near the folk park*,
is world famous and, though rather
small, is packed with atmosphere.

Castleconnell
13 km (8 miles) NE of Limerick.
Walks along both banks of the Shannon
in this famous fishing village. **Pink
Cottage** has local arts and crafts.

Cratloe
11 km (7 miles) W of Limerick.
Extensive woodland walks. The 17th c.
Cratloe Woods House *open 2pm-6pm*

Mon-Fri, June-Sept, tel. (061) 327028.

Crauggaunowen
*13 km (8 miles) NE of Shannon air-
port. Sixmilebridge. Tel. (061) 361511.*
Fascinating recreation of Ireland's
ancient history. Highlights include a
ring fort, man-made islands (or cran-
nogs) and the replica of the leather-
hulled boat in which St Brendan
reputedly discovered America.

Croom
11 km (7 miles) SE of Adare.
Pleasant town on the banks of the River
Maigue. **The Mill**, *open 10am-6pm
Mon-Thurs, 10am-9pm Fri-Sun, all
year. Tel. (061) 397130.* Restored as a
heritage project and includes a five-
storey granary. Exhibition section.
Visitors can grind their own corn.

Curraghchase
18 km (11 miles) W of Limerick. Open 9am-9pm daily, all year.
The estate of 19th c. poet and author Aubrey de Vere is now a national park. The big house, together with its priceless works of art, was destroyed in an accidental fire in 1941. See the tombstones of de Vere's pets and the earth mound where he sat to write. Gardens, arboretum.

Drumcollogher
40 km (25 miles) SW of Limerick.
Irish Dresden factory, *open 9am-5pm, Mon-Fri, all year. Tel. (063) 83030.* Fine porcelain products and Dresden figurines. **Dairy Co-Op Museum**, *open 10am-6pm daily, May-Sept, tel. (063) 83113,* details the history of Ireland's first co-operative creamery. Also **Springfield Castle Deer Farm**, *tel. (063) 83162.*

Foynes
37 km (23 miles) W of Limerick.
Flying Boat Museum, *open 10am-6pm daily, Mar 31-Oct 31, tel. (069) 65416,* has fascinating displays on this intriguing era of aviation on the Shannon estuary during World War II. A small 1940s style cinema shows newsreels from the period, while the café is also decorated in period style.

Glenstal Abbey
14 km (9 miles) W of Limerick. Open by arr, tel. (061) 386103.
This Benedictine college has attractive grounds and chapel. The monks work at a variety of crafts, including beekeeping, sculpture, silverware and stone-cutting. Scenic walks nearby through the Clare Glens.

Kilmallock
34 km (21 miles) S of Limerick.
A monastery town founded in the 7th c., many of its medieval structures still survive, including two town gates, part of the town wall and the early 14th c. Dominican friary. **Kilmallock Museum**, *open 1.30pm-5.30pm Mon-Fri, 1pm-5pm Sat, Sun. Tel. (063) 91300.* The museum aims to reflect farm, social and shop life in the 19th and earlier 20th c.
The young Eamon de Valera, later a President of Ireland, went to school at nearby **Bruree**, *6 km (4 miles) W of Kilmallock.* The old schoolhouse has

been turned into a **Museum**, *open 9am-4pm Tues-Fri, 2.30pm-5pm Sat, Sun. Tel. (063) 90717.* See also three 14th c. de Lacy castles and the waterwheel at the mill by River Maigue.

Limerick
198 km (123 miles) SW of Dublin. Pop. 52, 000. TIO Arthur's Quay, tel. (061) 317522.
The fourth largest city in Ireland and an important market and manufacturing centre, Limerick has made substantial progress in recent years in preserving its historical heritage and developing facilities for visitors. **King John's Castle**, *beside the River Shannon, open 9.30am-5.30pm daily, Apr-Oct, 12 noon-4pm Sat, Sun, Nov-Mar. Tel. (061) 361511.* Built in the 13th c., the castle has been extensively restored. It now houses a large scale historical exhibition and audio-visual show on the city and county. On the opposite side of the river, across the bridge, is the **Treaty Stone**, the place where the Treaty of Limerick was said to have been signed in 1691.

St Mary's Cathedral (CI) was built in the late 12th c. by Donal O'Brien, the last king of Munster. The interior has been extensively restored and the many interesting monuments and 15th c. choir stalls should not be missed. Nearby is the old **Custom House**, which has been restored to hold much of the outstanding Hunt Collection of Irish antiquities and medieval art and the National Self-portrait Collection. Due to open in 1995.

Portions of Limerick's medieval walls remain near **St John's Cathedral (C)**, a 19th c. Gothic building which has the tallest spire in Ireland. Ask at the Presbytery to see the 15th c. mitre and cross. The **Dominican Church (C)**, *Baker Place, Pery Street,* has an impressive 17th c. statue of Our Lady of Limerick, while the modern **Church of the Holy Rosary** *Ennis Road* has Stations of the Cross made by the craftsmen of Oberammergau in Bavaria.

Limerick City Museum, *John's Square, 10am-5pm Tues-Sat, all year, tel. (061) 417826.* The museum has much material on local events and personalities, including archaeological finds, trade history and details of the Limerick Soviet declared in 1919. The houses and church in the surrounding square have been restored. **Limerick**

City Art Gallery, *Pery Square, ope daily, except Sun, all year. Tel. (06 310633.* On the edge of the city's 18 c. Georgian district, the gallery displa works by many leading Irish artist including Percy French, Charles Lam Walter Osborne and Camille Soute Frequent exhibitions. **Belltable Ar Centre**, *69 O'Connell Street, ope daily, except Sun, tel. (061) 31986* Frequent exhibitions, other cultur events, theatre. Coffee shop. Limeri lace is an age-old tradition and can b seen at the **Good Shepherd Conven** *Dublin Road,* where purchases ca also be made. *Open 10am-4pm Mo Fri, all year.*

Lough Gur
16 km (10 miles) SE of Limerick.
Remarkable series of prehistor remains, including dolmens. The stor circle is the largest in Ireland. Ruins two medieval Desmond castles. Wall by lakeside. **Interpretative Centr** *open 10am-6pm daily, May-Sept, te (061) 85186/361511.*

Newcastle West
42 km (26 miles) SW of Limerick.
Bustling market town with a 12th Desmond castle in the town squa which is currently being restored. Se also tower house of **Glenquin Castl** 15th c. Enjoyable walks in the demesn

Rathkeale
29 km (18 miles) SW of Limerick.
Castle Matrix, *open 12 noon-5p daily, May-Sept, tel. (069) 64284. Th* Castle dates back to 15th c. and no has a vast library with many rai editions, fine furnishings, objets d'ai historic documents. Home of **Iris International Arts Centre**.

Shannon Airport
24 km (15 miles) W of Limerick.
Aviation hall of fame, shops, bar restaurant. Nearby **Ballycasey Cra Centre** has a variety of craft workshop including jewellery and pottery.

The West

The West of Ireland conjures up images of great heather-clad boglands, mountain peaks, small seaside villages and the sandy beaches of Connemara. Clifden, the 'capital' of Connemara, has tweed weaving, turf-smoke in the air and turf-coloured water. Islands off the coast, like Inishbofin and the three, mainly Irish-speaking, Aran Islands, offer a relaxing and traditional way of life. Further north, spectacular landscapes continue to unravel: the cliffs and beaches of Mayo and Sligo, the great Slieve League cliffs in south Donegal, reputedly the highest in Europe, and Ireland's most remote island, Tory.

Travel south from Connemara and Galway and another of Ireland's botanical mysteries comes into view, the Burren, with its lunar limestone landscape and exotic flora. Caves, too, at Ailwee. The man-made sits sympathetically with these primitive landscapes: Kylemore Abbey in Connemara, W.B. Yeats' castle near Gort, Co. Galway, Galway city itself, buzzing with western culture and 'craic', and the stately town of Westport.

The Burren and the Cliffs of Moher

Ailwee Caves
3 km (2 miles) SE of Ballyvaughan. Open 10am-6pm daily, Mar-June, 10am-7pm daily, July-Aug, 10am-6pm daily, Sept-Nov. Tel. (065) 77036.
This strange subterranean landscape includes stalactites and stalagmites, all dazzlingly lit. The cave centre at the entrance is shaped like a Stone Age cairn and contains a restaurant and craft shop.

Ballyvaughan
16 km (10 miles) NE of Lisdoonvarna.
Pleasant seaside village with pier, facing Galway Bay. Fine drive to Lisdoonvarna and Corkscrew Hill. Good views over Galway Bay, especially when the sun's going down.

Burren
N of Corofin, E of Lisdoonvarna.
Huge limestone plateau covering a vast area of north Clare. Mile after mile of stark rock resembling a lunar landscape, full of history and prehistory, from huge dolmens and cairns to round towers and celtic crosses. Also an area of remarkable flora and fauna with arctic, alpine and mediterranean plants growing together. Now a National Park, with controversial interpretative centre under construction.

Cliffs of Moher
10 km (6 miles) NW of Lahinch. TIO, tel. (065) 81171, Apr-Oct.
Extending for 8 km (5 miles), these majestic cliffs are among the most outstanding natural features of the West of Ireland. Best seen from **O'Brien's Tower**, *open 10am-6pm daily, May-Sept.* The **Information**

Centre, *open 10am-6pm daily, all year, tel. (065) 81171,* also contains the TIO and has full details of the area. Craft shop, restaurant.

Corofin
15 km (8 miles) N of Ennis.
Clare Heritage Centre *in converted Church of Ireland church, open 10am-7pm daily, Apr-Oct, 10am-5pm Sat-Sun, Nov-Mar. Tel. (065) 27955.*
The centre has a fine museum on 19th c. life in the county, besides genealogical records. **Dysert O'Dea Castle** has an **Archaeology Centre**, *open 10am-7pm daily, May-Sept, tel. (065) 27722,* with an audio-visual show, local history exhibition and museum. Nearby is the **White Cross of Tola** and round tower.

Doolin
8 km (5 miles) SW of Lisdoonvarna.
Small fishing village on sandy bay, famous for its folk music. Trips to Aran Islands in fine weather.

Ennis
233 km (145 miles) SW of Dublin. Pop. 14,000. TIO tel. (065) 28366.
An interesting town set on the banks of the River Fergus, with narrow, winding streets. Besides being the birthplace of Harriet Smithson, wife of the French composer Hector Berlioz, the town also saw such electoral firsts as the elections of Daniel O'Connell, in 1828, and Eamon de Valera, in 1917.
Ennis Friary, *open 9.30am-6.30pm daily, May-Sept.* This 13th c. Franciscan foundation was established by the O'Briens, Kings of Thomond. The ruins are well-preserved and the most outstanding features are a series of 15th and 16th c. sculptures. **De Valera Museum and Library**, *open 11am-5.30pm Mon-Fri, all year, tel. (065) 21616,* has many historic relics of the district, including the spade with which Charles Stewart Parnell turned the first sod of the West Clare railway. **O'Connell Monument**, town centre, is on the site of the 1828 meeting at which Daniel O'Connell was nominated to stand for Clare. Also see new de Valera statue. Railway station has old locomotive from the long closed West Clare Railway.

Ennistymon
3 km (2 miles) E of Lahinch.

Delightfully set in wooded vall◌ beside the River Cullenagh cascad◌ The **Falls Hotel**, overlooking th◌ waterfalls, generates its own electric◌ from water power. The Main Street h◌ interesting old-style shop facade◌ some with their names in tradition◌ Irish lettering.

Kilbaha
Near end of Loop Head Peninsula.
From its tiny harbour, road climbs we◌ very unevenly, for 5 km (3 miles) ◌ Loop Head lighthouse. Superb view◌

Kilfenora
11 km (7 miles) SE of Lisdoonvarn◌
Burren Display Centre *open 10a◌ 6pm daily, Mar-May, 10am-7pm dail◌ June-Aug, 10am-6pm daily, Sept-O◌ Tel (065) 88030.*
A fine introduction to the Burren, wi◌ its models of species and landscape◌ historical detail and library. Staff w◌ suggest scenic routes across the Burre◌ for drivers, cyclists and walkers. Cra◌ shop. Almost adjacent is **St Fachnan◌ Cathedral (CI)**. The nave is used as ◌ church, but the rest of the building ◌ roofless.

Kilkee
65 km (35 miles) SW of Ennis. TIO te◌ (065) 56112, June-Sept.
Popular seaside resort with long, sa◌ sandy beach stretching for 1.5 km ◌ mile). Children's amusement park. Th◌ **Duggerna Rocks**, beyond the beac◌ form a striking natural amphitheat◌ that is used for bathing and sometime◌ outdoor concerts. Nearby **Looko◌ Hill** gives excellent views. **Heritag◌ Centre**, *open 11am-5pm Mon-Fri, Jul◌ Aug, tel. (065) 56169,* has artefacts ar◌ photographs of the area.

Kilrush
43 km (27 miles) SW of Ennis. TIO te◌ (065) 51577, May-Sept.
This striking market town, enliven◌ by weekly horse fairs, has seen rece◌ tourism developments, including ◌ large marina. **Scattery Island Info◌ mation Centre**, *Merchant's Qua◌ open 9.30am-6.30pm daily, June-Se◌ Tel. (065) 52139/52144.* Gives detai◌ of the monastery founded on Scatte◌ Island in the 6th c. by St Ciaran ◌ Clonmacnois. Also details of the area◌ wildlife. The **Kilrush Heritage Centr◌ Town Hall, open 9.30am-5.30pm dail◌**

Poulnabrone dolmen, Co. Clare

ay-Sept, tel. (065) 51577/51047, depicts the town's history, including the Vandaleur family and their part in its 18th c. development.

Knappogue Castle
10 km (6 miles) SE of Ennis. Open 9.30am-5pm daily, Apr-Oct, tel. (061) 368102.
Built in the late 15th c. and the seat of the McNamara family until 1815. Restored in recent years to its medieval splendour, including a forge, orchard and gardens. Medieval banquets nightly during summer.

Lahinch
25 km (16 miles) NW of Ennis.
Popular resort with 1.5 km (1 mile) long beach. Promenade, sea-water swimming pool. Merriman Summer School, held in Aug, commemorates the author of the *Midnight Court*, a bawdy 18th c. Irish language epic.

Leamaneh Castle
6 km (4 miles) E of Kilfenora.

Amalgam of 1480 residential tower and early 17th c. fortified house, making striking ruins, which can only be seen from the road. The interior is closed, as the building is in a dangerous condition.

Lisdoonvarna
37 km (23 miles) NW of Ennis.
A leading spa town. The **Spa Wells Health Centre** has a sulphurous spring, with pump house and baths, an excellent way of removing late night impurities from the system. *Open daily, June-Oct, tel. (065) 74023.* **Lisdoonvarna Fair**, Sept, brings together bachelors in search of spouses. An interesting 3 km (2 miles) circular walk along the 'Bog' road via the Spectacle Bridge to SW of the town.

Milltown Malbay
32 km (20 miles) W of Ennis.
A former resort in an area of cliffs and sandy beaches, the town now hosts the annual Willie Clancy Summer School in July, a must for traditional musicians

worldwide. To the west, **Spanish Point** marks the wreck of Armada warships. The top of **Slieve Callan**, to the east, offers fine views of the surrounding countryside.

Quin Abbey
10 km (6 miles) E of Ennis.
Well preserved and extensive ruins of early 15th c. Franciscan friary. Remains of a Norman castle were used to build the friary and three of its towers still stand.

Scattery Island
3 km (2 miles) offshore from Cappagh Pier. Boat service and guided tours, summer only, details, Kilrush TIO.
The island's monastic settlement includes five churches and one round tower.

Lough Key, Co. Roscommon

Shannonside

Arigna Mountains
W of Lough Allen.
A scenic route through the mountains is clearly signposted. Superb views of Leitrim countryside.

Athlone
125 km (78 miles) W of Dublin. TIO Athlone Castle, tel. (0902) 94630/ 92856, May–mid-Oct.
This historic town, set halfway on the Shannon river system, also marks the boundaries between the provinces of Connacht and Leinster. The castle was built in the 13th c. and was extensively renovated in 1991, the 300th anniversary of its siege. The **Museum**, *open 10am-4.30pm daily, May-Sept. Tel. (0902) 72107*, houses artefacts related to Athlone's colourful history and is linked to an interpretative centre, which depicts the Battle of Athlone in 1691, the flora and fauna of the Shannon and the life of the town's most famous son, Count John McCormack, the tenor, who was born just across the river from the castle. An extension to the museum and also a military museum are planned. Also on the west bank of the River Shannon, near the castle, the church of Saints Peter and Paul, is marked by twin spires and dome. Trips on the Shannon, aboard the MV Ross, are run daily in the summer from the marina. *Tel. (0902) 72892.* On-board bar and coffee shop.

Boyle
14 km (9 miles) W of Carrick-on-Shannon. TIO tel. (079) 62145, May-Sept.
Boyle Abbey, *open 9.30am-6.30pm daily, mid-June–mid-Sept.* This 12th c. Cistercian monastery is one of the most impressive foundations of its kind in Ireland. **King House**, *tel. (079) 6324,* has a museum and audio-visual presentation on local clan and military history. **Lough Key Forest Park**, *3 km (2 miles) NE of Boyle* has many amenities, including cruising and forest walks, shop, restaurant.

Carrick-on-Shannon
48 km (30 miles) SE of Sligo. TIO The Marina, tel. (078) 20170, Apr-Sept.
The town is a renowned cruising base for the upper reaches of the River Shannon. The **Costello Chapel**, *Bridge Street, open daily, all year*, is considered to be the second smallest in the world. A new museum dedicated to the history of the famine in the area should be ready for 1995.

Carrigallen
24 km (15 miles) NE of Mohill.
This tiny Co. Leitrim village has two outstanding attractions, the **Teach**

Duchais Folk Museum, *open 10am-4pm Mon-Fri, 2pm-5pm Sun, all year, tel. (049) 33055* and the **Corn Mill Theatre and Arts Centre**, *tel. (049) 39612.*

Centre of Ireland

There are several contenders for this title including a tower-like structure on a hill, 3 km (2 miles) north-east of Glasson, and a stone pillar on an island off the western shore of Lough Ree, 6 km (4 miles) north-east Athlone, directly opposite Hodson Bay Hotel.

Clonalis House

0.8 km (0.5 mile) W of Castlerea. Open 11am-5.30pm Mon-Sat, 2pm-6 pm Sun, June–mid-Sept, tel. (0907) 20014.
The ancestral seat of the O'Connor Don clan, the present house was built in an Italianate-Victorian style in the late 19th c. The drawing room, library, bedrooms and chapel are some of the interior highlights. The billiard room has many archives, besides Carolan's harp.

Clonmacnois

5 km (4 miles) N of Shannonbridge. Open 10am-5pm daily, Nov mid-Mar, 10am-6pm daily, mid-Mar–mid-May, Sept-Oct, 9am-7pm daily, mid-May-early Sept. Tel. (0905) 74195.
This 6th c. monastic site, beside the River Shannon, has cathedral, churches, round tower and high crosses. The visitor centre has the original high crosses and graveslabs. Audio-visual show, exhibitions.

Clonmacnois & West Offaly Railway

Near Shannonbridge. Open 10am-5pm daily, Mar-Oct. Tel. (0905) 74114/74172.
Narrow gauge railway trundles through the bogland for 8 km (5.5 miles) in a fascinating hour-long trip, with plenty of sights of flora, fauna and distant mountains beyond the flat bogland.

Dromod

19 km (12 miles) SE of Carrick-on-Shannon.
It is hoped that in 1995 there will once again be steam trains on a restored 0.8 km (0. 5 mile) section of narrow gauge track. It's part of the former Cavan/Leitrim railway. Also railway memorabilia. Tel. (078) 38599.

Drumshanbo

12 km (9 miles) N of Carrick-on-Shannon.
This small town at the south end of Lough Allen is a noted fishing centre. **Lough Allen Heritage Centre**, *open daily in summer. Tel. (078) 41475.* Audio-visual presentation.

Elphin

13 km (8 miles) SW of Carrick-on-Shannon.
Small, but lively, cathedral town. The nearby **Smith Hill** is held to be the birthplace of Oliver Goldsmith.

Erne-Shannon Waterway

Tourist information, Mrs E. Smyth, High Street, Ballinamore, Mrs E. Mooney, Carrick Road, Drumshanbo.
Stretching for 56 km (35 miles), it connects the Shannon and the Erne river systems and opens up whole new boating and cruising vistas in a previously neglected but attractive part of the country. Boats can now sail from Killaloe right into the heart of the Lough Erne lakeland. In the £30 million project to restore the canal, 34 bridges were rebuilt and 16 locks reconstructed. Smart cards, like phone cards, are used to open them.

Frenchpark

13 km (8 miles) SW of Boyle.
Douglas Hyde, the Protestant founder of the Gaelic League, was the first President of Ireland. He was born at **Ratra House**, near here, which is now ruined and he is buried in the old graveyard at Frenchpark. **Douglas Hyde Interpretative Centre** is *open daily in summer.*

Hill of Rathcroghan

10 km (6 miles) SE of Frenchpark.
The ancient palace of the Kings of Connacht once stood here. A short distance from the central mound is an enclosure called **Roilig na Ri** (Burial Place of the Kings), where legend has it that the three Tuatha De Danaan queens, Eire, Fodhla and Banba are buried. They gave their names to prehistoric Ireland. Nearby is the grave of Dathi, the last pagan monarch of Ireland. His burial place is a smaller enclosure with a tumulus and extraordinary red pillar.

Killaloe

21 km (13 miles) NE of Limerick. TIO Heritage Centre, tel. (061) 376866, June-Sept.
The old, narrow 13 arch bridge across the River Shannon from the small village of Ballina marks the southern limit of navigation on the Shannon system. **St Flannan's Cathedral (CI)**, built late 12th c. has various interior attractions, including an ogham stone and an oratory in the grounds. **St Molua's Oratory** is in the grounds of **St Flannan's Cathedral (C)**, in the heights of the town. It was moved here in 1929 from Friar's Island in Shannon prior to flooding for the hydro-electric scheme. The new **Lough Derg Heritage Centre**, *open 10am-6pm daily, June–mid-Sept, tel. (061) 376866,* traces the history of Ireland's inland waterways, including the Shannon, and details the ESB hydro-electric power station at Ardnacrushna, downstream from Killaloe.

Derg Line, *tel. (061) 376364,* has cruisers for hire and runs daily boat trips on Lough Derg. The Arra mountains are on the east side of Lough Derg and the road between Ballina and Portroe gives good views of the lake. The **Graves of the Leinstermen**, on slopes of Touninna, the highest mountain in the range, are a long line of vast prehistoric slate slabs.

Lough Derg

Extends for 32 km (20 miles) NE from Killaloe to Portumna.
Vast lake on River Shannon. **Holy Island**, *off W shore of lake, 26 km(16 miles) N of Killaloe,* has round tower and extensive remains of 7th c. monastery. Boats from Mountshannon, Tuamgraney.

Lough Ree

Extends for 19 km (13 miles) north from Athlone to near Lanesborough.
Two good viewing points are Ballykeeran – a hill overlooking Killinure Lough in the south-east corner of the lake, and the **Hill of Ardagh,** *6 km (4 miles) SW of Edgeworthstown.* The country between Auburn and Ballymahon on the east shores of the lake is **Goldsmith's Place**; so named because Oliver Goldsmith, the 18th c. poet and playwright, spent his boyhood here.

Lough Rynn
11 km (7 miles) NE of Roosky. Open 10am-7pm daily, May–mid-Sept, tel. (078) 31427.
Fine estate includes three walled gardens, arboretum, dairy yard, coach yard, farm yard. Craft shop, restaurant.

Mountshannon
8 km (5 miles) NE of Scariff.
An attractive, lakeside village. A plaque on the post office wall commemorates Ireland's last manually operated telephone exchange which was closed in 1987.

Portumna
N end of Lough Derg.
Portumna Castle, *open 9.30am-5.30pm daily, mid-June–mid-Sept. Tel. (0509) 41658.* A great semi-fortified house built before 1618, with formal and geometrically laid out gardens in the Jacobean style.

Roscommon
43 km (27 miles) S of Carrick-on-Shannon. TIO tel. (0903) 26342, June-Sept.
Attractive market town. At the top of the main street, in the square, see the facade of the old town jail, which once had a hangwoman, "Lady Betty", the last of her ilk in Ireland. Ruins of 13th c. Dominican friary just south of town.

Shannon Harbour
32 km (20 miles) W of Tullamore.
At the junction of Grand Canal and the River Shannon, the harbour is used for mooring cruisers. The place is now something of a ghost town with ruins of hotels, deserted quaysides and empty warehouses – sad reminders of its former glory as a major commercial centre.

Source of the Shannon
From Dowra, near NE corner of Lough Allen, take the R207 N for about 6 km (4 miles), following the signposts, continue down track for a further 3 km (2 miles), then climb for 0.8 km (0.5 mile).

Strokestown
19 km (12 miles) S of Carrick-on-Shannon.

Left: Clonmacnois and the river Shannon, Co. Offaly

An attractive village, said to have Ireland's widest main street, designed to match the Ringstrasse in Vienna for width. At the top of the main street is the **St John's Heritage Centre** in a former Church of Ireland church, *open 9am-5pm Tues-Fri, 2pm-6pm Sat-Sun, May–Sept, tel. (078) 33380.* Genealogical research, audio-visual presentations, exhibitions. At the other end of the main street, a long driveway leads through the estate grounds to **Strokestown Park House**, a fine 1730s edifice built in the Palladian style. Much restoration work has been carried out in recent years. Reception rooms, upstairs school room and nursery room, restaurant in old kitchens. A new **Museum**, *open 11am-5pm Tues-Sun, all year, tel. (078) 33013,* has been built in the old stables and explores the many aspects of the great famine of the late 1840s, using a variety of presentation methods.

Tuamgraney
34 km (21 miles) N of Killaloe.
The small church (CI) in the village is believed to be oldest in Ireland still used for worship, with western parts dating back to the late 10th c. **Heritage Centre**, *open 10am-6pm Mon-Sat, 1pm-5pm Sun, Easter – mid-Sept.* Displays on local history, video presentation on the village. **Folk Museum** displays include old household items, old newspapers.

Galway's Claddagh and Corrib

Aran Islands
16 km (10 miles) S of the Connemara coast. TIO Kilronan, Inishmore, tel. (099) 61263, May-Sept. Ferry services, tel TIO, and daily air services link the mainland and each of the islands.
Three islands set in the Atlantic, the best time to visit the islands is in May or early June, when the Burren-like flora can be seen to its best advantage. During July and August the bulk of the islands' annual visitors, over 100,000, arrive making them feel distinctly over-populated.

Inishmore, the largest island, with a population of about 900, has a new **Interpretative Centre** *at Kilronan, open 11am-5pm Apr-May, 10am-7pm daily, June-Oct.* The centre gives a good view of the islands' culture and history. On the road out of Kilronan, you will see the many small fields divided by dry stone walls. On the western side of the island, Inishmore's biggest attraction is **Dun Aengus** – a prehistoric fort, set on the edge of a cliff. Half the site, consisting of three concentric enclosures, has fallen into the sea, but what's left makes a fascinating sight.

Inishmaan, the middle island, is where the traditional Aran lifestyle is most apparent. **Conor Fort** is a smaller version of Dun Aengus. **John Millington Synge's Cottage**, *open Mon-Fri, June-Sept.* The cottage has a fascinating collection of memorabilia. The island has fine cliff walks.

Inisheer, by far the smallest of the islands, can be explored in an afternoon, but the sheer tranquillity of the place may tempt you to stay longer.

Athenry
24 km (15 miles) E of Galway.
The Norman walls are among the best preserved in Ireland, with five of the original six wall towers surviving. However, only one of the five medieval entrances to the town still exists – the North Gate. The three-storey **Athenry Castle**, completed about 1250, is being restored and should be open for visitors in 1995. See also the ruins of the Dominican friary, dating from 13th c., beside Clarinbridge River, on east side of the town.

Aughrim
9 km (6 miles) SW of Ballinasloe. TIO tel. (0905) 73939, Apr-Oct.
Interpretative Centre, *open 10am-6pm daily, Easter-Sept, tel. (0905) 73939.* Has a good deal of information on the Battle of Aughrim, 1691, between the armies of James II and William, an important date in European history. Also prehistoric relics from the area and old household utensils. Audio-visual presentation.

Ballinasloe
64 km (40 miles) E of Galway. TIO (0905) 42131, July-Aug.
Best-known for its annual horse fair in October – an eight day carnival that's one of the largest and liveliest events of its kind in Europe. **St Michael's Church (C)** is 19th c. and has stained-glass by Harry Clarke. Ruins of 14th c. **Ballinasloe Castle** overlook the River Suck.

Coole Demesne
3 km (2 miles) N of Gort. Open 10am-5pm Tue-Sun, Easter–mid-June, Sept, 9.30am-6.30pm, daily. Tel. (095) 41054/ 41005.
The house where Lady Gregory once held literary court is long since gone, but visitors can enjoy walks through the demesne to Coole Lake, which still has its swans. The "autograph tree" where her writer guests carved their initials can still be seen. Audio-visual show in the visitor centre, tearooms.

Clarinbridge
13 km (8 miles) S of Galway.

This small village is renowned for its oysters.

Clonfert Cathedral
24 km (15 miles) NE of Portumna.
The original monastery founded by St Brendan the Navigator in 563 was destroyed six times before becoming an Augustinian priory. The late 12th c. doorway is finest example of Romanesque style in Ireland.

Kinvarra
27 km (17 miles) S of Galway. SE Galway Bay.
This attractive fishing village makes an ideal base for exploring the Gort area and the Burren. **Traught Strand** is a fine sandy beach stretching for 7 km (4 miles). **Dunguaire Castle**, *open 9.30am-5.30pm daily, Apr-Sept.* Nightly entertainment during the summer. This striking 16th c. castle is set overlooking Galway Bay and has been well restored.

Galway
217 km (135 miles) W of Dublin. Pop.

O'Brien's castle, Inisheer, Aran Islands

The Claddagh, Galway city

50,000. *TIO Victoria Place, Eyre Square, tel. (091) 583081, all year.* The West's major town, Galway is set at the mouth of the River Corrib, near the Western Gaeltacht (Irish-speaking areas). The city grew rich on fishing and trade and its merchant class commissioned many fine buildings in the city. It is long since recovered from the vicissitudes of the mid-19th c. famine and is now a prosperous city, well-endowed with facilities for visitors.

Cultural traditions and activities are very strong in this city which is keenly aware of its Irish identity. The two main events in Galway's social calendar, both very lively indeed, demanding much stamina, are the **Galway Races** on the August bank holiday and the **Oyster Festival** at the end of September.

Eyre Square in the centre of Galway has a memorial garden to the late John F. Kennedy, who as President of the US, visited the city in June, 1963. Other monuments include a sculpture of Padraic O Conaire, a noted early 20th c. Irish language writer. The **Bank of Ireland**, *19 Eyre Square*, has some

fine Irish silverwork, including a 1710 Mace. The Great Southern Hotel, facing the square, has photographs and other relics of old Galway. Nearby, at the corner of Shop Street, a branch of Allied Irish Bank is housed in Lynch's Castle, late 15th c., one of Ireland's finest surviving town castles. Inside, explanatory photographs and text. **The Collegiate Church of St Nicholas** (CI) was built in early 14th c. and later enlarged, it houses many fine carvings and relics.

In the centre of Galway, doorways and windows from 17th and 18th c. merchants' houses can be seen in Abbeygate Street, Middle Street, Shop Street and St Augustine Street. The **Spanish Arch** was built in 1594 to protect the quay where Spanish ships unloaded their wares; four centuries ago, the city had a thriving trade with mainland Europe. Just past the arch, **Galway Museum**, *open 10am-1pm daily, June-Aug,* has many fascinating relics, including photographs of the old tramway system that once ran between Galway and Salthill. James Joyce's wife,

Nora Barnacle, was brought up in the tiny, authentically restored house at *8, Bowling Green, open 10am-5pm Mon-Sat, mid-May – mid-Sept, tel. Sheila Gallagher on (091) 584743.*

The **Taibhdhearc na Gaillimhe** in *Middle Street*, stages regular Irish language performances and popular presentations of song, music and dance in summer. **The Druid Theatre**, *Chapel Lane, tel. (091) 588617* is Galway's other theatrical institution, with regular lunchtime and evening performances. The **Jesuit Hall**, *Sea Road*, has plays and entertainment in English. **Nun's Island Arts Centre**, *tel. (091) 585886,* also has regular performances and exhibitions.

Galway is an excellent shopping city with many long-established outlets such as McCambridges in Shop Street, which is an outstanding delicatessen and wine shop. As befits its cultural tradition, Galway is well-stocked with bookshops, including the venerable **Kenny's Bookshop and Art Gallery** in *High Street, tel. (091) 582739/581014/581021,* which has a very large selection of Irish interest material, new and antiquarian. It also specialises in bookbinding. The **Sheela-na-Gig** bookshop in *Middle Street* deserves browsing time, as does **Galway Irish Crystal**, *Merlin Park, open 9am-8pm Mon-Fri, 9am-6pm Sat-Sun, all year.* **Royal Tara China**, *Tara Hall, Mervue,* makes fine bone china, decorated and gilded. *Factory tours, 11am-3pm Mon-Fri, all year. Shop open 9am-9pm daily, all year.*

There are many pleasant walks in Galway. A stroll from the city centre to the salmon weir, will give you a good view of the salmon making their way upstream to Lough Corrib during mid-Apr – July. The busy harbour area makes for some interesting walks, down to the seaward end of **Nimmo's Pier**, or on the opposite side, by the Long Walk. Alternatively walk along Upper Canal Road to Lower Canal Road via Dominick Street to **The Claddagh**. This area was an Irish-speaking fishing district, which retained its own strong identity until early this century. Its traditional thatched cottages were levelled in the 1930s to make way for more comfortable but infinitely less appealing local authority housing. Sadly all that's left of the area's traditions today is the Claddagh ring also known as the Galway wedding ring. The design depicts two hands clasped in friendship, around a crowned heart, symbolising the sentiment "let love and friendship reign". Reproduction pieces are popular souvenirs.

Loughrea
32 km (20 miles) E of Galway.
Delightfully set on the north shore of Lough Rea. **St Brendan's Cathedral (C)** has fine examples of modern Irish ecclesiastical art.

Lough Corrib
Starts 3 km (2 miles) N of Galway.
The second largest lake in Ireland and dotted with numerous small islands which vary in size from the truly minute to larger islands like Inchagoill, which once had a monastery.

Oughterard
27 km (17 miles) NW of Galway. TIO tel. (091) 82808, all year.
Fine village beside the western shores of Lough Corrib, which is often

described as the gateway to Connemara. Popular fishing spot. The 16 km (10 mile) drive from here to Maam Cross has amazing variety of scenery, from bog, lake and moorland to mountains. Sections of the old Galway-Clifden railway line are suitable for walking. In Oughterard, the **V'Soske-Joyce factory**, which makes exquisite carpets, rugs and wall-hangings by hand, can be seen by arr, *tel. (091) 82113/82140.* **Aughnanure Castle**, *open 9.30am-6.30pm daily, mid-June – mid-Sept, tel. (091) 82214,* was built by the O'Flahertys about 1500. The four-storey tower house is idyllically set beside Lough Corrib.

Salthill
6 km (4 miles) SE of Galway city centre.
This western suburb of Galway city is one of Ireland's leading seaside resorts, with excellent walks along the breezy promenade. **Leisureland** *open daily, tel. (091) 590455,* has a full range of indoor activities, including a swimming pool.

Spiddal
19 km (12 miles) W of Galway.
Connemara village on north shore of Galway Bay. **Craft Village/Animal Farm** *open daily in summer, tel. (091) 83372,* has thatched cottage and traditional farm implements.

Thoor Ballylee
6 km (4 miles) NE of Gort. Open 10am-6pm daily, Apr-Oct. Tel. (091) 31436.
W. B. Yeats bought this Norman tower in 1916, as a ruin, for £35. After restoring it, he and his wife George, lived there occasionally until 1928. Now fully-restored, with interpretative centre on Yeats' life and work.

Tuam
24 km (15 miles) NW of Galway.
Small market town that was once a major ecclesiastical centre. The **Cathedral of the Assumption (C)** was built in the 1830s and has many fine carvings. **St Mary's Cathedral (CI)** dates from the 1860s and incorporates 12th c. and 14th c. features. **St Jarlath's churchyard**, west of the town centre, has yews growing among the grave-stones and surrounds the ruins of a 13th c. parish church. See also the 12th c. cross in the town square and the **Mill**

Museum, *west of the North Bridge, open 10am-6pm Mon-Sat, 2pm-6pm Sun, June – mid-Sept, tel. (093) 24463.* This converted 17th c. corn mill now houses a milling museum, with three sets of mill wheels and audio-visual presentation on locality's history. **Tuam Arts Centre** has regular functions. Railway station has a steam locomotive dating from 1875, rebuilt and in use, plus other engines.

Turoe Stone
5 km (3 miles) W of Loughrea. Open 10am-8pm Mon-Fri, May-Sept, 10am-5pm Mon-Fri, Oct-Apr, 10am-5pm Sat-Sun and bank holidays. Tel. (091) 41580.
Prehistoric pillar stone, decorated with Celtic inscriptions, one of the most significant monuments of its kind in Ireland. The **Pet Farm and Leisure Park**, near the stone, has rare animals and birds, duck pond, old farm machinery.

Connemara

Cashel
22 km (14 miles) SE of Clifden.
Attractive fishing and shooting centre at the head of Cashel Bay.

Clifden
79 km (49 miles) W of Galway. Pop 900. TIO tel. (095) 21163 May-Sept.
The capital of Connemara, Clifden has a wonderfully rangy, spacious feel to it, full of fresh air and turf smoke. The journey from Galway, which can take about two hours by bus or car, is an excellent introduction to the scenic glories of this part of Ireland. A highlight in the Clifden social calendar is

In Clifden, Co. Galway

the **Connemara Pony Show** in August.

Clifden has two churches, a Church of Ireland one built in 1820, five years after Clifden was founded, and the striking Catholic edifice built 10 years later. The best way to see the seashore is to walk along the quay road, through the grounds of the ruined **Clifden Castle**, built by John D'Arcy, the founder of the town.

To savour Clifden's alpine air, take the well-named **Sky Road** out of Clifden for 5 km (3 miles) to get excellent views of Clifden Bay. See the railway station; the line from Clifden to Galway was in use between 1885 and 1935. Millar's shop in the Main Street gives fine insights into the makings of local tweeds. **Derrygim-lagh Bog**, *6 km (4 miles) S of Clifden*. Foundations and some relics of the Marconi radio station destroyed during the civil war. Nearby is the site where Alcock and Brown landed after making the first trans-Atlantic flight in June, 1919. A cairn shaped like a plane is 3 km (2 miles) away.

Connemara National Park

Open 10am-5.30pm daily, May, Sept, 10am-6.30pm daily, June, 9.30am - 6.30pm July-Aug. Tel. (095) 41054.
Near Letterfrack, the park covers a vast area of Connemara, including the slopes of the Twelve Bens. Attractions include exhibitions, nature trails, audio-visual show, tearooms.

Coral Strand

6 km (4 miles) SW of Clifden.
One of the many fine strands in Mannin Bay.

Derryclare Lough

20 km (12 miles) E of Clifden.
Breathtaking drive from Ballynahinch Lake, east of the Twelve Bens. Continue past Lough Inagh and Kylemore. Mountains rise up on both side of the valley.

Inishbofin Island

19 km (12 miles) NW of Clifden. Regular sailings daily, all year, from Cleggan harbour on the mainland. Tel. (095) 45806.
Tremendous seascapes, safe beaches and plenty of very fresh air, straight from the Atlantic. Many varieties of wild flowers. Ideal for water sports and walking. Hotel accommodation for visitors.

Killary Harbour

24 km (15 miles) NE of Clifden.
Long, deep fjord-like inlet stretching inland for 16 km (10 miles). The road on the south side of the harbour, through Leenane, gives tremendous views. **Leenane Cultural Centre**, *open 10am-6pm daily, Apr-Sept, tel. (095) 42323/42231*, details the history of wool and sheep, with video presentations. Visitors can feed the lambs, or, if they're really plucky, try their hand at sheep shearing.

Kylemore Abbey

Between the Twelve Bens and the Dorraugh Mountains. Open 9.30am-5.45pm daily, Mar-Oct. Tel. (095) 41146.
The abbey was built as a private home in 1864, later becoming a Benedictine convent. The nuns runs a girls' boarding school here. The grounds are freely accessible. Also craftshop, pottery and restaurant.

Letterfrack

13 km (8 miles) NE of Clifden.
Founded in 19th c. by Quakers as a mission settlement. Excellent bathing strands at nearby Barnaderg Bay. **Diamond Hill**, *just E of Letterfrack*, offers marvellous views of the Connemara coast from its summit (445 m / 1,460 ft high).

Mweenish Island

Near Kilkieran.
Sandy beaches. Connected to the mainland by a bridge.

Omey Island

9 km (6 miles) SW of Cleggan.
Can be reached on foot at low tide. Fine beaches. Ruins of 7th c. religious buildings can be seen in the sandhills on the north side of the island.

Renvyle Peninsula

NW of Letterfrack.
Renvyle House Hotel was run for many years by Oliver St Gogarty, writer, wit and contemporary of James Joyce. Excellent beaches nearby, views from **Renvyle Hill**.

Rosmuck

32 km (20 miles) SE of Clifden.
See the cottage where Patrick Pearse, 1916 leader, stayed to improve his Irish. He also wrote most of his work

here. It is now the **Pearse Museum**, *open 9.30am-6.30pm daily, mid-June–mid-Sept. Tel. (091) 74292.*

Roundstone

22 km (14 miles) SE of Clifden.
Quiet fishing village built in the early 19th c. by Alexander Nimmo, a Scottish engineer who worked for years in the West of Ireland. **Dog's Bay** and **Gurteen Bay**, *3 km (2 miles) SW of Roundstone*, offer fine, sandy beaches.

Mayo's Mountains and Islands

Aasleagh Waterfall

32 km (20 miles) SW of Westport.
Peat-stained falls on the Erriff River, flanked by masses of rhododendrons.

Achill Island

West Mayo
Connected to the mainland by a bridge, Achill is the largest island in Ireland, natural and unspoiled, mainly mountain, bog and heather. In fine summer weather the place is a joy to visit, but when it's wet, it can be miserable, since so much of its enjoyment is based on outdoor activity. The main road runs to Keel, which has a 3 km (2 mile) long beach. The amazing cliff formations are like natural cathedrals carved by nature from the rock. The longer **Atlantic Drive** also gives good vistas of the island. On the seaward side of **Croghaun mountain**, near Keem, the cliff falls nearly 600 m (2,000 ft) to the sea. Keem Strand is a popular bathing place; sometimes, basking sharks come close to shore. **Slieve-more village**, *2.5 km (1.5 miles) north of Keel* is a ruin of this once thriving

Sunset over Achill island, Co. Mayo

village which lost its population at the time of the mid-19th c. famine.

Ballina

65 km (41 miles) NE of Westport. TIO (096) 70848, May-Sept.
The centre of Ballina is straggling and uninspiring, but the quayside walks beside the River Moy are pleasant. The **Cathedral of St Muiredach (C)** on the east bank dates from the 19th c. See also the **Dolmen of the Four Maols** near the railway station.

Ballintubber Abbey

13 km (8 miles) S of Castlebar. Open daily.
A 13th c. foundation, it was largely destroyed by Cromwellians in 1653. The abbey church was marvellously restored in the early 1960s. Nearby are ruins of **Moore Hall**, birthplace of George Moore, noted late 19th/early 20th c. writer.

Ballycastle

26 km (16 miles) NW of Ballina
Pleasant village in the Ballinglen valley, with attractive coastal scenery and good beaches and walking nearby.

Bellacorick

17 km (11 miles) W of Crossmolina, on the road to Bangor Erris.
You can play a tune on the **Musical Bridge** by rubbing a stone along the north parapet. However, don't attempt to complete bridge. According to local legend, a sudden end awaits anyone who tries.

At the Bord na Móna works, a tourist train takes visitors around a narrow gauge railway network through the boglands, which provide fuel for the nearby power station. Visitors can also see the nearby **Wind Farm**, *tel.* (096) 53002, with 21 wind turbines. It is the only one of its kind in Ireland.

Belmullet

63 km (39 miles) W of Ballina.
This small town, enchantingly set, is the entrance to the Mullet peninsula, a desolate but beautiful place. The road runs south from Belmullet to Blacksod Point, at the southern end of the peninsula. The **Danish Cellar**, *8 km (5 miles) north of Belmullet*, is a fine looking bay fringed with cliffs. **Elly Bay** on the east side of the peninsula has a magnificent strand. **Doonamo Point**, *8 km (5 miles) north-west of Belmullet*, has the ruins of a prehistoric fort situated on the cliff edge. Stupendous views out to **Eagle Island** with its lighthouse.

Benwee Head

40 km (24 miles) W of Ballycastle.
This north-western tip of Co Mayo has outstanding cliffscapes and views out to the **Stags of Broad Haven**, a cluster of rocks 3 km (2 miles) out to sea.

Castlebar

18 km (11 miles) E of Westport. TIO tel. (094) 21207, Apr-Sept.
A much improved town in recent years. The green sward of the Mall was once the cricket pitch of the 19th c. Lord Lucan. A plaque in the Mall commemorates Margaret Burke-Sheridan, the internationally famous prima donna who was born here, while one in the

Main Street marks the birthplace of Louis Brennan, who invented the torpedo and the monorail. The exhibition centre in the Town Hall has regular exhibitions, arts and crafts events.

Ceide Fields
8 km (5 miles) W of Ballycastle.
A spectacular setting on the north Mayo coast for the equally striking pyramid-shaped **Visitor Centre**, *open 10am-5pm daily, mid-Mar – May, Oct, 9.30am-6.30pm daily, June-Sept, tel. (096) 43325.* Details the surrounding Stone Age settlement, said to be the largest of its kind in the world. The flora of the bog is equally important, and the centre has displays, exhibitions and video presentations.

Clare Island
The largest island in Clew Bay (there are said to be 365 in total – one for each day of the year!), Clare Island has a hotel and offers peace, solitude and walks around the 15th c. **Clare Abbey**. Fine views of Clew Bay and Connemara and Mayo mountains. Boats from Roonagh Quay, near Louisburgh. *Tel. Aine O'Malley (098) 21129.*

Cong
9 km (6 miles) SW of Ballinrobe.
The legendary Maureen O'Hara/John Wayne film, *The Quiet Man*, was partly made on location here. The 19th c. **Ashford Castle**, now a luxury hotel with interesting historical material, is open to non-residents. It was originally occupied by members of the Guinness family.

Croagh Patrick
8 km (5 miles) W of Westport.
Ireland's holy mountain is a steep but rewarding climb at any time, but if you're really devout and want to do it the hard way, try the annual pilgrimage on the last Sunday in July. Views from the summit are heavenly.

Crossmolina
13 km (8 miles) W of Ballina.
Beautifully set on River Deel in the shadow of Nephin Mountains, less than 2 km (1 mile) from Lough Conn, in the heart of fabulous salmon and brown trout fishing country. **North Mayo Heritage Centre**. *Open daily. Tel. (096) 31809.* Old artefacts and farm implements on display, genealogical research.

Foxford
16 km (10 miles) S of Ballina.
The century old **Foxford Woollen Mills**, *open 10am-6pm, Mon-Sat, all year, 12 noon-6pm, Sun, Apr-Sept, 2pm-6pm, Sun, Oct-Mar. Tel. (096) 43325.* Has an outstanding and absorbing presentation on its history and the effects of the famine on the locality. Products from the mills, other local crafts, on sale. Art exhibitions. Also see the birthplace in the town of Admiral Brown, founder of the Argentinian Navy in early 19th c.

Inishturk
13 km (8 miles) SW of Roonagh Quay.
Small but interesting and inhabited island, measuring just 5 x 2.5 km (3 x 1.5 miles). Boats from Roonagh Quay.

Killala
11 km (7 miles) NW of Ballina.
The small cathedral (CI) has fine paintings and many historical records. Also a round tower. Excellent walks on quayside and pier. Boats to the secluded Bartragh island at mouth of River Moy.

Kiltimagh
24 km (15 miles) E of Castlebar.
Many 19th c. buildings in the town have been restored, along with blacksmith's forge. The goods store in the railway station is now a museum of old farm implements and household utensils. Exhibitions staged in **Station Master's House**, *open 12 noon-6pm Mon-Sat, 2pm-6pm Sun, during the summer.*

Knock
11 km (7 miles) NE of Claremorris. TIO tel (098) 88193, May-Sept.
Knock is a major pilgrimage centre, attracting over 2 million people a year. Magnificent new basilica next the old church where the famous apparition was seen in 1879. **Our Lady's Domain** is finely landscaped parkland, with trees, shrubs, roses. **Folk Museum**, *open 10am-7pm daily, May-Oct, tel. (094) 88100.* Has many relics of old-style life in Co Mayo.

Louisburgh
19 km (12 miles) W of Westport.
Delightful small village near south-west corner of Clew Bay and good, sandy beaches. **Granuaile Centre**, *open daily, May-Sept, tel. (098) 66195.* Set in the former St Catherine's Church details the life of this western queen of the sea.

Mulrany
29 km (18 miles) NW of Westport.
Attractive village between Clew Bay and Blacksod Bay. Mild climate encourages giant fuchsias and rare plants such as Mediterranean heather. Good bathing beach.

Murrisk Abbey
8 km (5 miles) W of Westport.
Ruins of 15th c. abbey, in fine setting overlooking Clew Bay.

Newport
12 km (8 miles) N of Westport.
Fronted by Clew Bay and sheltered to N by Nephin Beg mountain range. **St Patrick's Church** has Harry Clarke windows showing the Last Judgement. An abandoned seven arch railway bridge, once part of the old Westport-Achill Island railway, spans the river and is now part of a linear park. **Salmon World Visitor Centre**, *open daily, June-Aug. Tel. (098) 41107.* This salmon research centre has audio-visual presentation on the salmon, together with a photographic record of the centre's work.

Sheeffry Hills
22 km (14 miles) SW of Westport.
The two main peaks are worth climbing for the views from the top.

Straide
9 km (6 miles) S of Foxford.
Michael Davitt Museum, *open 2pm-6pm Tues-Sat. Tel. Nancy Smyth (094) 31022.* Has archive material, including photographs and documents, on the founder of the Land League and founding patron of the Gaelic Athletic Association.

Westport
260 km (162 miles) NW of Dublin. Pop 3,700. TIO tel (098) 21711 all year.
The most attractive town in Co Mayo, Westport was planned by an 18th c. architect, James Wyatt, who had been employed to finish Westport House. The result is a town planned with natural symmetry, divided by the Mall that runs along both banks of the rushing Carrowbeg River, spanned by

Westport House, Westport, Co. Mayo

a hump-backed bridge. The atmospheric **Olde Railway Hotel** on the Mall has many interesting mementoes of the town and well-known people who have visited Westport over the years.

From the river, the streets rise up to the **Octagon**, the focus of the town's commercial centre. Westport has an intriguing mix of old-style shops, modern emporia and continental-style cafés. A traditional farmers' market is held in the Octagon every Thursday morning. Down by the harbour is the Museum which details local history and maritime matters.

Westport House, *2.5 km (1.5 miles) W of Westport. Open 2pm-5pm Mon-Sat, Apr-May, Sept, 12 noon-5pm Mon-Fri, 2pm-6pm Sat-Sun, June, 10.30am-6pm Mon-Sat, 2pm-6pm Sun, July-Aug. Tel. (098) 21430.* Stately home built in late 18th c., with fine late Georgian and Victorian furnishings. The dungeons have video games to keep younger members of the family happy, while many attractions have been devised for the surrounding parkland, including a children's zoo

and a narrow gauge steam railway. Visitors can miss the bustle of children by coming early in the day.

Yeats Country

Ballymote
22 km (14 miles) S of Sligo.
Ballymote Castle was built by Richard de Burgh, Red Earl of Ulster, extensive ruins flanked by six towers. Ruins of Franciscan friary. Remains of the house

of the 14th c. Knights of St John can be seen on the shores of **Templehouse Lough**, *3 km (2 miles) SW of village.* **Irish Falconry Centre**, *tel. Michael Devlin (071) 83211.* The medieval sport of falconry has been revived here.

Ben Bulben
N of Sligo.
This dramatic mountain, which dominates the surrounding countryside, features prominently in Irish mythology and also offers some decent walking.

Bricklieve Mountains
10 km (6 miles) SE of Ballymote.
A whole day can be spent exploring these remote mountain tops and the prehistoric burial cairns dating back to 2,000 BC.

Creevykeel Court Cairn
24 km (15 miles) N of Sligo, near Cliffony.
Some of the best megalithic remains in Ireland. The cairn is impressively sited, with mountains to the south and east.

Drumcliffe

6 km (4 miles) N of Sligo.
W. B. Yeats is buried in the churchyard (CI), beneath Ben Bulben. Yeats died at Roquebrune in the South of France in 1939, but his remains were not brought home until 1948. On his tombstone are carved the immortal words:

> Cast a cold eye
> On Life, on Death,
> Horseman, pass by!

Enniscrone

55 km (34 miles) W of Sligo.
Popular resort with 5 km (3 miles) long sandy beach, seaweed baths (very therapeutic), fine walks.

Glencar Lake

11 km (7 miles) NE of Sligo.
Scenic lough in a tranquil landscape with impressive waterfalls – the highest is an unbroken fall of over 15 metres (50 feet), and pleasant walking.

Gleniff Horseshoe

Near Cliffony, midway between Sligo and Bundoran.

Ben Bulben, Co. Sligo

The route along the glen forms one of the most spectacular tours in the north-west.

Innisfree

20 km (12 miles) E of Sligo.
To find the island that Yeats immortalised, take the R287 through Dromahair, along the south side of Lough Gill. It is signposted.

Innismurray Island

6 km (4 miles) offshore from Streedagh Point.
2 km (1 mile) from end to end, this low lying island has substantial early Christian monastic remains. The island's 50 inhabitants left in Oct 1947. Boats from Mullaghmore, Rosses Point, Streedagh.

Knocknarea

6 km (4 miles) SW of Sligo.
This cone-shaped limestone mountain dominates the surrounding area. From the summit you can enjoy tremendous views. The south eastern side of the mountain presents an easy climb.

Carrowmore Megaliths, *3 km (2 miles) SW of Sligo. Open 9.30am-6.30pm daily, May-Sept. Tel. (071) 61534.* Over 60 Bronze Age tombs are set at the foot of Knocknarea, making the site the largest such concentration in Ireland and one of the largest in Europe. A restored cottage has a small exhibition detailing the site.

Lissadell House

6 km (4 miles) NW of Drumcliffe. Open 10.30am-4.30pm Mon-Sat, June-Sept. Tel. (071) 63150.
This 1834 aristocratic mansion has been in the Gore-Booth family since it was built. It was the childhood home of Countess Markievicz, a leader in the 1916 Easter Rising and her sister Eva Gore-Booth. W. B. Yeats had many links with the family and the house and regularly slept in the bedroom above the porch. Tours of the house include the fine dining and music rooms. Impressive gardens, full of daffodils in spring. The woods on the estate are now a forestry and wildlife reserve.

Lough Arrow
32 km (20 miles) SW of Sligo.
Peaceful and picturesque lough dotted with islets. Nearby **Curlew Hill** offers some good walking and great views.

Lough Gill
3 km (2 miles) E of Sligo.
This wonderfully situated lake with its 22 islands rivals Killarney's lake district. Daily cruises in summer, *tel. George McGoldrick (071) 62000.* Also **Wild Rose Waterbus service**, *tel. (071) 54266.*

Mullaghmore
16 km (10 miles) N of Sligo.
Pleasant town with tranquil harbour and good beach in the shadow of **Classiebawn Castle**.

Parke's Castle
On Sligo-Dromahair R286 road, NE of Lough Gill. Open 10am-5pm Tues-Sun, Apr-May, Oct, 9.30am-6.30pm daily, June-Sept. Tel. (071) 64149.
Restored early 17th c. plantation castle and courtyard. Exhibitions, audio-visual show, tearooms.

Rosses Point
8 km (5 miles) NW of Sligo.
Small but attractive seaside resort on north side of Sligo Bay, with two excellent beaches.

Sligo
217 km (135 miles) NW of Dublin. Pop 17,500. TIO Temple Street, tel. (071) 61201, all year.
This old, flourishing town on the Garavogue River, with Ben Bulben to the north and a fine coastline nearby, deserves exploration. Its many Yeatsian links add strong cultural qualities. The **County Library and Museum**, *Stephen Street, library open 10am-5pm Tues-Sat, also 7pm-9pm on Tues and Thurs, museum open 10.30am-4.30pm Tues-Sat, June-Sept. Tel. (071) 42212.* Has special W. B. Yeats section, including first editions, his 1923 Nobel Prize for Literature and the Irish tricolour flag that draped his coffin. The art gallery section has Ireland's largest collection of works by Jack B. Yeats, W. B.'s brother.

Yeats Memorial Building, *at Hyde Bridge, open 10.30am-5pm Mon-Fri, all year. Tel. (071) 42693.* This is the centre for the Yeats annual internation-al summer school held in August. Audio-visual shows on the great poet's life and times. As a boy, Yeats spent many a happy hour in the **Watch Tower** *on the corner of Adelaide Street and Wine Street*, where his grandfather kept sight of his sailing ships entering and leaving Sligo harbour.

Hawk's Well Theatre has frequent performances, *tel. (071) 61518/61526.* **Sligo Abbey** dates from 13th c. and has almost perfect cloisters on three sides. **Hargadon's Bar**, O'Connell Street, has changed little over the century – all mirrors and mahogany. Guided walking tours of Sligo town, daily during the summer.

Strandhill
6 km (4 miles) W of Sligo.
Another pleasant seaside resort, this time on the southern shores of Sligo Bay. When the tide is out, you can follow the pillars from here to **Coney Island**, in the middle of the bay. The island has a fine sandy setting, with excellent sea views.

Streedagh
3 km (2 miles) W of Grange.
During low water at spring tide, you can sometimes see the wrecks of three Spanish Armada galleons, which sank here in 1588. Only one sailor survived.

Donegal Highlands & Islands

Ardara
39 km (24 miles) NW of Donegal.
One of Donegal's main tweed weaving centres, which is reflected in the **Ardara Heritage Centre**, *open daily,* *tel. (075) 41262.* The **Church of the Holy Family (C)** has an Evie Hone stained-glass window in western nave, depicting the Word of God.

Arranmore Island
5 km (3 miles) offshore from Burtonport.
Largest island off the west coast of Donegal, with just over 700 inhabi-tants. Magnificent caves, cliffs and strands, including **Aphort**, on the south of the island, which is Arran-more's largest beach. Striking little villages, like Illion, where houses rise up from the chapel on the strand. Lough Shure, in the north of island, is Ireland's only rainbow trout lake. Regular daily sailings from Burtonport; the trip is an excitement in itself, tel. Tom Gallagher (075) 20521.

Ballyshannon
24 km (15 miles) SW of Donegal.
The steep, narrow streets of this 17th c. town impart a fine historic atmos-phere. The poet William Allingham was born at a house in The Mall in 1824. He died in 1889 and is buried in **St Anne's Churchyard**, *off the Main Street.* **Donegal Parian China**, *open 9am-6pm Mon-Fri, all year, tel. (072) 51826.* Delicate china and porcelain. Video, factory tour, showroom.

Bloody Foreland
20 km (12 miles) W of Falcarragh. NW Donegal.
One of the best vantage points in the county, with views out to Tory Island. **Teach Mhuiris** is a traditional thatched cottage with a heritage centre and tea shop.

Bunbeg
15 km (10 miles) N of Dungloe.
Tiny restful fishing village with pretty harbour and extensive sandy beach to the north.

Bundoran
30 km (19 miles) S of Donegal.
Premier holiday resort in the north-west, with a fine strand backed by a promenade. **Waterworld Centre**, *open daily, tel. (072) 41172,* has range of water-based leisure activities, incorp-orating the existing swimming pool on the front. The headlands and cliffs near the town give fine walks and views.

Burtonport
8 km (5 miles) NW of Dungloe.
Small fishing village noted for its lobster and salmon.

Carrigart
23 km (15 miles) N of Letterkenny.
Quiet resort with good fishing and beach at base of the wonderful Rosguill peninsula.

Church Hill
16 km (10 miles) W of Letterkenny.
Angling centre near beautiful shores of Gartan Lough. **Colmcille Heritage Centre**, *open 11am-6.30pm Mon-Sat, 1pm-6.30pm Sun, May, Sept, Oct, 10am-6.30pm Mon-Sat, 12 noon-6.30pm Sun, June-Aug. Tel. (074) 21160.* Interpretative centre on life and times of St Colmcille (Columba of Iona), who was born in nearby Gartan in 521. Details of manuscript production.

Creeslough
10 km (6 miles) S of Dunfanaghy.
Attractive village on high ground overlooking an inlet from Sheephaven Bay.

Cruit Island
5 km (4 miles) N of Burtonport.
This small island, with wild bog and reed beds, makes for a memorable visit. Connected to the mainland by a bridge. Outstanding views, especially south to Arranmore island.

Donegal Town
30 km (19 miles) NE of Bundoran.
Magee Tweed Factory, *open Mon-Fri, all year, tel. (073) 21100*, welcomes visitors, also restaurant. Craft Village houses some new craft shops. **St Patrick's Church of the Four Masters (C)** is strikingly modern, dating from 1935. **Donegal Castle**, built in the 15th c., is being restored, but should be open in 1995.

Dunfanaghy
13 km (8 miles) NE of Falcarragh.
Popular resort near Horn Head, one of the most attractive locations anywhere in Co Donegal. Magnificent strands in vicinity. One of last places in Ireland where the corncrake can be heard in its natural environment. A famine museum has been developed.

On the road near Falcarragh, Co. Donegal

Dunlewy
11 km (7 miles) E of Gweedore
Enviously placed on the shores of Lough Nacung and at the foot of Mount Errigal, Dunlewy is a good base from which to explore the fantastic **Poisoned Glen** and **Derryveagh Mountains**. **Lakeside Centre**, *open 11.30am-6pm Mon-Sat, 12.30pm-7pm Sun, June-Sept. Tel. (075) 31699.* Museum based on the life of a local weaver, Manus Ferry. His house has been reconstructed as an interpretative centre giving the flavour of early 20th c. Donegal home life. Demonstrations of woollen trade skills. Boat trips on lake, tea room, craftshop.

Fahan
6 km (4 miles) S of Buncrana.
Attractive village by shores of Lough Swilly with delightful beach.

Falcarragh
35 km (22 miles) NW of Letterkenny.
Bi-lingual village near the east end of the north-west Donegal Gaeltacht. **Oldphert House and Gardens, Ballyconnell Estate**, are being developed as a visitor centre.

Fanad Peninsula
Begins 10 km (6 miles) N of Letterkenny.
This peninsula offers some of the best scenery in north Donegal. Head north for Ramelton and take in the three-mile long stretch of perfect beach at Ballymastocker Bay, the slightly dilapidated resort of Portsalon and the wonderfully-positioned lighthouse at Fanad Head.

Glencolumbkille
56 km (35 miles) NW of Donegal.
This fascinating self-help co-operative community was inspired by the late Fr James McDyer. As he said: "If you like wild, rugged scenery, uncluttered beaches, a secluded area where you can unwind from modern city life, then Glencolumbkille is for you". **The Folk Village and Museum**, *open 10am-5.30pm Mon-Sat, 12 noon-6.30pm Sun, June-Oct, tel. (073) 30017*, has a series of buildings that include a school, shebeen (pub) and craft shop. Also a group of traditional thatched cottages.

Glengesh Pass
Begins 5 km (3 miles) E of Adara.
Between Ardara and Glencolumbkille, it rises spectacularly to 274 m (900 ft) before plunging to the valley. Excellent views.

Glenties
30 km (19 miles) NW of Donegal.
Striking small town set amid woods where two glens meet. **St Conal's Museum**, *open 10am-5pm Mon-Fri, 11am-2pm Sat, May-Aug, tel. (075) 51277.* Has large collection of railway memorabilia.

Glenveagh National Park
W of Letterkenny. Open 10am-6.30pm daily, Apr-May, 10am-6.30pm Mon-Sat, 10am-7.30pm Sun, June-Sept, 10am-6.30pm Sat-Thurs, Oct. Tel. (074) 37090.
This vast area of mountains, glens, lakes and woods has its own herd of deer. **Visitor Centre**, has audio-visual show on the park. **Glenveagh Castle**, built 1870-1873, is open, but only for tours. **The Glebe House and Gallery**, *open 11am-6.30pm daily, Apr, 11am-6.30pm Sat-Thurs, May-Oct. Tel. (074) 37071.* This Regency house, set in woodland gardens, is exquisitely decorated with over 300 modern works of art, including Picasso and Kokoschka, plus many Irish and Italian artists.

Grianan of Aileach
11 km (7 miles) S of Fahan.
Remarkable circular stone fort, in almost perfect condition, dating from about 1,700 BC. Very similar to Staigue Fort in south Kerry. Excellent views from top. See striking modern church at Burt, nearby.

Inch Island
8 km (5 miles) S of Buncrana.
Despite its name, the "island" is actually part of the mainland! **Inishowen Heritage and Genealogical Centre**, *open daily*, details local history.

Inishowen Peninsula
Begins 15 km (9 miles) N of Derry.
This NE corner of Co Donegal provides many fine views and interesting places to visit. Buncrana has a **Vintage Car and Carriage Museum**, *open 10am-8pm daily, during summer, daily by arr in winter, tel. (077) 61130.* A fine collection of old cars, Victorian bicycles, model cars and trains. **Tullyarvan Mill Interpretative Centre**,

open 10am-6pm Mon-Sat, 12 noon-6pm Sun, Easter-Sept. Tel. (077) 61613. Details of 250 years of textile production in the area. Also local wildlife, craft and souvenir shop.

National Knitting Centre, open daily, Jan-Sept, Mon-Fri, Oct-Dec, tel. (077) 62355. Details of Donegal's handknitting cottage industry. **Fort Dunree Military Museum**, open 10am-6pm Tues-Sat, 12 noon-6pm Sun and bank holidays, Easter-Sept, tel. (074) 21160. Once a coastal fort with commanding views, the museum details military history going back to Napoleonic times.

There are many fine strands on the peninsula, including Pollan Strand near Ballyliffen. **Leisureland, Redcastle, Moville**, open daily, Easter-Sept, tel. (077) 82306, has fun and entertainment for children of all ages. The tiny town of Malin is most attractive. From here, the road leads to Malin Head, the most northerly point, not only of the Inishowen Peninsula, but of all Ireland. Boats cross from the small harbour to the deserted island of **Inishtrahull**, abandoned over 60 years ago.

Killybegs
27 km(17 miles) W of Donegal.
Arguably Ireland's most important fishing port, set on a fine natural harbour. The place buzzes when the fishing fleet returns and the air is thick with gulls. Major annual sea-angling festival in August.

Kilmacrennan
11 km (7 miles) N of Letterkenny.
Ruins of a 15th c. Franciscan friary. Lough Slat, near the village, is a very scenic area. **Lurgyvale Thatched Cottage**, open 10am-7pm Mon-Sat, 11am-7pm Sun, May-Sept. Tel.(074) 39216. This 150 year-old thatched cottage recreates simple lifestyle of the early 19th c. Displays of farm implements, nature walk along river bank, craft shop, tea room, traditional music sessions weekly in summer.

Letterkenny
34 km (21 miles) W of Derry. TIO Derry Road, tel. (074) 21160 all year.
Donegal County Museum in former workhouse, open 11am-4.30pm Tues-Fri, 1pm-4.30pm Sat, all year, tel. (074) 24613. Exhibits ranging from Stone and Bronze Ages to early Christian era. **St Eunan's Cathedral (C)** is a modern building in the Gothic style with richly decorated ceilings and striking windows. Its spire is a landmark for miles around.

Lifford
24 km (15 miles) SW of Derry.
Cavanacor House, open daily, Easter-Sept, tel. (074) 41143, is one of Donegal's oldest inhabited houses, dating back 300 years. It was the ancestral home of James Knox Polk, US President 1845-1849. Apart from the house there is a museum, art gallery with contemporary paintings and sculptures, pottery, craft shop, tearoom. **Lifford Visitor Centre**, located in the restored basement of courthouse, open daily, all year, tel. (074) 41228.

Lough Derg
16 km (10 miles) E of Donegal.
St Patrick's Purgatory in the middle of the lake has been a place of pilgrimage since early Christian times. The octagonal church was built in 1921. Boat trips on the lake, Easter-Sept, tel. (072) 61518/61550.

Lough Eske
8 km(5 miles) NW of Donegal.
The 15-mile drive round the shore of the beautiful lough offers views of some of Ireland's most seductive scenery.

Narin/Portnoo
13 km (8 miles) N of Ardara.
The chief attraction of these twin villages is Narin's wonderful mile-long beach. At low tide you can walk to the offshore island of Innisheel, where there are remains of 12th c. churches.

New Mills
5 km (3 miles) W of Letterkenny. Open daily, all year. Tel. (074) 21160.
Old corn and flax mill, up to four centuries old, has been recently restored and is a fascinating piece of early industrial archaeology. The millrace and mill wheels have also been restored.

Ramelton
13 km (8 miles) N of Letterkenny.
The **Old Meeting House**, open 9am-5pm daily, July-Aug, tel. (074) 51266. The house has been restored and contains a library and geneaologica centre. Rev Francis Makemie, a rector here, emigrated to America in 1683 and founded the first Presbyterian Church in Virginia. The 'Pool' here is a famous cast for salmon on the River Lennon Walks by the old quayside warehouses

Rathmullan
24 km (15 miles) NE of Letterkenny.
Once an anchorage for the British flee during World War I, the town's solid villas are a reminder of those far-of days. The **Flight of the Earls Interpretive Centre**, open 10am 6pm Mon-Sat, 12 noon-6.30pm Sun mid-May – Sept. Tel. (074) 58178, 58131. It commemorates the last two great Celtic chieftains, Hugh O'Donnel and Hugh O'Neill, who departed from the harbour here in 1607, creating a great turning point in Irish history. Fine beach, pier.

Rossguill Peninsula
35 km (21 miles) NW of Letterkenny.
This wonderfully scenic peninsula can be seen to best advantage by taking the Atlantic Drive. A truly spectacular road it runs right round the peninsula starting at Downings, and affords stunning coastal views.

Rossnowlagh
17 km (11 miles) SW of Donegal Town.
Abbey Assaroe Mills and Waterwheels, open daily in summer. Waterwheels and site restored to form interpretative centre with audio-visual presentation on Cistercian history Franciscan friary has grounds that are ideal for strolling, while viewpoint at the west end of the grounds overlooks the great sweep of Rossnowlagh strand. **Donegal Historical Society's Museum**, open daily, all year, tel. (072) 51342. A fine repository of local artefacts and historical detail.

Sheephaven Bay
N Donegal, due W from Rosguill Peninsula.
Attractions on west side of bay include the ruins of **Doe Castle**, early 16th c. now ruined, **Ards Forest Park**, the seaside villages of Portnablagh and Dunfanaghy and great stretches of sandy beach, including **Marble Hill strand**.

Portsalon strand, Co. Donegal

Slieve League

SW Donegal, 20 km (12 miles) W of Killybegs.

The majestic cliffs here are the highest sea cliffs in Europe and are a truly awesome sight. Provided suitable care is taken, the climb to the summit of Slieve League will be suitably rewarding. The slopes are home to many seabirds.

St John's Point

20 km (12 miles) S of Killybegs. S of Dunkineely.

This peninsula stretches for about 8 km (5 miles) into Donegal Bay. A road covers almost the entire distance. One of Donegal's finest beaches – and that's saying something!

Tory Island

11 km (7 miles) off the NW Donegal coast. Tel. Eamonn Heaney (Co-op Manager) on (075) 20521.

Reached by regular ferry service from Magheraroarty on the mainland. The island is a haven of solitude, craft working, primitive painting and bird watching. Historic features on the island include a round tower and the ruins of two churches, probably once part of the 6th c. monastery founded by St Colmcille. Visitors can now stay in comfort on Tory Island at the new hotel.

Thatching, Co. Donegal

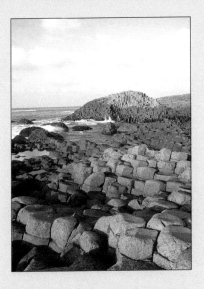

Northern Ireland

Of all the spectacular natural formations in Ireland, nothing can excel the Giant's Causeway on the north Antrim coast, its octagonal basalt columns testimony to some unknown upheaval of the earth countless aeons ago. Northern Ireland abounds with such places of outstanding natural beauty and interest. Off the north coast of Antrim lies the island of Rathlin, remote but rewarding to the visitor who takes a boat across from the unspoiled, peaceful town of Ballycastle. The Glens of Antrim are verdant and magnificent, while on the other side of Northern Ireland, the endless waterways of the Erne system offer paradise to boating enthusiasts who may now also take the new canal that links the Erne system with the River Shannon. In the south-east, the Mountains of Mourne, which dominate the surrounding countryside, offer wonderful climbing and walking possibilities. Northern Ireland is rich not just in unspoiled, natural landscapes, but in man-made places too. Armagh has its ecclesiastical and ancient history, the city of Derry has been revitalised in recent years, while Belfast is full of attractions and facilities for its many visitors.

Greater Belfast & the Lagan Valley

Belfast
Pop. 300,000. TIO St Anne's Court, 59 North Street, Belfast BT1 1NB, tel. (01232) 231221, all year.
The capital of Northern Ireland is attractively situated on the Lagan estuary, at the foot of the Antrim plateau. Despite its relative decline as an industrial centre and the toll taken by the so-called "Troubles" since 1969, the city is still thriving. Facilities for visitors, places to shop, eat and visit have been expanded considerably, to keep up with the increasing numbers of tourists, both from the United Kingdom and further afield, who visit the city each year.

Belfast is a vigorous, no-nonsense city and its people are famed for their wry humour and wit. Much of the city's wealth came from the linen industry in the 1800s and this is evident in the city buildings – it is very much a Victorian city with some impressive architecture, notably the stately City Hall in the centre of town. It also has a very fine cultural tradition; its art galleries and museums, including some recent arrivals, well repay closer inspection.

Access to the city is easy whether you arrive by air at the Belfast International Airport at Aldergrove or Belfast City Airport; by car on the clearly marked and easy to use motorway system; by ferry or Seacat at the docks, or by rail (the Dublin-Belfast line is currently being upgraded and should be fully operational in 1996).

Major annual festivals in Belfast include: Belfast Arts Festival, a three week long cultural extravaganza in November; the Royal Ulster Agri-cultural Society Show in May; Orange parades on July 12; Ancient Order of Hibernian parades on August 15.

CATHEDRALS AND CHURCHES

Over 70 churches were built in the latter half of the 19th c. as Belfast expanded dramatically. Among the most notable are **Fitzroy Presbyterian** built in 1872 and **St Mark's**, *Dundela* (1878). **St Malachy's (C)**, *Alfred Street*, has an excellent fan-vaulted ceiling, while **St Patrick's (C)**, *Upper Donegall Street*, has a chapel decorated by the esteemed painter, Sir John Lavery. The **Unitarian Church**, *Rosemary Street*, also has fine plaster and woodwork. **St Anne's Cathedral (CI)**, *Lower Donegall Street*, is a modern Romanesque building. The mosaic roof of the baptistery is made up of 150,000 pieces of glass, symbolising the Creation. The tomb of the Ulster Unionist leader, Lord Carson is in the nave of the cathedral.

NOTABLE BUILDINGS

City Hall
Donegall Square. Open (for guided tours only) 10.30am Wed. Tel. (01232) 320202, extn 2618.
Handsome structure with fine marble interior, wall murals and excellent city views from the dome.

Harbour Office
Corporation Square. Open by arr. Tel. (01232) 234422
Recollections of Belfast's strong maritime tradition.

Custom House
High Street.
Majestically proportioned building. The writer Anthony Trollope worked here as a surveyor's clerk in 1841.

Royal Courts of Justice
Chichester Street
A substantial structure, built in Portland stone which was a gift from Westminster, the courts opened in 1933.

Queen's University of Belfast
University Road.
Founded in 1849, the university is a leading centre for many branches of scientific research. The library has ov 750,000 books, many collections a rare editions.

MUSEUMS AND LIBRARIES

Ulster Museum and Art Gallery
Stranmillis Road. Open Mon-Fr 10am-5pm, Sat, 1pm-5pm, Sun, 2pr 5pm, all year. Tel. (01232) 381251.
Noted for its Irish antiquities and a collections. The Museum hous treasures from the *Girona*, a Spani Armada galleon wrecked off the nor Antrim coast. Among the distinguishe Irish artists represented are Willia Conor, Jack B. Yeats, Colin Middlet and George Campbell. Sculpto represented include Henry Moor Barbara Hepworth and F.E. McWilliar Frequent visiting exhibitions. Engine ing hall has working examples of o machinery. Shop, café.

Malone House
Barnett's Demesne, Upper Malor Road. Open 10am-4.30pm Mon-Sat, d year. Tel. (01232) 681246.
This early 19th c. building has permanent exhibition on Belfast park

Royal Ulster Rifles Museum
War Memorial Building, 5 Warin Street. Open 10am-4pm Mon-Fri, a year. Tel. (01232) 232086.
Relics of the regiment and i predecessors.

Linen Hall Library
17 Donegall Square North. Tel. (0123. 321707.
Established in 1788, the library has fine collection of Irish publishe material. Reading room, café.

Central Library
Royal Avenue. Tel. (01232) 243233.
Collection of early Belfast printe books, photographs, maps, exh bitions.

GALLERIES

Arts Council Gallery
56 Dublin Road. Tel. (01232) 32140.

Donegall Place, Belfast

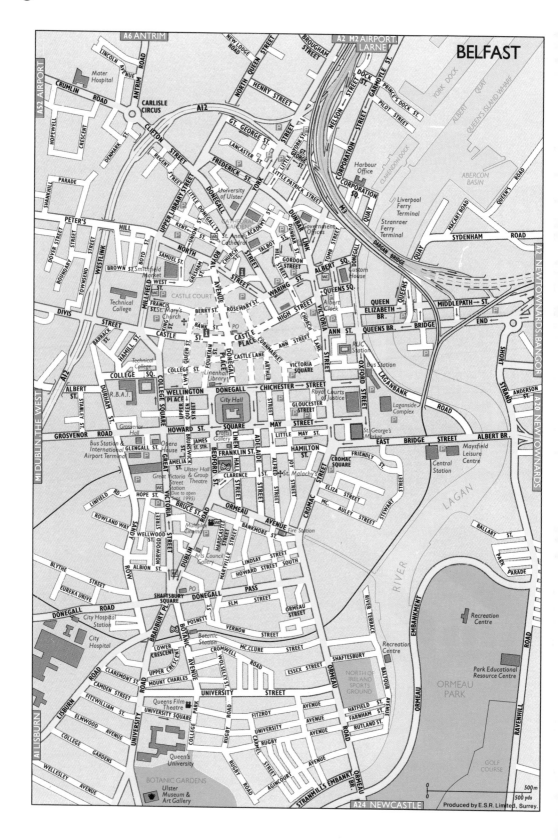

BELFAST

s Council Sculpture Park
Stranmillis Road
rks by noted local sculptors in a
den setting.

1 Gallery
Adelaide Park. Tel. (01232) 662998.
licated to Irish artists.

n Caldwell Gallery
Bradbury Place. Tel. (01232) 323226.
ibitions of living Irish artists.

vehill Gallery
Old Cavehill Road. Tel. (01232)
784.
h artists.

kin Gallery
Lisburn Road. Tel. (01232) 668522
h artists.

deresky Gallery at Queens
er Crescent. Tel. (01232) 235245
ntemporary art.

scent Arts Centre
niversity Road. Tel. (01232) 242338
ntemporary work, craft demonstra-
ns.

e old **Ormeau Baths** in south
fast are due to open in 1995 as a
jor new contemporary art venue.

EATRES AND CONCERT HALLS

and Opera House
at Victoria Street. Tel. (01232)
919.
nd style Victorian theatre, present-
wide variety of entertainment.

s Theatre
anic Avenue. Tel. (01232) 324936.
ular productions.

ic Theatre
geway Street. Tel. (01232) 381081.
formances of Irish drama, including
w works, international theatre.

up Theatre
dford Street. Tel. (01232) 329685.
cal amateur dramatics society
ductions.

d Museum
lege Square. Tel. (01232) 235053.
w plays and experimental theatre.

Ulster Hall
Bedford Street. Tel. (01232) 323900.
Everything from rock bands to
symphonies performed by the Ulster
Orchestra.

King's Hall
Lisburn Road. Tel. (01232) 665225.
Large exhibition and concert venue.

ROUND & ABOUT

Bass Ireland Brewery
*Glen Road. Open by arrangement
only.*
Has audio-visual presentation on
brewery's history. Viewing of
production processes.

Belfast Zoo
*Antrim Road. Open 10am-5pm daily,
Apr-Sept, 10am-3.30pm daily, Oct-Mar.
Tel. (01232) 776277.*
The zoo has new pens allowing visitors
to view sea lions and penguins under
the surface of the water. Land-based
species vary from bears and gorillas to
marmosets. Restaurant, tea house.
Hazelwood Park, beside the zoo, is a
delightful area, featuring a lake.

Belvoir Park
*Newtownbreda, 6 km (4 miles) S of
Belfast city centre.*
Extensive parkland, with Norman
motte and ruins of the 14th c. Breda
Old Church.

Botanic Gardens
*University Road. Open 10am-5pm
Mon-Fri, 2pm-5pm Sat-Sun and bank
holidays, Apr-Sept, 10am-4pm Mon-
Fri, 2pm-4pm Oct-Mar. Tel. (01232)
324902.*
Dates back to 1828 and features a rose
garden and herbaceous borders. The
Palm House was built in 1839 and has
been restored, while the Tropical
Ravine, completed 1889, is a fine
example of horticultural Victoriana.

Cave Hill Country Park and Belfast Castle.
Climb Cave Hill for panoramic views
from MacArt's Fort, where the United
Irishmen planned a rebellion in 1795.
Belfast Castle, with its immaculate
gardens, has a new **heritage centre**,
open 9am-6pm daily, all year. The
park is accessible at all times.

Colin Glen Forest Park
*Stewartstown Road, west Belfast. Tel.
(01232) 614115.*
At the foot of the Black Mountain. The
Park has a waterfall, mill race, nature
trails, wildlife pond, restored aque-
duct, heritage centre, audio-visual
presentation. Café.

Crown Liquor Saloon
*Great Victoria Street. Open 11.30am-
11pm Mon-Sat, 12.30pm-2.30pm, 7pm-
10pm Sun, all year.*
This magnificent high-Victorian pub, is
richly ornamented with fine woodwork, glass and tiles.

Falls Road/Shankill Road
The infamous Nationalist Falls and
Unionist Shankill have considerable
personality and are not without appeal.

Giant's Ring
*1.5 km (1 Mile) S of Shaw's Bridge, on
S outskirts, Belfast. Freely accessible.*
Most impressive prehistoric earthwork
over 200m (600ft) in diameter, with
dolmen in centre. There are excellent
views of Belfast from the nearby
ancient earthwork on a hilltop.

Harland & Wolff Shipyard
*Docks, town centre. Can be visited by
written arrangement with the public
relations department.*
This world renowned shipyard was
where the Titanic and Canberra were
built, among many others. It now
houses two of the worlds largest cranes
– 'Samson' and 'Goliath'.

Kelly's Cellars
Bank Place, off Royal Avenue
One of Belfast's oldest pubs, dating
back 200 years.

Lagan Valley Regional Park
Comprises 16 km (10 miles) of towpath
walks beside the River Lagan, starting
at Stranmillis and ending in Lisburn.
The **Lagan Lookout Visitor Centre**,
*open 11am-5pm Mon-Fri, 12 noon-
5pm Sat, 2pm-5pm Sun, Mar-Sept,
10am-5pm bank holidays. Tel. (01232)
315444.* Extensive riverside developments underway beside the River
Lagan will mean many new facilities for
visitors.

Redburn Country Park
Old Holywood Road, E outskirts of

Stormont, Belfast

Belfast.
Woodland walks, fine views of Belfast hills and lough.

Sir Thomas & Lady Dixon Park
Upper Malone Road. Open dawn to dusk, daily, all year. Tel. (01232) 611506/320202.
Has Japanese garden. The City of Belfast International Rose Trials are held here. Restaurant.

SPORT

Ravenhill Road is the main rugby venue in Belfast, while **Windsor Park** is Northern Ireland's premier football stadium. The city has nearly 20 leisure centres, four swimming baths and eight golf courses.

Crumlin
16 km (10 miles) W of Belfast.
A pleasant village at the head of the wooded Crumlin Glen. Good walks beside the small Crumlin River, which

forms cascades after the weir. **Talnotry Cottage Bird Garden**, *2 Crumlin Road, open daily, all year, tel. (01849) 422900.* This 200 year-old walled garden is a sanctuary for sick and injured birds. Former **US Air Force Base**, *open 12 noon-6pm Sat-Sun, all year, tel. (01849) 422128.* Station 597 was a US 8th Army Air Force base in World War II. Memorabilia, audio-visual presentation. Shop, café.

Down Royal Racecourse
The Maze, near Lisburn. Tel. (01846) 621256.
Regular horse races, including the Ulster Harp Derby in July.

Dundonald
8 km (5 miles) E of Belfast.
Dundonald Old Mill, *open 10am-5.15pm Mon-Sat, 11am-5.15pm Sun, all year. Tel. (01232) 480117,* has Ireland's largest water wheel, which dates from 1752. Displays, craft shop, restaurant. **Streamvale Open Dairy Farm**, *open 2pm-6pm Wed, Sat, Sun and bank holidays, Feb-May, Sept-Oct,*

12 noon-6pm daily, June, 10.30a 6pm daily, July-Aug. Tel. (0123 483244. **Dundonald Ice Bowl**, *(01232) 482611.* The centre offers i skating, ten-pin bowling and children's adventure playground.

Hillsborough
5 km (3 miles) S of Lisburn.
Charming village with steep m Street, an antiques and crafts cent **Hillsborough Fort**, *open 10am-7 Tues-Sat, 2pm-7pm Sun, Apr-Se, 10am-4pm Tues-Sat, 2pm-4pm Su Oct-Mar. Tel. (01846) 6832* **Shambles Arts Centre**, *tel. (018- 682946:* summer exhibitior **Hillsborough Parish Church (** dates from 1773, it is an impos building with approaches to match. Hamilton Harty, composer a conductor, is buried here.

Lisburn
13 km (8 miles) SW of Belfast.
Christchurch Cathedral (CI) da from early 18th c. and is a most intere ing building. **Lisburn Museu**

embly Rooms, Market Square, has
ch material on local history and
haeology, including railway items.
gallery, exhibitions.
The major new development here
the **Irish Linen Centre**, *open*
0am-5.30pm Mon-Sat, 2pm-5.30pm
1, Apr-Sept, 9.30am-5pm, Mon-Sat,
n-5pm, Sun, Oct-Mar, tel. (01846)
3377. Details the history and heri-
e of what was once Ulster's greatest
ustry. Weaving workshop has hand
oms. Audio-visual presentations.
op, restaurant.

ira
km (7 miles) SW of Lisburn.
John's Parish Church (CI) is
uated at the head of an imposing
enue leading from the wooded park.
ilway station is oldest surviving
lway building in Northern Ireland;
ates from 1841.

trangford &
lorth Down

llycopeland Windmill
5 km (1 mile) W of Millisle. Open
am-7pm Tues-Sat, 2pm-7pm Sun,
ster-Sept, 10am-4pm Sat, 2pm-4pm
n, Oct-Mar. Tel. (01247) 861413.
e late 18th c. windmill was in use
til 1915 and is still in working order.
e miller's house has been turned
o a visitor centre, with an electrically-
erated model of the mill.

llyhalbert
km (10 miles) S of Donaghadee.
shing village on east coast of Ards
eninsula, with small harbour and
ore walk for 2 km (1.5 miles) to **Burr**
oint, Ireland's most easterly point.

Ballywalter
8 km (5 miles) S of Millisle.
Small fishing village with good beaches
and harbour. The coastal road in
vicinity offers good views.

Bangor
21 km (13 miles) NE of Belfast. TIO 34
Quay Street, tel. (01247) 270069, June-
Sept.
North Down Heritage Centre, *Castle*
Park Avenue. Open 10.30am-4.30pm
Tues-Sat, 2pm-4.30pm Sun, Sept-June,
10.30am-5.30pm Mon-Sat, 2pm-
5.30pm Sun, July-Aug. Tel. (01247)
271200. All kinds of memorabilia, including toys and railway memorabilia.
Vintage film of Pickie Park, observation
beehive in summer.
   Bangor Abbey, at entrance to town,
just off the Belfast Road, has traces of
the original monastery, but most was
incorporated in the present church
which was built in 1617. **Pickie Family
Fun Park**, on the promenade, *open*
10am-sunset daily has swan pedal
boats, paddling pools, miniature train
and café. **Bangor Marina** has some
lovely walks along the promenade.
Ward Park, *open daily, all year*, has a
nature trail, children's zoo, bowls and
putting green.

Castle Ward
*1.5 km (1 mile) W of Strangford
village. Estate open dawn to dusk,
daily, all year. House open 1pm-6pm
Sat-Sun, Apr, Sept, Oct, daily, Easter,
daily except Thurs, May-Aug. Tel.
(01396) 881204.*
Vast country estate with woodlands,
lake and seashore. The 18th c. house
has façades in two different styles, one
Classical, the other Gothic. Formal
gardens, wildfowl collection, theatre in
stable yard, cornmill used for
exhibitions.

Comber
6 km (4 miles) SW of Newtownards.
Fine central square and village green.
Some pubs may have a few precious
bottles left of Comber whiskey, from
the local distillery which closed down
after World War II. **Castle Espie
Centre**, *open 10.30am-5pm Mon-Sat,
11.30am-5pm Sun, all year. Tel.
(01247) 872517.* Ireland's largest
collection of ducks, geese and swans,
can be viewed from hides. Waterfowl
gardens, woodland walks. Nature

centre, shop, coffee room.

Copeland Islands
5 km (3 miles) N of Donaghadee.
Now deserted, but outstanding bird
sanctuary. Boats from Donaghadee
harbour.

Donaghadee
10 km (6 miles) SE of Bangor.
Most attractive seaside town, built
around an imposing harbour. Grace
Neill's bar, facing the harbour, dates
from 1611. Peter the Great of Russia
was entertained here in 1690s, while
the poet Keats also paid a visit.
Laneways in the town centre add
atmosphere. **Summer cruises**, *from
harbour, tel. (01247) 812215.* Three
hour cruises of Belfast Lough on
former Scilly Isles lifeboat, *tel. (01247)
883403.*

Downpatrick
*14 km (9 miles) W of Strangford. TIO
74 Market Street, tel. (01396) 612233,
all year.*
Down County Museum, *open 11am-
5pm Mon-Fri, 2pm-5pm Sat-Sun, July-
mid-Sept, 11am-5pm Tues-Fri, 2pm-
5pm Sat, mid-Sept – June. Tel. (01396)
615218.* Located in a restored jail, the
museum has Stone Age artefacts and
Bronze Age gold found locally. St
Patrick's story is told in one of the
gatehouses. The saint is said to have
been buried in the grounds of the
cathedral. **Saul Church** also has an
exhibition commemorating St. Patrick.
   Downpatrick Steam Railway,
Market Street, tel. (01396) 615779 has
trains on 1.5 km (1 mile) of former
branch line, restored signal cabin,
displays in station house. Walks in
Georgian mall. **Quoile Countryside
Centre**, *open 11am-5pm daily, Apr-
Sept, 1pm-5pm Sat-Sun, Oct-Mar. Tel.
(01396) 615520.* Inspect fish and
wildlife in Quoile Pondage, guided
walks, trails, lectures, fishing jetty and
the ruins of a 16th c. castle.

Greyabbey
*13 km (8 miles) SE of Newtownards.
Open 10am-7pm Tues-Sat, 2pm-7pm
Sun, Apr-Sept.*
Ruins of 12th c. Cistercian abbey in fine
parkland setting, medieval 'physick'
garden, visitor centre.

oomsport
m (3 miles) E of Bangor.
d-world village with beach,
omenade and summer displays of
ork by local artists.

len's Bay
m (3 miles) W of Bangor.
all resort on southern shore of
elfast Lough. Pleasant walk from
ronial-style railway station to beach.
nearby **Crawfordsburn** the country
rk offers beaches and coastal and
erside walks. The Crawfordsburn
n dates from 1614.

ch Abbey
*5 km (1 mile) NW of Downpatrick.
en 10am-7pm Tues-Sat, 2pm-7pm
n, Apr-Sept.*
e ruins of this island monastery are
ached by a causeway. The abbey is
stercian and was founded in the late
th c.

llyleagh
*shore of Strangford Lough, 24 km
5 miles) NW of Downpatrick.*
easant walks around Killyleagh's
oad streets and up to gates of the
stle. Interesting harbour area.
elamont Country Park, *3 km (2
iles) S of Killyleagh. Open 9am-10pm
ily, Apr-Sept, 9am-5pm Oct-Mar. Tel.
1396) 828333.* Restored walled
rden, heronry, woodland walks, fine
ws over Strangford Lough, tea room.

ount Stewart
*km (5 miles) SE of Newtownards.
ouse open 1pm-6pm daily, except
es, May-Sept. Garden open 10.30am-
m daily, Apr-Sept. Temple of the
inds, open 2pm-5pm daily, except
es, May-Sept. Tel. (012477) 88387.*
fine 18th c. house with 19th c.
dditions. Rooms include the blue
emed "Rome" bedroom. The Temple
the Winds overlooks Strangford
ugh. The gardens, with their rare and
usual plants, formal and informal
sits, are among the finest in these
lands. Shop, tea room.

ewtownards
km (6 miles) S of Bangor.
rk Open Farm, *open 10am-5.30pm
on-Sat, 2pm-6pm Sun, Mar 17-Oct,
l. (01247) 812672/820445,* has many

rangford

---

rare breeds, including Vietnamese pot-
bellied pigs, Nigerian pygmy goats,
llamas. **Ulster Flying Club**, *tel.
(01247) 813327*, pleasure flights from
an airfield just outside Newtownards.
Scrabo Country Park, *open 11am-
6.30pm daily, except Fri, June-Sept, tel.
(01247) 811491.* Woodland walks,
wildlife. Climb the 122 steps to the top
of **Scrabo Tower** for fine views of the
surrounding countryside.

Portaferry
40 km (25 miles) SE Belfast.
Attractive seaside village facing
Strangford village across the lough.
Long waterfront has mix of Scots-style
cottages and Georgian houses. Boats
leave from the quays for trips around
the lough. **Exploris** in *Rope Walk,
Castle Street, open 10am-6pm Mon-Fri,
11am-6pm Sat, 1pm-6pm Sun, all year.
Tel. (01247) 28062.* This is a new high-
tech aquarium with impressive
displays. Visitors can sit in a cave
beneath the open sea tank and watch
sharks and other giants of the deep.
The anemone tank shows off these
creatures from Strangford Lough.

Seaforde
13 km (8 miles) SW of Downpatrick.
Seaforde Gardens Butterfly House,
*open 10am-5pm Mon-Sat, 2pm-6pm
Sun, Easter-Sept. Tel. (01396) 87225.*
Has hundreds of exotic butterflies, also
reptiles and insects. Maze with viewing
tower, shop, tea room.

Somme Heritage Centre
*4 km (2.5 miles) N of Newtownards.
Open 10am-6pm Tues-Sat, 11am-6pm
Sun, Apr-Sept, 10am-5pm Tues-Sat,
11am-5pm Sun, Oct-Mar. Tel. (01247)
823202.*
Audio-visual recreation of the Battle of
the Somme, World War I. Computer-
ised information service, original artefacts, lecture theatre, shop, restaurant.

Strangford
11 km (7 miles) W of Downpatrick.
Attractively situated, facing Portaferry
across the mouth of Strangford Lough
(regular car-ferry crossings). A couple
of miles to the south, **Kilclief Castle**
is one of Ireland's earliest tower
houses.

Struell Wells
2 km (1.5 miles) E of Downpatrick.

17th c. wells and bath houses, on a site
closely associated with St Patrick.

Ulster Folk & Transport Museum
*Cultra, near Holywood. Open 9.30am-
5pm Mon-Fri, 10.30am-6pm Sat, 12
noon-6pm Sun, Apr-June, Sept,
10.30am-6pm Mon-Sat, 12 noon-6pm
Sun, July-Aug, 9.30am-4pm Mon-Fri,
12.30pm-4.30pm Sat-Sun, Oct-Mar. Tel.
(01232) 428428.*
This outstanding museum provides a
very full day out. It is a treasury of
Ulster's economic and social history. A
gallery houses displays of 19th c.
domestic objects, furniture, crafts,
photographs and William Conor paintings. In the surrounding park, many
buildings have been reconstructed
from their original sites, including a
weaver's house, a linen scutch mill, a
blacksmith's forge, even city streets of
old. In the transport section, all modes
are represented, from donkey creels to
pony traps, old aircraft to the *Result*
schooner, built in Carrickfergus in
1893.
The railway collection that once
graced the Witham Street Museum in
east Belfast has been moved to Cultra.
Highlight is the *Maeve*, the largest
steam locomotive ever built in Ireland
for the old Great Southern Railways.
Horse and carriage rides on the estate
(Easter-Sept). Tea room.

The Mountains of Mourne

Annalong
13 km (8 miles) S of Newcastle.
The Mountains of Mourne make a
spectacular backdrop to this agreeable
fishing village and its harbour that is

often filled with fishing boats. **The Cornmill**, *open 2pm-6pm daily, June-Aug, tel. (013967) 68736*, built about 1830 and powered by a waterwheel, has flour-making exhibition. Herb garden and café.

Ardglass

32 km (20 miles) NE of Newcastle.
An important fishing port in Co Down, with walks around both the inner and outer harbours. **Jordan's Castle**, *open 10am-7pm Tues-Sat, 2pm-7pm Sun, July-Aug.* The largest of a cluster of castles, this is a well-preserved four storey tower house.

Bessbrook

5 km (3 miles) NW of Newry.
Founded in 1845 by a Quaker linen manufacturer, so it has no pub, though the adjacent village of Camlough makes up for this deficiency by having six! Walks around College and Charlemont squares. See the huge old mill, with dam, sluices and weirs.

Brontë Homeland Interpretative Centre, Drumballyroney

5 km (3 miles) NE of Rathfriland. Open 11am-5pm Tues-Fri, 2pm-6pm Sat-Sun, Mar-Oct. Tel. (018206) 31152.
Centre details life and times of Brontë family. School and church where Patrick Brontë, father of the novelist sisters, taught and preached, are preserved. His birthplace is one of many sights on the 13 km (8 miles) signposted drive which starts at the centre.

Castlewellan

8 km (5 miles) NW of Newcastle.
Pleasant market town with broad main street and two squares. **Forest Park**, *open 10am-dusk daily, all year, tel. (013967) 78664.* The arboretum was begun in 1740, old courtyards, tropical birds in glasshouses and a 5 km (3 mile) sculpture trail around the lake. Visitor centre, café. Five good fishing lakes within 8 km (5 mile) radius of Castlewellan.

Dundrum

5 km (3 miles) N of Newcastle.
Small seaside village with the substantial ruins of the castle built by Normans in late 12th c. Views to sea and the Mountains of Mourne. **Dundrum Bay** has sandy strand, while

Minerstown Beach on the east side of the bay continues into the 6 km (4 miles) long **Tyrella strand**, where the sand is firm enough for driving. **Murlough Nature Reserve**, *3 km (2 miles) south of Dundrum*, is rich in terms of botanic and wildlife interest. **Visitor Centre** *open 10am-5pm daily, June – mid-Sept, tel. (013967) 51467.*

Greencastle

6 km (4 miles) SW of Kilkeel.
See the ruins of the **13th c. castle**, *north entrance to Carlingford Lough, open 10am-7pm Tues-Sat, Apr-Sept, 10am-4pm Sat, 2pm-4pm Sun, Oct-Mar.*

Hilltown

13 km (8 miles) N of Rostrevor.
Its numerous pubs are a reminder of the village's old days of brandy smuggling. Attractive tree-lined square. At "Bush Town", 5 km (3 miles) east of Hilltown on the B27, the fairy thorn tree at the junction of the Bryansford and Kilkeel Road, is the largest in the North of Ireland.

Katesbridge

Between Castlewellan and Banbridge.
Delightful little village on banks of Upper River Bann.

Kilkeel

16 km (10 miles) E of Rostrevor.
The main fishing port of Co Down. Winding streets, stepped footpaths, many old houses of great character and an enjoyable harbour area all add-up to make Kilkeel an interesting resting point for visitors. In addition, the water in the granite trough at 14th c. church ruins in town centre is said to cure warts!

Legananny Dolmen

7 km (4 miles) S of Dromara on the slopes of Cratlieve Mountain.
Widely considered to be the most graceful Stone Age monument in Northern Ireland.

Mountains of Mourne

The mountains rise up in spectacular fashion from Newcastle and Annalong. Minor roads lead into the Mournes, but since none cross the centre of the range, you must walk to see the main peaks at close quarters. **Slieve Donard**, 850 m (2,796 ft), the highest mountain,

is well worth climbing for the spectac lar views on a clear day, when you c. see as far as Donegal and Wicklow Ireland, the Isle of Man, north-we England and north Wales. The clin takes about two hours from Newcast At the summit, you will see the remai of the 5th c. oratory built by Domhanghort, who gave the mounta its name.

The **Mourne Coastal Path** ru south for 6 km (4 miles) along t seashore from Bloody Bridge, at t foot of Slieve Donard, while anoth path follows the course of Bloody Riv up into the mountains.

The **Silent Valley** and **Ben Cro** reservoirs supply water to Belfast an Co Down. Surrounding parklan crafts shop, café and **Visitor Centr** *open 10am-6.30pm daily, Easter-Sep 10am-4.30pm daily, Oct-Mar. T (01232) 746581.*

On the western edges of tl Mournes, near the **Spelga Dam**, 6 k *(4 miles) west of Hilltown*, you ca experience a similar 'magnetic mil effect to that in **Gortin Forest Par** where your car appears to be goin uphill when it's actually pointir downhill and vice versa! Besides tl strange optical effects, the landscap views are quite stunning.

Newcastle

21 km (13 miles) SE of Downpatric TIO Newcastle Centre, 10-14 Centr Promenade, tel. (013967) 22222, a year.
One of Northern Ireland's top seasic resorts, magnificently situated, with : vast sandy beach backed to the imm diate south by the towering Sliev Donard mountain, one of tl Mountains of Mourne. In recent year visitor facilities in the town have bee much extended. **Newcastle Centr** *open daily, tel. (013967) 25034*, has ; impressive range of indoc entertainments, including tl Tropicana swimming pool, sports ha lounge and café. It is ideal fc occupying children during a spell c wet weather.

Mourne Countryside Centr *Central Promenade, open dail summer, tel. (013697) 24059, h; displays, maps and other materi;

Near the Silent Valley, Mourne Mountain Co. Down

tailing the Mournes.

Grant Gallery, *open 2pm-5pm on-Sat, tel. (013697) 22349*, has Irish d international paintings, sculptures. ewcastle Art Gallery, *18-22 Main eet, open daily, tel. (013697) 23555.* r Lady of the Assumption Church), *near the north end of Downs Park*, a modern, circular and striking ilding.

The **Promenade Gardens** have a untain commemorating Percy ench, composer of the song The untains of Mourne. **Castle Park** has de range of sporting activities, mmer concerts, open-air entertain-ent. **Donard Park** rises up the lower pes of Slieve Donard.

wry
km (10 miles) NW of Rostrevor.
e town has many interesting features d good shopping. The Clanrye River d the canal bisect the town. The nal quaysides have some original th c. warehouses. **Cathedral of St trick and Colman** (C) in *Hill Street*, tes from 1825 and has unusual ined-glass windows and mosaics. **St trick's Church (CI)**, *Church Street*, cludes part of a 16th c. tower.

Newry Arts Centre, *Bank Parade, '. (01693) 61244*, stages a variety of ltural events. **Newry Museum**, cated in the arts centre, open 11am-m Mon-Fri, 10am-1pm Sat, all year, '. (01693) 66232. Has archaeological ms, the table used by Nelson on MS Victory and material on the "Gap the North". A special feature of the useum is the restored 18th c. room th period furniture.

thfriland
km (4 miles) S of Katesbridge.
nall plantation town set on a hill. The eep streets rise to the square. Old ildings include a Quaker meeting use.

strevor
km (9 miles) SE of Newry.
small and delightfully nostalgic aside town, where Victorian elegance ll lingers. Just behind the town, strevor Forest offers gentle walking d more arduous mountain top mbing.

e Mall, Armagh city

Scarva
6 km (4 miles) SW of Banbridge.
New **Interpretative Centre**, *Main Street, open 11am-5pm Tues-Fri, 2pm-5pm Sat-Sun, Mar-Oct, tel. (01762) 832163.* Details the history and development of the Newry canal and also the history of Scarva, which developed because of the canal.

Tullymore Forest Park
3 km (2 miles) E of Newcastle. Open 10am-dusk daily, all year. Tel. (013967) 22428.
Numerous stone follies and bridges, sequoia tree in arboretum, wildlife and forestry exhibits. Pony trekking, fishing, walking, café.

Warrenpoint
5 km (3 miles) W of Rostrevor.
Spacious resort with fine square and tree-lined promenade. The two piers are ideal for fishing and walking. Summer boat excursions across Carlingford Lough to Omeath. The **Burren Heritage Centre**, *Bridge Road, open 11am-5pm Tues-Fri, 2.30pm-5.30pm Sat-Sun, Apr-Oct, Nov-Mar, tel. (016937) 73378.* Interprets the history of the Burren district of south Down from prehistory to the 16th c. Video presentation. Craft shop, coffee shop.

Armagh's Orchard Country

Ardress House
8 km (5 miles) E of Moy. Open 2pm-6pm Sat-Sun and bank holidays, Apr-June, Sept, 2pm-6pm daily except Tues, July-Aug. Farmyard also open 12 noon-4pm weekdays May-June, Sept. Tel. (01762)851236.

17th c. farmhouse with 18th c. additions. Neo-classical plasterwork in drawing room, good furniture and pictures. Farm implements, livestock, garden, woodland walks, playground.

Armagh
59 km (37 miles) SW of Belfast. Pop 12, 700. TIO Old Bank Building, 40 English Street, tel. (01861) 527808, all year.
For 1,500 years, Armagh has been the ecclesiastical capital of Ireland. Today, it retains much of its historic atmosphere, but many new visitor attractions have been added. The Mall is a pleasant tree-lined oasis in the city centre. **St Patrick's Cathedral (C)** is set on a hilltop and is reached by a fine flight of steps, it is 19th c. Byzantine in style and has lavish interior decoration. Red hats of cardinals hang from the ceiling of the Lady Chapel. **St Patrick's Cathedral (CI)** is largely an early 19th c. restoration of a 13th c. building. Tablet outside the north transept marks the reputed grave of Brian Boru.

St Patrick's Trian, *open 10am-7pm Mon-Sat, 1pm-7pm Sun, Apr-Sept, 10am-5pm Mon-Sat, 2pm-5pm Sun, Oct-Mar. Tel. (01861) 527808.* Tells the story of Armagh's history and details Jonathan Swift's association with Armagh and the writing of Gulliver's Travels. Audio-visual theatre, exhibi-tion, craft shop, café.

Palace Stables Heritage Centre, *open 10am-7pm Mon-Sat, 1pm-7pm Sun, Apr-Sept, 10am-5pm Mon-Sat, 2pm-5pm Sun, Oct-Mar. Tel. (01861) 522722.* Shows how life was in Armagh in 1776. Visits to the archbishop's chapel, ice-house and walks in the demesne. **County Museum**, *open 10am-5pm Mon-Sat. Tel. (01861) 523070.* Material on history of the county, railway material and an art gallery. The **Royal Irish Fusiliers Regimental Museum**, *open by arr. tel. (01861) 522911*, includes a 1943 Christmas card from Hitler. **Robinson Library**, *open 10am-4pm Mon-Fri, all year, tel. (01861) 523142*, has books, manuscripts and registers going back to medieval times.

Armagh Planetarium. *Open 11.30am-5pm Mon-Fri, 1.30pm-5pm Sat-Sun, all year. Tel. (01861) 522928.* Regular star shows. New attractions include the **AstroPark**, featuring a model solar system and a 17th c.

telescope; the **Eartharium**, which shows the earth on three levels; and the interactive laser **Encyclopaedia Galactic**. Observatory grounds have sundial and audio-visual presentation of the work of the observatory.

New **Navan** exhibition at the **Armagh Centre**, *open 10am-7pm Mon-Sat, 11am-7pm Sun, Apr-Aug, 10am-5pm Mon-Sat, 11am-5pm Sun, Sept-Mar. Tel. (01861) 525550.* The exhibition details, in impressive style, the history and archaeology of one of Europe's most important Celtic sites. It was the seat of the ancient Kings of Ulster and the setting for the legends of Cuchulainn. Stunning visual and interactive displays.

Craigavon
22 km (35 miles) SW of Belfast.
'60s architect's dream 'new town' yet to come true. Named after Northern Ireland's first Prime Minister. **Tannaghmore Gardens and Farm**, *open daily, tel. (01762) 343244.* Victorian and rose gardens. Rare farm breeds, including Kerry cattle, Jacob and Soay sheep, saddleback pigs.

Fews Forest
15 km (9 miles) S of Armagh.
Great walking through forests and along moorland tracks. Fine views over counties Armagh and Down from some picnic sites.

Gosford Forest Park
3 km (2 miles) NE of Markethill. Open daily.
Walled garden, mock Norman castle, round tower built by German prisoners-of-war during World War II. Traditional poultry breeds, pigeons.

Keady
13 km (8 miles) S of Armagh.
Heritage Centre due to be completed in a restored mill in the town centre. It will include a history of local linen and other textile making.

Loughgall
8 km (5 miles) NW of Armagh.
The centre of the county's apple growing district. **Orange Order Museum** recalls founding of the order here in 1795.

Lough Neagh Discovery Centre
Oxford Island, S shores of Lough Neagh, 5 km (3 miles) N of Lurgan. Open 10am-7pm Mon-Fri, 10am-8pm Sat, 12 noon-8pm Sun. Tel. (01762) 322205.
History of the lough, "working water" computer, wildlife exhibition. Bird-watching, walks, boat trips and café.

Mullaghbawn Folk Museum
Between Crossmaglen and Camlough, S Armagh. Open 11am-7pm Mon-Sat, 2pm-7pm Sun, May-Sept, 2pm-7pm Sun, Oct-Apr. Tel. (01693) 888278/838762.
Thatched roadside museum in the style of a traditional farmhouse. Exhibitions, craft demonstrations and coffee shop.

Portadown
43 km (27 miles) SW Belfast. TIO Tel. (01762) 332499
Market town on the River Bann, and a major coarse fishing centre. Indoor, heated swimming pool. Learner and competitive pools. **Portadown Golf Club**, 18 holes, *tel. (01762) 335356.* **Moneypenny's Lock**, *3 km (2 miles) S of Portadown, open 2pm-5pm Sat-Sun, Easter-Sept. Tel. (01762) 322205.* Restored lock-keeper's house and stables on the Newry canal. Exhibitions on the old lightermen, canal and lock, wildlife.

Slieve Gullion Forest Park
8 km (5 miles) SW of Newry. Open 10am-dusk daily, Easter-Aug. Tel. (016937) 38284.
Scenic 13 km (8 miles) drive around this well-wooded park. Mountain top trail gives excellent views to the Mountains of Mourne. Visitor centre has exhibitions and a walled garden.

Fermanagh Lakelands

Belleek Pottery
38 km (24 miles) NW of Enniskillen Open 9am-6pm Mon-Fri, 10am-6pm Sat, 2pm-6pm Sun, Mar-June, Sep 9am-8pm Mon-Fri, 10am-6pm Sc 11am-8pm Sun, July-Aug, 9am-5.30pm Mon-Fri, 10am-5.30pm Sat, 2pm-6pm Sun, Oct, 9am-5.30pm Mon-Fri, O Feb. Tel. (01365) 658501.
Visitors can see how this lustro Parian ware is made. Productic started here in 1857. Audio-visu presentation is followed by facto tour. Visitor centre has products f sale and a restaurant.

Boa Island
N side of Lower Lough Erne, 33 km (miles) NW of Enniskillen.
Joined to the mainland by a bridge. C the western side of the island, near t ancient cemetery, you can see two ve strange old stone figures called "Jan statues" because they have a face e each side. Boats to **Lusty Beg Islan** a noted holiday spot, from the jetty c the eastern side.

Castle Archdale Forest Park
5 km (3 miles) S of Kesh. Open 11am 7pm daily, June-Sept. Tel. (01365 21333/21588.
Enchanting country park with ruins **Castle Archdale**, pony trekking a nature trails. Three offshore islan form a nature reserve. Natural histo old farm machinery exhibits. Sho café.

Castle Coole
3 km (2 miles) SE of Enniskillen. Ope

Near Carrickreagh, Co. Fermanagh

pm-6pm Sat-Sun and bank holidays, Apr-May, Sept, 1pm-6pm daily, except Thurs, June-Aug. Tel. (01365) 322690. This great Palladian house, begun in 1790 and completed in 1798, is the stateliest of all the National Trust houses in Northern Ireland. Fine interior fittings and furnishings, include the State bedroom. Stables and coach house. Mature oak woodland, parkland running down to Lough Coole, with its flock of greylag geese. Shop and tearooms.

Crom Estate
5 km (3 miles) W of Newtownbutler. Open 10am-6pm Mon-Sat, 12 noon-6pm Sun, Apr-Sept. Tel. (01365) 738118.
Vast wood, farmland, loughs with rare plants and wildlife. Ruins of early 17th c. Crom Castle. Visitor centre. Nature trails, walks.

Derrin Lough
3 km (2 miles) NW of Tempo.
Shore walks, lake views. Nearby Topped Mountain has path to the summit and its Bronze Age cairn.

Devenish Island
5 km (3 miles) NW of Enniskillen.
Best-known of the 97 islands in Lower Lough Erne. The well-preserved round tower can be climbed by means of internal ladders. Early Christian religious ruins. Daily boats from Trory Point, Lower Lough Erne, Easter-Sept.

Enniskillen
138 km (86 miles) SW of Belfast. Pop 10,500. TIO Wellington Road. Tel. (01365) 323110, all year.
Enniskillen, the county town of Fermanagh in the heart of Ulster's lakelands, is well set on an island between the two channels of the river linking Upper and Lower Lough Erne.
Enniskillen County Museum is devoted to the history and archaeology of Co Fermanagh, with models and dioramas. The story of the Maguire family, who had their headquarters here, is told in audio-visual form. The Regimental Museum, open 10am-5pm Tues-Fri, 2pm-5pm Sat, 2pm-5pm Sun, May-Sept, 10am-5pm, Tues-Fri, 2pm-5pm, Mon, Oct-Apr. Tel. (01365) 325000, details the history of the Royal

Marble Arch Caves, Co. Fermanagh

Inniskilling Fusiliers.
Ardhowen Theatre and Arts Centre, Dublin Road, tel. (01365) 325400. Theatre and other performance events plus exhibitions. St MacCartan's Cathedral (CI), Church Street, dates largely from the early 19th c. but has parts of the original 17th c. building. The old colours of Enniskillen regiments are laid up here. Convent Chapel (C) in Belmore Street has remarkable nave windows. The Methodist Church in Darling Street has some interesting features – the bulges in the balcony were designed to take crinolines! Forthill Park, on the east side of town, has good walks and views. Climb the 108 steps to the top of the Cole Monument for an excellent panorama of the town and surrounding lakelands. Summer cruises on Lough Erne, daily, tel. TIO.

Florence Court
13 km (8 miles) SW of Enniskillen. Open 1pm-6pm Sat-Sun and bank holidays, Apr-May, Sept, 1pm-6pm Wed-Mon, June-Aug. Tel. (01365) 348249.
Three-storey 18th c. mansion linked to flanking pavilions by open arched corridors. The house has Rococo plasterwork and a collection of Irish furniture. The grounds have a summer house, ice house, pleasure gardens and a water-powered sawmill. Many specimen trees in demesne including a yew tree that is said to have been the stock from which all Irish yews have been cultivated. Tea room and shop.

Inishmacsaint
W shore of Lower Lough Erne, 5 km (4 miles) W of Killadeas.
A place of great solitude, with High Cross and the remains of a 6th c. monastery. Boat from Killadeas.

Lisnaskea
19 km (12 miles) SE of Enniskillen.
One of Fermanagh's few substantial towns. Castle Balfour is firmly Scottish in character. The town library has a small, but interesting, folklife display.

Lough Navar Forest Park
19 km (12 miles) NW of Enniskillen. Open 10am-dusk, all year.
Vast expanse of woodland best approached from Derrygonnelly. Scenic drive concludes at summit viewpoint from which you get excellent

views over Lower Lough Erne, most of south Donegal and north Sligo.

Marble Arch Caves
5 km (3 miles) W of Florence Court. Open daily, mid-Mar – Sept, weather permitting. Tours 11am-4.30pm. Tel. (01365) 348855.
Extensive caves open to the experts and general visitors alike. For the latter, the tour begins with an underground boat trip past the stalactites.

Monea Castle
10 km (7 miles) NW of Enniskillen.
Well-preserved, 17th c. castle, handsomely set at the end of a tree-lined lane. Like Castle Balfour in Lisnaskea, it is another plantation castle showing strong Scottish influences.

Roslea
51 km (32 miles) SE of Enniskillen.
The Heritage Centre, open 9am-5pm Mon-Fri, 4pm-6pm Sat-Sun, Apr-Sept. Tel. (013657) 51750. Located in a late 19th c. schoolhouse, the centre has traditional farm implements, old crochet work. Genealogy service. Shop and tearoom.

White Island
16 km (10 miles) NW of Enniskillen.
This island set in Castle Archdale Bay, has eight inscrutable statues, not unlike those on Easter Island, and equally mysterious in their origins. Summer ferry service from Castle Archdale Marina.

Mid-Ulster

Ardboe Cross
W shores of Lough Neagh 16 km (10 miles) E of Cookstown.

Well preserved 10th c. **High Cross** in remote setting. Ruins of old churches and a 6th c. abbey are nearby.

The Argory
6 km (4 miles) NE of Moy. Open 2pm-6pm Sat-Sun and bank holidays, Apr-June, Sept, 2pm-6pm daily, except Tues, July-Aug. Tel. (01868) 784753.
Fine early 19th c. house set in wooded countryside, overlooking the River Blackwater. The house has been little changed since early this century. Stable yard, sundial garden, extensive walks. Shop and tea room.

Beaghmore Stone Circles
22 km (14 miles) NW of Cookstown.
Six stone circles and some cairns, dating back 4,000 years. Their origins and purpose are unclear.

Benburb
14 km (9 miles) S of Dungannon.
Benburb Valley Heritage Centre, open 10am-5pm Tues-Sat, 2pm-5pm Sun, Easter-Sept, tel. (01861) 549752, set in a former linen mill with much of the machinery intact, the centre tells the story of linen making here. **O'Neill Historical Centre**, *Servite Priory, tel. (01861) 548187.* **Benburb Valley Park**, with walks beside the River Blackwater, overlooked by clifftop ruins of **Benburb Castle**.

Clogher
12 km (8 miles) SW of Ballygawley.
Clogher Cathedral (CI) was built on a hilltop in 18th c. and dominates the village. It claims to be the oldest bishopric in Ireland. The nearby village of Augher is set on a fine-looking stretch of the River Blackwater.

Coalisland
6 km (4 miles) NE of Dungannon.
An early centre of the industrial revolution in the North of Ireland. Coal has been mined here, on and off, for the past 200 years. The **Coalisland Corn Mill**, *open 10am-8pm Mon-Fri, 10am-6pm Sat, 12 noon-6pm Sun, Apr-Oct, 10am-6pm Mon-Fri, Nov-Mar. Tel. (018687) 48532.* The mill details the town's industrial history with audio-visual techniques, old photographs and personal recollections. The nearby **Weaving Factory Museum** concentrates on this aspect of local industrial history.

Cookstown
74 km (46 miles) W of Belfast. TIO, 48 Molesworth Street, tel. (016487) 66727 June-Sept.
A restored station is the setting for both the TIO and the **Museum** which details local heritage. *Open 9am-5pm Mon-Fri, Easter-Sept, 9am-12pm Sat, July-Aug. Tel. (016487) 66727.* The town has one of the longest and widest main streets in Ireland and some agreeably old-fashioned pubs. **Killymoon Castle**, in the grounds of the golf club, and **Derryloran Parish Church (CI)**, in the town, were both designed by John Nash, architect of Brighton Pavilion. The spire of the Catholic church in the town centre, is a landmark for miles around.

Davagh Forest Park
13 km (8 miles) NW of Cookstown.
You can see most of Northern Ireland from the summit of **Beleevnamore Mountain** given a clear day.

Dungannon
69 km (43 miles) W of Belfast.
Tyrone Crystal began here in 1971, exactly 200 years after a previous crystal glass making factory had started production in the vicinity. Today, visitors can take a tour of the modern factory to see all stages of production. *Guided tours, Mon-Fri, May-Sept, tel. (018687) 25335.* **Peatlands Park**, *open 2pm-6pm Sat-Sun and bank holidays, Easter-Sept. Tel. (01762) 851102.* Visitor centre details peatland ecology. Video, outdoor exhibits. Rail trip on narrow gauge railway formerly used in peat workings.
 Donaghmore Heritage Centre, *6 km (4 miles) NW of Dungannon. Open 9am-5pm Mon-Thurs (4.30pm Fri), 11am-4pm Sat, May-Aug, all year. Tel. (01868) 767039.* This converted late 19th c. national school has historical material on local industries. See also the high cross nearby. **Parkanaur Forest Park**, *5 km (3 miles) W of Dungannon. Open daily, all year.* Woodland trails and deer park. Farm buildings restored to original character.

Fivemiletown
32 km (20 miles) E of Enniskillen.
Two transport museum collections in the area. The **Blessingbourne Museum**, *open daily, Easter-Sept, tel. (013656) 21221.* Has some coaches and carriages. Fivemiletown Library ha a small display of local railwa memorabilia.

Gortin Glen Forest Park
11 km (7 miles) N of Omagh. Oper 9am-dusk daily, all year. Tel. (016626 48217.
The 8 km (5 miles) forest drive ha viewpoints, sika deer, wildfowl, a visitor centre and a café.

Moneymore
6 km (4 miles) NW of Cookstown.
Handsome plantation town with wide main street, reconstructed by the Draper's company in 1817. A numbe of nearby plantation towns are also o interest: Draperstown (also founded by the Drapers) and Magherafelt, granted to the Salters' Company by James I.

Omagh
54 km (34 miles) S of Derry. TIO, Market Street, tel. (01662) 247831 247832, all year.
Quiet market town where the rivers Camowen and Drumragh meet Hometown of noted author, Ben Kiely The best view is from the top of the steep, wide main street which leads to the courthouse. Riverside walks along the banks of the River Camowen.

Sion Mills
5 km (3 miles) S of Strabane.
Originally a model linen village, Sion Mills boasts an exceptionally wide main street, and still exudes much charm.

The Sperrins
S of Derry.
These wild remote mountains offe wonderful views from their peaks and a fascinating array of wildlife. They also offer good walking, and the stunning Glenelly and Owenkillew river valleys attract both walkers and cyclists. In addition gold has recently been rediscovered in the mountains.
 Sperrin Heritage Centre, *9 miles east of Plumbridge. Open 11am-6pm Mon-Fri, 11.30am-6pm Sat, 2pm-7pm Sun, Easter-Sept, tel. (01662) 648142* Features natural history and gold-mining exhibits plus other Sperrin treasures. Try your hand at panning for gold.

Springhill House, near Moneymore, Co. Derry

pringhill

km (5 miles) NE of Cookstown. Open
pm-6pm Sat-Sun and bank holidays,
pr-June, Sept, 2pm-6pm daily, except
hurs, July-Aug. Tel. (016487) 48210.
7th c. whitewashed house built for a
ettler's family, complete with family
urniture, paintings, ornaments, curios,
itchen with old utensils. There is a
arge collection of costumes in the
utbuildings, together with walled
ardens, woodland walks, a shop and
earoom. Also one of Ulster's best
uthenticated ghosts!

trabane

0 km (14 miles) SW of Derry. TIO
bercorn Square, tel. (01504) 883735,
ll year.

iray's Printing Press at 49 Main
treet, open 2pm-5.30pm daily, except
hurs, Sun, Apr-Sept. Tel. (01504)
84094. See the display of 18th and
9th c. printing equipment. John
Junlap, who printed the first copies
f the American Declaration of Inde-
endence in 1776, began his appren-
iceship here. An audio-visual display
ells the story of printing. Also see the
ncestral home of Woodrow Wilson, US
resident 1913-1921, open daily, Apr-
ept, tel. (01662) 243292.

Ilster-American Folk Park

km (3 miles) N of Omagh. Open
1am-6.30pm Mon-Sat, 11.30am-7pm
un, Easter-Sept, 10.30am-5pm Mon-
ri, Oct-Easter. Tel. (01662) 243292.
his elaborate display tells the story of
migrant life on both sides of the
tlantic in the 18th and 19th c. Among
he many highlights are the emigration
nuseum, the ship and dockside gallery,
n American street, Pennsylvania log
arn and farmhouse and a Victorian
hemist's shop. Craft shop and café.

Jlster History Park

1 km (7 miles) N of Omagh. Open
0.30am-6.30pm Mon-Sat, 11.30am-
7pm Sun and bank holidays, Apr-Sept,
0.30am-5pm Mon-Fri, Oct-Mar. Tel.
01662) 648188.
Traces the story of settlement in Ireland
rom the Stone Age to the end of 17th
. Audio-visual presentations and
xhibition gallery in the new visitor
entre. Shop and café.

Derry city at dusk

Wellbrook Beetling Mill

6 km (4 miles) W of Cookstown. Open
2pm-6pm Sat-Sun and bank holidays,
Apr-June, Sept, 2pm-6pm daily, except
Tues, July-Aug. Tel. (01648) 751735.
This water-powered hammer mill was
used for the final stage in linen making;
the machinery is still in working order.
Walks by mill race and Ballinderry
River.

Derry City and County

Castlerock

13 km (8 miles) NW of Coleraine.
Bracing seaside village just W of Bann
estuary. Good beach. Open air swimming pool. **Castlerock Golf Club**, 18
holes. **Downhill Castle**, 13 km (8
miles) NW of Coleraine. Landscaped
estate laid out in late 18th c. by Frederick Hervey, Earl of Bristol and Angli-
can Bishop of Derry. The ruins of the
bishop's palatial house can still be
seen. Also gardens, fish ponds, woodland, glen and cliff top walks.
Mussenden Temple is perched on the
clifftop, open 12 noon-6pm Sat-Sun
and bank holidays, Apr-June, Sept, tel.
(01265) 848728. The grounds are open
at all times.

Coleraine

50 km (31 miles) NE of Derry. TIO
Railway Road, tel. (01265) 44723.
Easter-Sept.
Dating back to the 5th c., Coleraine is
a plantation town and boasts some fine
Georgian houses and streets. It is now
the location of the main campus of the
University of Ulster.

The **Riverside Gallery**, tel. (01265)
44141, has regular exhibitions, while

the **Riverside Theatre**, tel. (01265)
51388, stages regular productions. The
Wilson Daffodil Gardens, also on
campus, have rare Irish-bred daffodils
and narcissi. Best seen in April when
the flowers are in full bloom.

Derry

117 km (73 miles) W of Belfast. Pop
95,000. TIO, 8 Bishop Street, tel.
(01504)267284.
Although its official title is
Londonderry, this city set on both
banks of the River Foyle is often called
by the simpler, older title of Derry.
Derry hit the world headlines with the
famous civil rights march of October
1968. Then serious disturbances,
starting in 1969, put the Bogside on
the global agenda. A walk from the
Guildhall, through William Street, to
Free Derry Corner, with its
internationally known legend, "You are
now entering Free Derry", will give a
vivid illustration of the historical
turmoil of this intensely Irish city.

In recent years, Derry's prosperity
has improved and many new visitor
amenities have been opened. The
Walls of Derry, largely intact, but just
1. 6 km (1 mile) in circumference, and
complete with the **Roaring Meg**
cannon, are the best place to start a
city tour.

St Columb's Cathedral (CI), built
in 1628 and consecrated in 1634, has
many relics of the 1689 siege, which
was the political pivot of the city's
history and development, until the
events of 1968 onwards. The mortar
shell which contained the surrender
terms of the siege is preserved in the
cathedral porch, while the **Chapter
House** has other interesting relics of
the siege. **Long Tower Church (C)** to
the SW of St Columb's Cathedral, is the
oldest Catholic church in the city,
dating from the 1780s, and it has an
interesting Rococo interior. **St
Eugene's Cathedral (C)** is much more
recent, built in the Gothic style in the
late 19th c. and finally completed in
1903 with the addition of the cross on
top of the spire.

At the very centre of Derry is the
Guildhall. It was built in late Gothic
style in 1890 and is the venue for arts
events. Just round the corner from the
Guildhall is the **Harbour Museum** in
Harbour Square, open 10am-5pm
Mon-Sat, all year, tel. (01504) 365151,

which has a replica of the craft St Columba used to sail to Iona and many details of Derry's vital role as a port during World War II. The **Tower Museum** tells Derry's story from prehistory to the present, including the 1689 siege, in an exciting presentation. See also the craft village. The **O'Doherty Tower**, *above the museum, open 10am-5pm Tues-Sat, all year, tel. (01504) 372411*, has artefacts from the Spanish Armada ships wrecked off the Irish coast in 1588. **Ulster Science Centre**, *Foyle Street, tel. (01504) 370239*, has interactive exhibitions.

Foyle Valley Railway Centre, *beside Craigavon Bridge, open 10am-5pm Tues-Sat, all year. Tel. (01504) 265234*. Has much material on the narrow gauge systems of Co Donegal and Co Londonderry & Lough Swilly railways, which have long since closed down. Also operational models, audio-visual presentations and trips on diesel railcars on track running through **Foyle Riverside Park**, *(weekends only from May to Sept)*.

Earhart Centre, *Ballyarnet on the west bank of the Foyle, open 9am-4.30pm Mon-Thur, 9am-1pm Fri, all year, 9am-6pm, Sat, Sun, Jun-Sept, tel. (01504) 354040*. This is a cottage exhibition devoted to Amelia Earhart, the first woman to fly the Atlantic solo, who landed here in 1932. Adjoining **wildlife sanctuary**, *open 9am-dusk Mon-Fri, 10am-6pm Sat-Sun, tel. (01504) 353202*. **Hilltop Open Farm**, *Ballyarnet, open 1pm-6pm daily, Mar-Aug, 1pm-6pm Sun, Sept-Feb, tel. (01504) 354556*. Has exotic game birds, poultry, rare breeds of pigs, sheep and Highland cattle.

Gordon Gallery, *36 Ferryquay Street, open 11am-5.30pm Tues-Fri, 11am-1pm Sat, all year, tel. (01504) 266261*, has regular exhibitions by well-known Irish artists. **Orchard Gallery**, *Orchard Street, open 10am-6pm Tues-Sat, all year, tel. (01504) 269675*, has regular exhibitions and lectures. **Magee College**, *Northland Road*, has occasional theatre, film and other cultural events as does the **Foyle Arts Centre**, *Lawrence Hill, tel. (01504) 363166*. The **Heritage Library**, *14 Bishop Street, tel. (01504) 269792*, a reference library with reading room and genealogical research centre, also puts on exhibitions.

Draperstown
9 km (6 miles) SW of Maghera.
Named after the London Company of Drapers, which was part of the plantation of Derry city and county, this east Co Derry town is building a new heritage centre which will detail the often barbarous events of that plantation. Should be open in 1995.

Dungiven
32 km (20 miles) SE of Derry.
See the ruins of the 12th c. Augustinian priory, on the banks of River Roe. The ruins of the early Christian **Banagher Church**, *5 km (3 miles) south of the town*, while a similar distance to the north are the ruins of Bovevagh Church.

Eglinton
8 km (5 miles) NE of Derry.
This tree-lined village, near Derry airport, has a very English air. Enjoyable walks in the Muff Glen, just south of the village.

Garvagh
17 km (11 miles) S of Coleraine.
The **Folk Museum**, *open 2pm-5pm Thurs, Sat, June-Aug, tel. (01265) 57924*, has many artefacts on local history.

Hezlett House
8 km (5 miles) W of Coleraine. Open 1pm-5pm Sat-Sun and bank holidays, Apr-June, Sept, daily, July-Aug, except Tues. Tel. (01265) 848567.
Not so much a house as a 17th c. thatched cottage furnished in Victorian style. Also a small museum of farm implements.

Knockcloghrim Windmill
11 km (7 miles) N of Magherafelt. Open 9am-7pm Mon-Sat, Easter-Sept, 9am-5pm Mon-Sat, Oct-Mar. Tel. (01648) 44745.
The heritage centre is located inside this restored windmill, which was in working order until the Great Wind of 1895 blew off its sails! Local history, viewing gallery, working scale model.

Limavady
27 km (17 miles) E of Derry. TIO council offices, Benevenagh Drive, tel. (015047) 22226 all year.
Market town with plenty of Georgian style. The six-arched Roe Bridge dates back to 1700. In 1851, Jane Ross, a loc resident, noted down a tune played b a travelling fiddler which becam known later as the "Londonderry Air and later again as "Danny Boy".

Magilligan Strand
From near Eglinton to Magilliga Point.
This vast sandy strand, arguably th most impressive beach in Ireland stretches for some 24 km (15 mile along the east shores of Lough Foyle Tremendous views of the Inishowe Peninsula, across the estuary.

Mountsandel Fort
1.5 km (1 mile) SE of Coleraine.
A large oval mound, dominating th River Bann. See the site of the olde house in Ireland, lived in 9,000 year ago close by. Riverside walks.

Ness Country Park
11 km (7 miles) SE of Derry.
Broadleaved woodland walks. Natur trail. Path from car park leads to th highest waterfall in Northern Ireland about 12 m (39 ft).

Portstewart
6 km (4 miles) SW of Portrush. TI Town Hall, tel. (0126583) 2286.
The main streets of this attractiv Victorian-style town form an Atlanti promenade, winding round rocky bay with shore paths at each end Magnificent 3 km (2 mile) long stran between town and River Bann, backe by dunes.

Roe Valley Country Park
1.5 km (1 mile) S of Limavady. Ope 11am-4pm Mon-Fri, 10.30am-4.30pr Sat-Sun, Sept-June, 9am-9pm daily July-Aug. Tel. (015047) 22074.
The first domestic hydro-electric powe station in Northern Ireland, built i 1896 has been preserved, along wit the water wheels used for linen pro duction. Museum, exhibitions, rive side walks, café. Park always accessible

...king out towards Rathlin island, Co. Antrim

...ntrim Coast & ...lens

...*km (17 miles) NW of Belfast. TIO ...gue's Entry, Church Street, tel. ...849) 428331, Easter-Sept.*
...gue's Entry was the childhood ...me of Alexander Irvine, who became ...issionary in New York's Bowery and ...ote **My Lady of the Chimney ...rner** about the lives of Irish country ...k. The **Irvine House** is *open 10am-...n Mon-Fri, 10am-2pm Sat, all year, ...(01849) 428331/463113, extn 230.* ...e round tower in **Steeples Park** is ...out 1,000 years old and is well-...eserved and freely accessible. ...assereene Demesne, *tel. (01894) ...000*, is a restored 17th c. garden ...hioned in the Anglo-Dutch style, ...th wooded grove, ponds and walks. ...ane's Castle Railway, *open 12 ...on-6.30pm Sun and bank holidays, ...r-May, Wed, Sat-Sun, June, Sept,*

Tues-Thurs, Sat-Sun and bank holidays July-Aug. Tel. (01894) 63380. This narrow gauge steam railway runs along the lough shore for 2.5 km (1.5 miles). Also nature reserve, wildfowl refuge, deer park, small fairground and restaurant.

Ballintoy Harbour
8 km (5 miles) NE of Ballycastle.
North Antrim cliff path runs for 18 km (11 miles) from here to Runkerry taking in the **Giant's Causeway, Dunseverick Castle, White Park Bay**. The village has a most attractive harbour: white piers and a white beach make fine a contrast with the black cliffs. Parish church with beautiful resurrection window. Youth Hostel. Cliff-top walks. Boats to the cave below **Kinbane Castle** ruins.

Ballycastle
108 km (67 miles) NW of Belfast. Pop 3,300. TIO Sheskburn House, 7 Mary Street, tel. (012657) 62024, all year.
A most attractive seaside resort on the north Antrim coast, completely unspoiled. Ballycastle proper is 3 km (2 miles) inland and is connected to the harbour area by a broad tree-lined avenue. An ideal base for exploring the many delights of the Antrim coast and host to the lively two day **Oul' Lammas Fair**, which dates back to 1606, held on the last Monday and Tuesday in August. Bargains and banter are plentiful, as are the local delicacies of dulse (edible seaweed) and yellowman (a sticky honeycomb).

Ballycastle is the departure point for boats to **Rathlin Island**, which beckons invitingly across the sound. **Ballycastle Museum** *open 2pm-6pm July – mid-Sept, tel. (012657) 62024,* has folk and social history of the Glens, set in 18th c. schoolhouse. The **Marconi Memorial** on the seafront, marks the spot from which the inventor of wireless telegraphy made his first successful transmission in 1898, between Ballycastle and Rathlin Island.

Pans Rock, *east end of Ballycastle beach*, is an old salt drying pan and is reached by a footbridge. In the 18th c. extensive coal mining was carried out at Ballycastle and remnants of this mining can be seen along the coast and in the glens. Pony trekking in the glens is popular, try the **Watertop Trekking Centre**, *188 Cushendall Road, Ballycastle, tel. (012657) 62576.* **Bonamargy Friary**, *0.8 km (0.5 mile) E of Ballycastle.* Ruins of Franciscan friary built about 1500 on the banks of the River Margy. **Watertop Open Farm**, *9 km (6 miles) S of Ballycastle. Open 10am-5.30pm daily, July-Aug. Tel. (012657) 62576/63785.* Museum, ornamental game birds, farm tours, sheep shearing demonstrations (July-Aug), pony trekking, boating and fishing.

Ballymena
18 km (11 miles) N of Antrim.
The largest town in this area, Ballymena is a prosperous market town with a strong Scottish influence and a reputation for meanness!

lymoney
km (8 miles) SE of Coleraine.
interesting churches: our **Lady St Patrick (C)**, built of local basalt, stained glass windows and **Trinity sbyterian Church**, built in 1884 by me Rule advocate, Rev. J.B. Armour. useway Safari Park, open 10am-0pm Sat, Sun, Apr, 9 days at Easter, , May, Sept, daily, Jun-Aug. Tel. 2657) 41474. Drive-through closures housing lions and other tic wildlife species. Farmyard area, i zoo, amusement park with minia-e railway. Shops, bar and restaurant. lie Hill Heritage Farm Park, 1.5 (1 mile) W of Ballymoney. Open n-6pm Sun and bank holidays, Apr-, Sept, Sat-Sun, June, 11am-6pm n-Sat, 2pm-6pm July-Aug. Tel. 2656) 66803. Museum, rare breeds, r, ornamental fowl, gardens, lakes, ure trails, horse-trap and donkey es through 18th c. estate.

shmills
m (3 miles) S of Giant's Causeway. d **Bushmills Whiskey Distillery**, n Mon-Fri, all year, tel. (012657) 521. Attractively set by St Columb's l, Bushmills has the world's oldest iskey distilling licence, dating from 09. The Bushmills open-top bus vels the scenic route between shmills and Coleraine, taking in the nt's Causeway. Daily, July-Aug.

rnlough
m (3 miles) NW of Glenarm.
tty Glens of Antrim village, at the ad of Glencloy, constructed by the rquess of Londonderry in the mid-th c.

rrick-a-Rede
m (5 miles) W of Ballycastle.
is swinging rope-bridge spans the asm between the mainland and rrick-a-Rede Island. Not for the faint-arted, it is only in position in the mon fishing season (May-Sept).

rrickfergus
km (11 miles) NE of Belfast. TIO ight Ride, Antrim Street, tel. 19603) 66455, all year.
rrickfergus Castle, open 10am-n Mon-Sat, 2pm-6pm Sun, Apr-Sept, am-4pm Mon-Sat, 2pm-4pm Sun,

e Carrick-a-Rede rope bridge, Co. Antrim

Oct-Mar. Tel. (01960) 351273. Built in 1180 by John de Courcy, the castle had a garrison until 1928. Exhibition on castle's history, including audio-visual presentation, shop and café. Last admission 30 mins before closing. **St Nicholas Church (CI)**, off Market Place, dates from 12th c. and has interesting stained-glass windows. There is a small section of old town walls nearby. Louis MacNeice plaque in North Road, marks where the distin-guished poet lived from when he was two years of age until he went up to Cambridge University. His father was rector of St Nicholas.
Carrickfergus Gasworks, tel. (01960) 366455 was one of the last coal-fired gas-making operations in Ireland when it closed down in 1964. Exhibition of machinery and also domestic equipment worked by gas. Audio-visual presentation.
Knight Ride and Heritage Plaza. Open 10am-8pm Mon-Fri, 10am-6pm Sat, 12 noon-6pm Sun, Apr-Sept, 10am-4.30pm daily, Oct-Mar. Last admission 30 mins before closing. Tel. (01960) 366455. This is a monorail ride through the history of Carrickfergus from 531. Shops and café. The **Andrew Jackson Centre**, Boneybefore, open 10am-6pm Mon-Fri, 2pm-6pm Sat-Sun, all year. Tel. (01960) 364972. The centre commemorates the 7th US President and has exhibition devoted to the 1st Battalion, US Rangers which was raised in Carrickfergus in 1942. Rowing boats can be hired in harbour and there are walks along the wide promenade and Marine Gardens.

Cushendall
27 km (17 miles) SE of Ballycastle.
The "capital" of the Glens of Antrim, this village is one of the most distinctively Irish parts of Northern Ireland. The village was largely created by a 19th c. landowner Francis Turnly. Boats for hire from **Red Bay Boats**, which also has boat building yard. Tel. (012667) 71331.

Cushendun
8 km (5 miles) N of Cushendall.
The most northerly of the Glens of Antrim. Some cottages designed by Clough Williams Ellis, famed for the village of Portmerion in north Wales. He also designed nearby 'Glenmona' the home of Lord Cushendun. Many

delightful cliff walks in vicinity of Cushendun. **Loughareema Vanishing Lake**, beside the road from Ballycastle to Cushendun. This lake can dry up very quickly, as if someone had pulled the plug! **Ossian's Grave**, 5 km (3 miles) S of Cushendun. This megalithic tomb on the slopes of Tievebulliagh mountain is the burial place of the warrior-bard son of Finn McCool. Nearby, a modern bard is commem-orated; the cairn in memory of John Hewitt, a renowned 20th c. Ulster poet.

Dunluce Castle
5 km (3 miles) E of Portrush. Open 10am-7pm Mon-Sat, 2pm-7pm Sun, Apr-Sept, 10am-4pm Tues-Sat, 2pm-4pm Sun, Oct-Mar.
Dramatic ruins set on a craggy cliff. The castle dates mostly from 16th and 17th c. In 1639, part fell into the sea, taking with it several unfortunate servants who were in the kitchens at the time. The ruins are among the largest and most spectacularly set of any castle ruins in Ireland. Visitor centre, audio-visual presentation.

Dunseverick Castle
E end of Giant's Causeway.
Some slight ruins of one of Ireland's oldest castles, built around 500 A.D., perched on a high crag.

Fair Head
6 km (4 miles) NE of Ballycastle.
One of the most rugged and desolate spots on the north coast, with wonderful views of Rathlin island and south-west Scotland in clear weather.

Giant's Causeway
3 km (2 miles) N of Bushmills. TIO tel. (012657) 31855 all year. Giant's Causeway accessible to visitors at all times. Visitor Centre open daily, 10am-7pm daily, summer, 10am-4pm winter. The **Giant's Causeway**, with more than 40,000 hexagonal basalt columns, is a world heritage sight, and offers an extraordinary panorama. The **Visitor Centre** depicts the flora, fauna and geology of the area, together with a replica of the hydroelectric tram that ran between the Causeway and Portrush until 1951. Shop and tea room.
Causeway School Museum, next to Giant's Causeway Visitor Centre, open 11am-4.30pm daily, July-Aug, tel.

(012657) 31777. Originally a national school, designed by Clough Williams Ellis, the museum recreates the atmosphere of a 1920s classroom.

Glenariff Forest Park

Between Waterfoot and Ballymena. Open daily, all year. Tel. (012667) 58232.
Spectacular glen walk with three waterfalls. Scenic path runs round the sheer sides of the gorge. Walks and trails to mountain viewpoints. Visitor centre, shop, restaurant.

Glenarm

16 km (10 miles) N of Larne.
Delightful village in southern glens with park offering walks up the glen beside Glenarm river.

Gracehill

3 km (2 miles) W of Ballymena.
Model settlement founded by Moravians in the 18th c. The original square survives as do the separate buildings for men and women. German Christmas customs are still observed in the village church.

Islandmagee

Peninsula near Larne, stretching for 11 km (7 miles) and 3 km (2 miles) at its widest point.
Fine cliffs on the eastern side and bathing at **Brown's Bay** and **Ferris Bay**. **Ford Farm Park and Museum**, *open 2pm-6pm daily, all year, tel. (01960) 353264.* This small country museum features butter-making and sheep-shearing demonstrations.

Larne

34 km (21 miles) NE of Belfast. TIO Narrow Gauge Road, tel. (01574)260088, all year.
Larne & District Historical Centre, *Old Carnegie Library, 2 Victoria Road, open 2pm-5pm Tues-Sat, all year, tel. (01574) 279482.* Exhibits include turn-of-the-century country kitchen, milk house, blacksmith's forge, family history material. **Carnfunnock Country Park**, *5.5 km (3.5 miles) N of Larne. Open 10am-dusk, daily, Easter-Oct. Tel. (01574) 270541/250088.* Maze shaped like map of Northern Ireland, walled garden, adventure playground, golf, putting green and visitor centre. The **Antrim Coast Road**, which runs from Larne to Cushendun and on to Ballycastle, offers some of the most impressive coastal scenery in Ireland. The mountains roads leading off it, especially in the Cushendall area, offer good views.

Murlough Bay

5 km (3 miles) E of Fair Head.
Unspoiled bay in National Trust care. See monument to Sir Roger Casement on the way down to the shore.

Portballintrae

3 km (2 miles) SW of Giant's Causeway.
Pleasant, secluded seaside village with harbour and beach.

Port Braddan

15 km (9 miles) W of Ballycastle.
This tiny hamlet has Ireland's smallest church, a mere 3 x 2 m (11 x 6 ft).

Portrush

19 km (12 miles) N of Coleraine. TIO Dunluce Centre, Sandhill Drive, tel. (01265) 823333.
Dunluce Centre is a virtual reality entertainment centre that includes the high tech **Turbo Theatre**, the **Earthquest** interactive fun adventure, the **Myths & Legends** theatre, a viewing tower for superb views over Portrush and surrounding area, outdoor play-park for children. Shop and restaurant. *Tel. (01265) 824444.* **Waterworld** is a water-based leisure centre, *tel. (01265) 822001.* **Portrush Countryside Centre**, *open daily in summer, tel. (01265) 823600.* **Town Hall Theatre**, amusement arcades, seafront. Excellent beaches on east and west strands. Boat trips from harbour to see caves at **White Rock**, and to **The Skerries**, offshore islands home to multitude of sea birds.

Rathlin Island

13 km (8 miles) offshore from Ballycastle.
Northern Ireland's only inhabited island, with a population of about 100, has plenty of natural attractions. Nearly all the coastline is formed by cliffs, but the island itself is flat, making for easy walking. Near the **East Lighthouse** are cement blocks with title 'Lloyds' marked on them – the base of the wireless mast set up for Marconi's first radio transmission in 1898.

Brockley has the remains of a Stone Age settlement, wh **Knockanas**, between Brockley and harbour, has traces of an early Christ settlement. **Kebble National Natu Reserve**, *near the West Lighthouse* home to colonies of kittiwak razorbills and guillemots. The islan an ideal base for deep sea fishing a scuba diving. During summer there boats daily from Ballycastle, weat permitting. The mail boat runs th times a week, all year. Tel. (0126 62024/62225.

Templepatrick

8 km (5 miles) SE of Antrim.
Patterson's Spade Mill, *open 2p 6pm Sat-Sun and bank holidays, A May, Sept, daily (except Tues) Ju Aug, tel. (01238) 510721.* The l surviving water-driven spade mill Ireland which was in operation un 1990. All the original equipment been restored and there a demonstrations of spade making.

Torr Head

E end of Murlough Bay.
Approached by narrow road fr either Cushendun or Murlough B Desolate spot affording excellent vie over the North Channel. Scotland only 19 km (12 miles) away.

Waterfoot

1.5 km (1 mile) S of Cushendall.
Modest village at mouth of Glena river. The main appeal here is **Glena Glen**, known as the "Queen of the N Glens". Steep mountains rise on bo sides of the glen which narrows to deep wooded gorge. A path wi along, and a further path runs from head of the glen to Ballycastle.

Whitehead

8 km (5 miles) N of Carrickfergus.
Attractive seaside town with go walks along promenade. **Whiteh Excursion Station** has a uniq collection of Irish standard gau steam locomotives and coaches at t Headquarters of **Railway Preser tion Society of Ireland**. Regular ste events, *tel. (01960) 353567.*

White Park Bay

3 km (2 miles) W of Ballintoy.
The half-moon bay is one of the fin in the North, but it's not recommend for swimming because of the curren

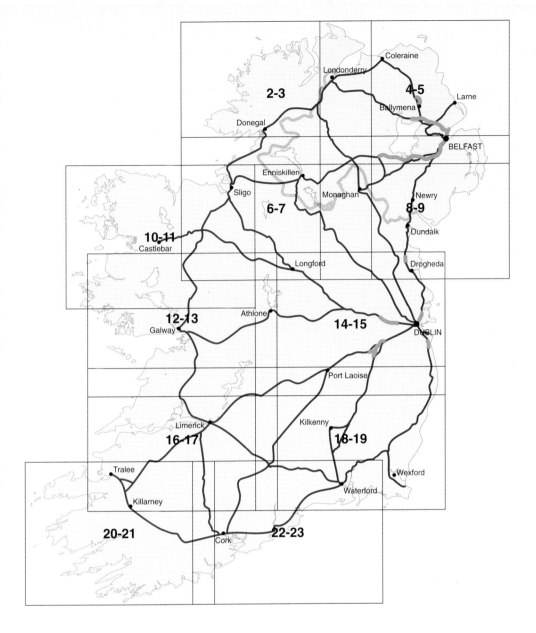

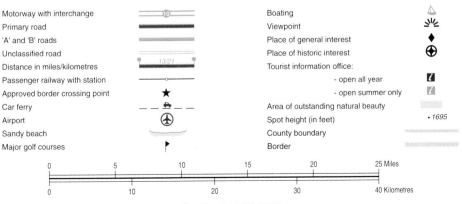

Legend of Map Symbols

Motorway with interchange	Boating	
Primary road	Viewpoint	
'A' and 'B' roads	Place of general interest	
Unclassified road	Place of historic interest	
Distance in miles/kilometres	Tourist information office:	
Passenger railway with station		- open all year
Approved border crossing point		- open summer only
Car ferry	Area of outstanding natural beauty	
Airport	Spot height (in feet)	• 1695
Sandy beach	County boundary	
Major golf courses	Border	

Scale 1:443 520

Digitally produced by E.S.R. Ltd., Byfleet, Surrey, England.

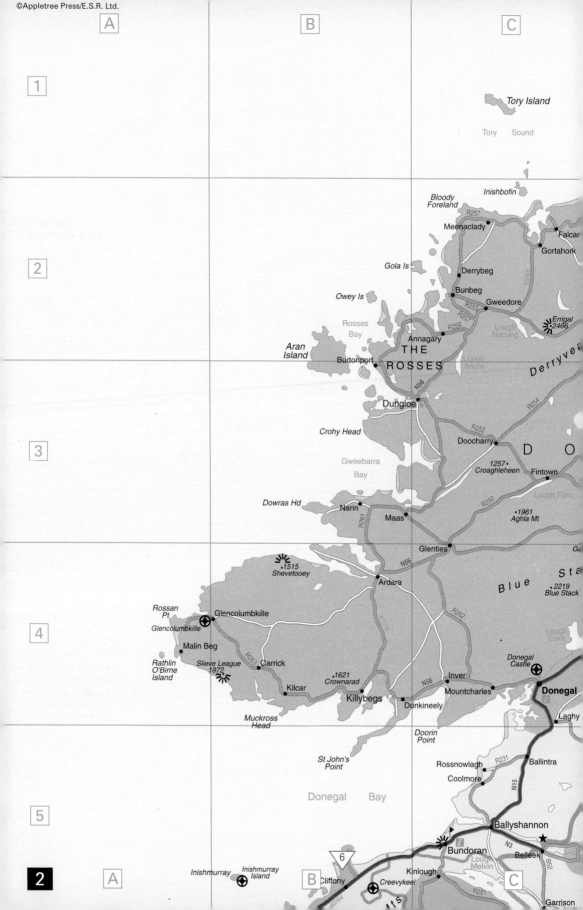

©Appletree Press/E.S.R. Ltd.

A   B   C

1

Tory Island

Tory Sound

Inishbofin

Bloody
Foreland

Meenaclady   Falcar

R257   Gortahork

Gola Is

Derrybeg

Owey Is   Bunbeg
                Gweedore

2   Rosses   R253
            Bay   R257   Errigal
                        R259   2466

Aran   Annagary   Lough
Island   Nacung
        Burtonport   THE
            ROSSES   Lough
                        Anure   Derryvea
            N56
            Dungloe   R254

        Crohy Head   R252   D   O

3   Doocharry
        Gweebarra
        Bay   1257   Fintown
                        Croaghleheen

        Dowras Hd   Lough Finn
            Narin
            Maas   R250
                        1961
                        Aghla Mt
    R261
                    Glenties   Ga

        1515   N56
        Shevetooey
                    Ardara   Blue   Sta

                                    2219
                                    Blue Stack

Rossan   R262
Pt   Glencolumbkille
Glencolumbkille   Lough
        Malin Beg   Eske
4   R263
Rathlin   Donegal
O'Birne   Slieve League   Carrick   Castle
Island   1972   Donegal
        Kilcar   1621
                Crownarad   Laghy
            Killybegs   N56   Inver
        Muckross   Dunkineely   Mountcharles
        Head
                    Doorin
                    Point

        St John's
        Point   Rossnowlagh   R231
                            Coolmore   Ballintra
                                    N15
        Donegal   Bay
5   Ballyshannon

                                    Bundoran   Belleek   B52
                            Kinlough   N3
Inishmurray   Inishmurray   6   Cliffony   Lough
            Island   Creevykeel   Melvin
                                        Garrison
2   A   B   C   R281

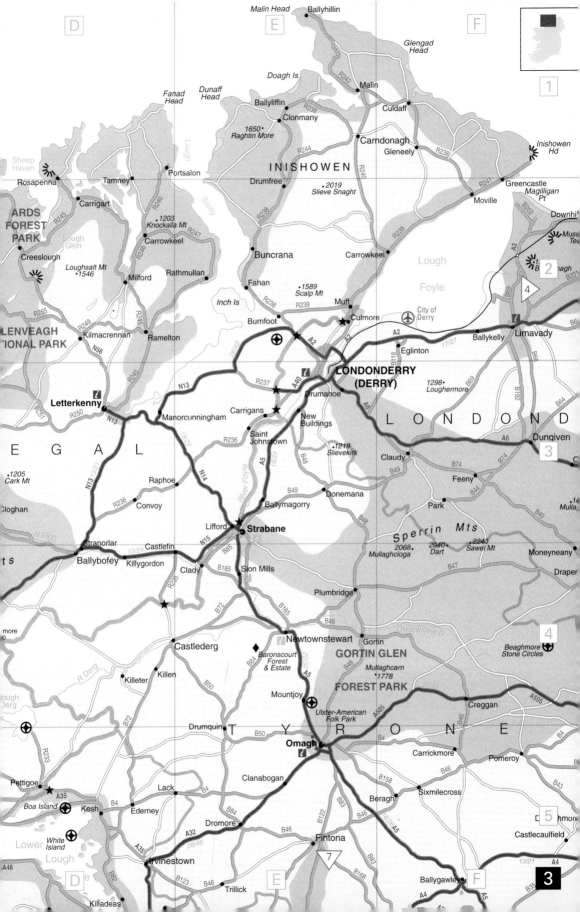

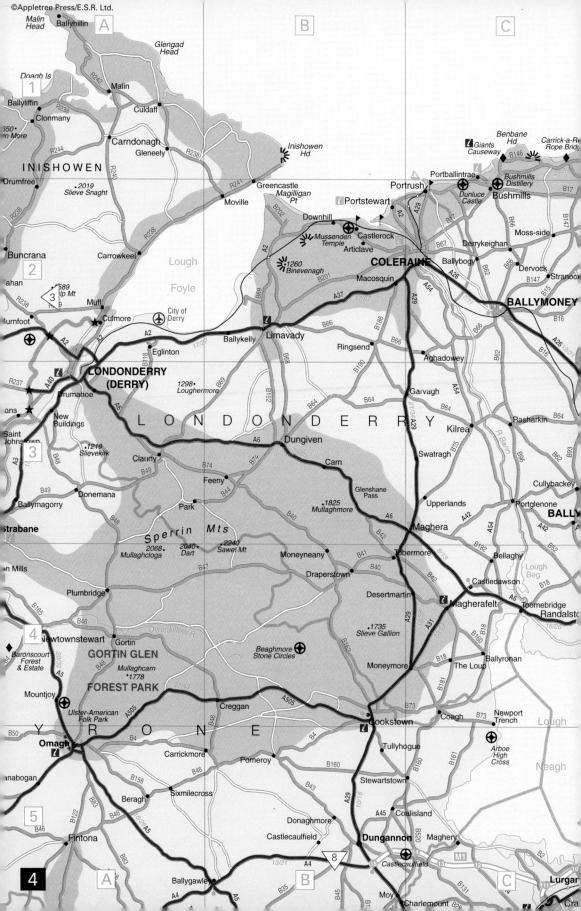

D   E   F

1

2

3

4

5

Rathlin Island

Fair Head

Ballycastle
Ballyvoy

Torr Head

Runabay Hd

A2

Cushendun

B92

Antrim

•1676
eveanarra

Cushendall

Waterfoot *Red Bay*

Garron Pt

1817•
Trostan B14

GLENARIFF
FOREST
PARK

Hills

B43

Carnlough Bay

Newtown-
Crommelin

A43

Carnlough

•1426
Collin Top

Glenarm

B97

A2

B94

The Sheddings

A42

Broughshane •1437
Slemish Mt.

Carncastle

Ballygalley

A2

A36

B148

LARNE

N   T   R   I   M

A36

Mullaghboy

Island Magee

Kells

Moorfields

B94

Glynn

B99

B100

Connor

B59

Glenoe

A2

B90

B150

Ballynure

Ballycarry

Black Hd

Ballyclare

Doagh

B58

B149

Whitehead

M2

Carrickfergus
Castle

A8

M2

Templepatrick

A6

B90

Eden

Carrickfergus

Glengormley

Belfast Lough

Whiteabbey

Ulster Folk &
Transport Museum

Groomsport

Mew I

Douglas

A26

B39

Newtownabbey

Whitehouse

Crawfordsburn

BANGOR

A2

Copeland I

Nutt's
Corner

A26

A52

Belfast
Harbour

Holywood

B170

Conlig

Donaghadee

Legoniel

BELFAST

1574•
Divis

B38

A501

Dunmurry

A3

Newtownbreda

Dundonald

A20

Newtownards

*Mount
Stewart*

Six Road Ends

A48

Millisle

B172

Glenavy

B101

M1

B23

Carryduff

A24

Moneyreagh

Comber

A22

A21

Greyabbey

A20

B5

Ballywalter

A2

ARDS

LISBURN

B178

A7

Ballygowan

A22

9

Kircubbin

B173

Ballyhalbert

A26

A3

Hillsborough

B6

Saintfield

PENINSULA

Portavogie

A49

B177

Ardkeen

Cairnryan Stranraer

Stranraer

NORTH CHANNEL

5

©Appletree Press/E.S.R. Ltd.

A   **B**   **C**

1

St John's Point

△2

Donegal   Bay

Rossnowlagh   R232   Ballintra
Coolmore   N15
Ballyshannon
Bundoran   N3
Belleek   B52
Lough Melvin
Inishmurray   Inishmurray Island
Kinlough
Cliffony
☗ Creevykeel   Garrison
Grange   Dartry Mts   R281
Rossinver
Lissadell House   •1722 Benbulben   •2113 Truskmore   R281
N15   Kiltyclogher
Carney   Drumcliff   ☗ Glencar Lake   R280   R283
Rosses Point   N16
Sligo Bay   R291   Shanvaus   Manorhamilton
Strandhill   R292   ⓘ SLIGO (SLIGEACH)   Leckaun   41/66   N16
Aughris Hd   Knocknarea Passage Grave   R286   Glenfarr
☗ Parke's Castle
Carrowmore   N4   Dromahair   R287   Killarga
Beltra   Lough Gill
Dromard   N59   Ballisodare   R287

Easky   R297
2 △11   Dromore West   Templeboy
nnishcrone   32/51   Owenbeg
Culleens
Pt   athle

Collooney   R290   LEITRIM   Dowra
Toberscanavan   R280   R200   Slie
Riverstown   R291   Drumkeeran   Ball
Bunnyconnellan   30/48   R293   N4   Lough Allen   R207
3   R294   S L I G O   Sliev
Cloonacool   N17   Ballymote Castle   Ballymote   Keshcorran Hill   Ballyfarnan   Drumshar
Mullany's Cross   R296   R295   Keadue   R20
Aclare   Tobercurry   R294   Bunnanadan   Ballinafad   LOUGH KEY FOREST PARK   Sliev

Slieve Gamph or Ox Mts
Lough Easky
•1788 Knockalongy

Curry   Doocastle
Bellahy   Gorteen   Boyle   ☗ Boyle Abbey   Leitrim
4   Swinford   Charlestown   Mullaghroe   R293   R361   51/51   Carrick-on-Shannon
24/39   N5   Horan International   N5   Lough Gara   N4   Jamestown
hola   N17   N370   R368   Drum
R321   R325   Bellaghadorreen   Lough Boderg
Ballyglass   Frenchpark   N61   R368
nagh   R322   Kilkelly   N83   Lisacul   R293   Elphin   R371
R323   26/42   Bellanagare   R369
R320   Mannin Lake   Loughglinn   R361
5 ⓘ Knock   R323   R293   R325   Tulsk   Strokestown   Scramoge
Ballyhaunis   Castlerea   Clonalis House   N5
Claremorris   N60   Ballinlough   43/69   N60   Castleplunket   11/18   R368
R327   N60   R357
Ballindine   Cloonfad   R360   Ballymoe   Ballintober   R O S C O M M O N   Ballyclare   Lar
N17   R328   R364   △13   Oran   N61   N60
1(329)   R360   R363   Roscommon Castle   Emmoo

6

A   **B**   **C**

A   **B**   **C**

1

2

3

4

5

Benwee Head

Porturlin

Belder

Erris Head

Broad Haven

Knocknalina

Belmullet

Binghamstown

Barnatra

Glenamoy

R314

12
Maum

Bunnahowen

R313

THE

Carrowmore Lough

R313

MULLET

Bangor Erris

N59

Bellacorick

Inishkea Nth

Aghleam

Gweesalia

R312

Inishkea Sth

•2369
Slieve Car

Black Rock

Duvillaun More

Blacksod Bay

Ballycroy

Nephin

•2065
Nephin Beg

2204•
Slieve More

Doogort

Castlehill

•2295
Birreencorra

Achill Hd

2192•
Croaghaun

Dooagh

Keel

R319

Annagh Is

R317

Range

•2343
Cushcamcarragh

Lough Feeagh

Lo

Achill Island

Achill Sound

Mulrany

N59

Newport

R311

CORRAUN PENINSULA

(Cai

Achillbeg Is

Clew Bay

Clare Is

Westport House
Westport

11/18

Westport Quay

N5

Louisburgh

R335

•2510
Croagh Patrick

Agha

Caher Is

Killadoon

Cregganbaun

Liscarney

N59

Inishturk

R335

Benbury
2610•

Partry

Inishbofin

•2688
Mweelrea

Ben Gorm
•2303

Benwee
2239•

•2207
Maumtrasna

Killateeau

Inishshark

Killary Harbour

Aasleagh

Glennagevlah

Leenane

Lough Nafooey

Lough Fee

N59

Maumturk

R336

JOYCE'S

Moyard

Letterfrack

Benbaun
•2993

2193

Maam

COUNTRY

Omey Is

CONNEMARA

The Twelve Pins

2307

R945

Corr

NATIONAL PARK

Clifden

Mts

CONNEMARA

•2236
Bencorr

Lough Inagh

Mannin Bay

Ballinaboy

Ballynahinch

12

Recess

N59

Maam Cross

Ballyconneely

Toombeola

R342

R340

Skye

10

A   **B**   **C**

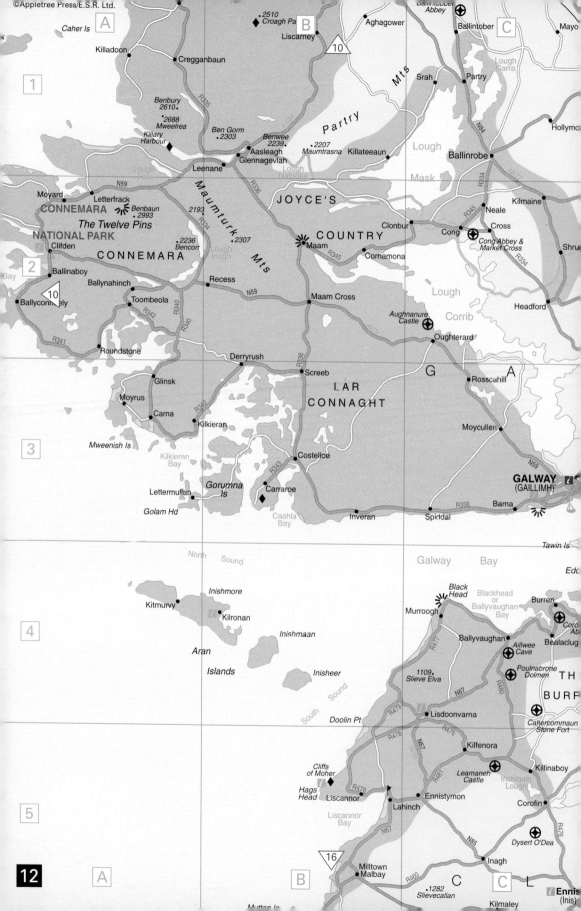

©Appletree Press/E.S.R. Ltd.

A **B** **C**

Caher Is

Killadoon

Cregganbaun

Croagh Pa 2510
Liscarney

Aghagower

Ballintubber Abbey
Ballintober

Mayo

1

Lough Carra

Hollymo

Benbury 2610

2688 Mweelrea

Ben Gorm 2303

Benwee 2239

Maumtrasna 2207

Killateeaun

Srah

Partry

Partry Mts

Ballinrobe

R334

Killary Harbour

Aasleagh
Glennagevlah

Leenane

N59

Lough Nafooey

Lough Mask

Lough

R334

Kilmaine

Moyard

Letterfrack

CONNEMARA

The Twelve Pins

NATIONAL PARK

Benbaun 2993

Maumturk Mts

2193

R334

JOYCE'S COUNTRY

Clonbur

Neale

Cross

Cong

R345

Cong Abbey & Market Cross

Shru

2

Clifden

Ballinaboy

CONNEMARA

2236 Bencorr

2307

Lough Inagh

Maam

R345

Cornamona

Lough

10

Ballynahinch

Recess

N59

Maam Cross

Corrib

Headford

Ballyconnely

Toombeola

R340

R342

R336

Aughnanure Castle

Oughterard

Roundstone

R341

Derryrush

Screeb

G **A**

Rosscahill

3

Glinsk

R340

LAR CONNAGHT

Moycullen

Moyrus

Carna

Kilkieran

R336

N59

Mweenish Is

Kilkieran Bay

Costelloe

R343

GALWAY (GAILLIMH)

Lettermullan

Gorumna Is

Carraroe

Barna

Golam Hd

Cashla Bay

Inveran

Spiddal

4

North Sound

Galway Bay

Tawin Is

Edd

Inishmore

Kitmurvy

Kilronan

Inishmaan

Black Head

Murroogh

Blackhead or Ballyvaughan Bay

Burren

Aran Islands

Inisheer

Ballyvaughan

Aillwee Cave

Bealaclug

R477

1109 Slieve Elva

Poulnabrone Dolmen

TH BURR

South Sound

Doolin Pt

R479

N67

Lisdoonvarna

Cahercommaun Stone Fort

5

Cliffs of Moher

Hags Head

Liscannor

R478

Kilfenora

Leamaneh Castle

Killinaboy

N67

Lahinch

Ennistymon

Corofin

Liscannor Bay

R481

Inchiquin Lough

R476

16

Milltown Malbay

R460

1282 Slievecallan

N85

Dysert O'Dea

Inagh

C **C** **L**

Mutton Is

Kilmaley

Ennis (Inis)

12

A **B** **C**

10

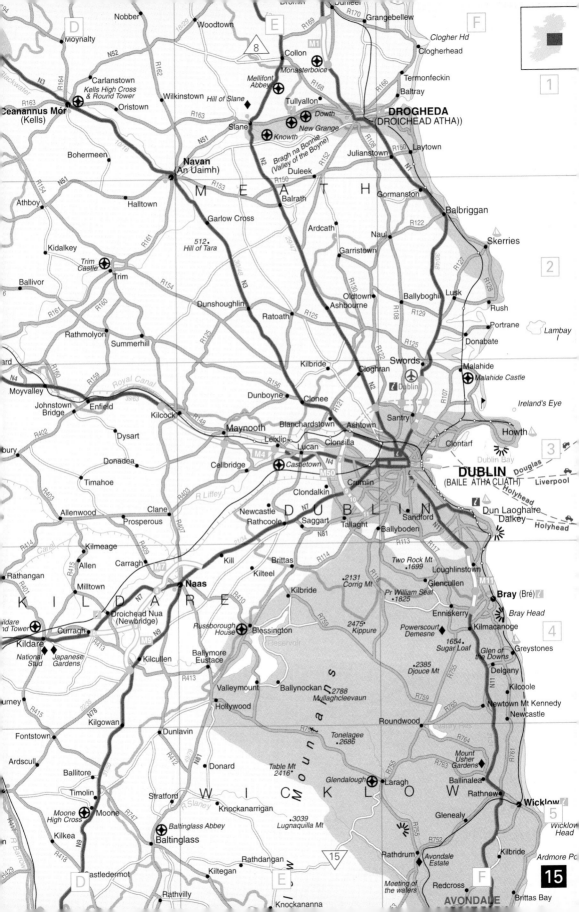

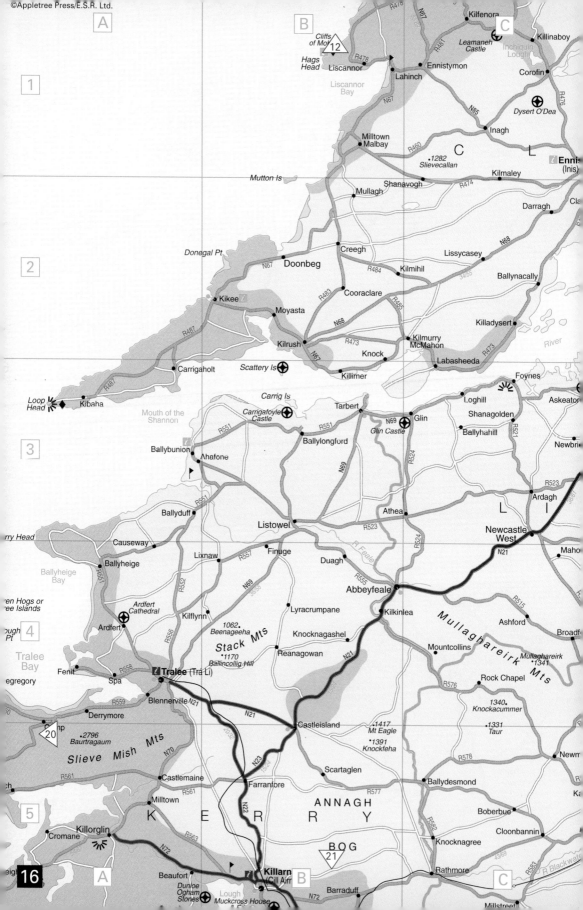

©Appletree Press/E.S.R. Ltd.

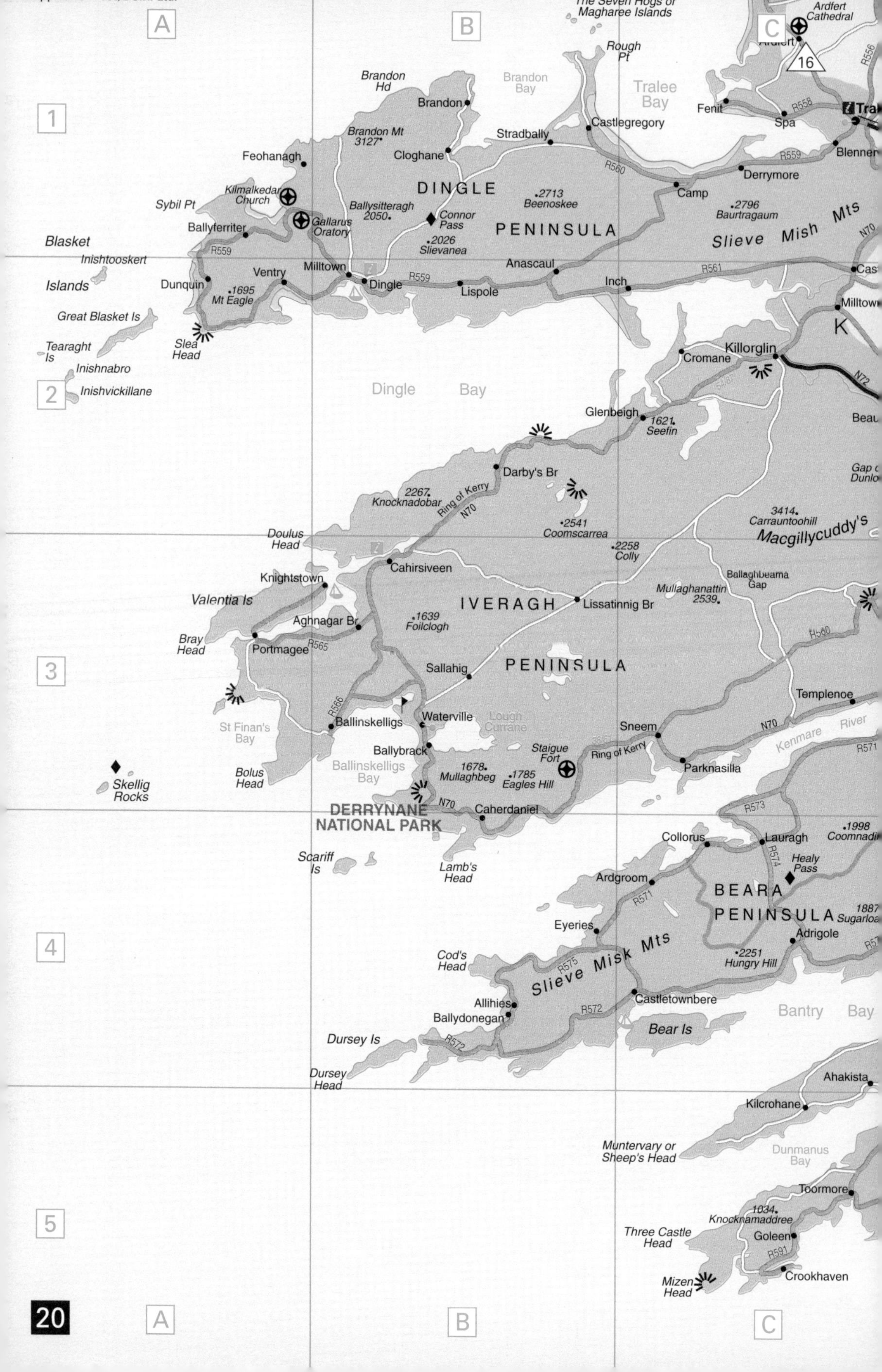

The Seven Hogs or
Magharee Islands

Ardfert
Cathedral

Rough
Pt

Ardfert

16

R556

1

Brandon
Hd

Brandon

Brandon
Bay

Tralee
Bay

Fenit

R558

Tra

Brandon Mt
3127

Cloghane

Stradbally

Castlegregory

Spa

Blenner

Feohanagh

R560

Derrymore

DINGLE

.2713
Beenoskee

Camp

.2796
Baurtragaum

Sybil Pt

Kilmalkedar
Church

Ballysitteragh
2050.

Connor
Pass

PENINSULA

Slieve Mish Mts

N70

Ballyferriter

Gallarus
Oratory

.2026
Slievanea

Blasket

R559

Ventry

Milltown

Anascaul

R561

Cas

Inishtooskert

Dunquin

Dingle

Lispole

Inch

Milltow

Islands

.1695
Mt Eagle

R559

K

Great Blaskel Is

Killorglin

Tearaght
Is

Slea
Head

Dingle   Bay

Cromane

N72

Beau

2

Inishnabro

Inishvickillane

Glenbeigh

.1621
Seefin

Gap
Dunlo

Darby's Br

.2267
Knocknadobar

Ring of Kerry

N70

.2541
Coomscarrea

3414.
Carrauntoohill

Doulus
Head

.2258
Colly

Macgillycuddy's

Knightstown

Cahirsiveen

IVERAGH

Ballaghbeama
Gap

Valentia Is

.1639
Foilclogh

Lissatinnig Br

Mullaghanattin
2539.

R560

Bray
Head

Aghnagar Br

R565

PENINSULA

Templenoe

Portmagee

R566

Sallahig

N70

River

R571

3

St Finan's
Bay

Ballinskelligs

Waterville

Lough
Currane

Sneem

Kenmare

Ballybrack

.1678
Mullaghbeg

Staigue
Fort

Ring of Kerry

Parknasilla

Bolus
Head

Ballinskelligs
Bay

N70

.1785
Eagles Hill

Skellig
Rocks

DERRYNANE
NATIONAL PARK

Caherdaniel

Collorus

Laugh

.1998
Coomnadi

Scariff
Is

Lamb's
Head

Ardgroom

R571

R573

R574

Healy
Pass

BEARA

Eyeries

PENINSULA

.1887
Sugarloa

4

Cod's
Head

.2251
Hungry Hill

Adrigole

Slieve Misk Mts

R575

Allihies

R572

Castletownbere

Bantry   Bay

Ballydonegan

Dursey Is

R572

Bear Is

Ahakista

Dursey
Head

Kilcrohane

Muntervary or
Sheep's Head

Dunmanus
Bay

Toormore

5

.1034
Knocknamaddree

Three Castle
Head

Goleen

R591

Mizen
Head

Crookhaven

20

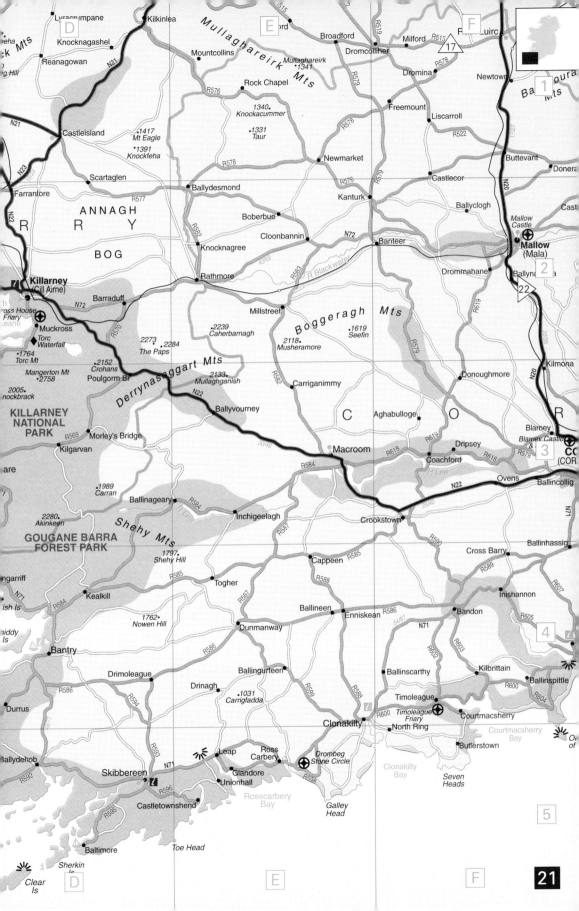

Index

This index lists places included in both the gazetteer and the road atlas. Page numbers in **bold type** immediately after a name indicate an entry in the gazetteer. Page numbers and map references in roman type refer to the road atlas: a name may appear more than once on the atlas, but the index lists only the best presentation.

D

E

F

G